D0780369

NOTHING IS BEYOND OUR REACH

NOTHING IS BEYOND OUR REACH

AMERICA'S TECHNO-SPY EMPIRE

KRISTIE MACRAKIS

Georgetown University Press | Washington, DC

Library of Congress Cataloging-in-Publication Data

Names: Macrakis, Kristie, author.
Title: Nothing is beyond our reach: America's techno-spy empire / Kristie Macrakis.
Description: Washington, DC: Georgetown University Press, 2023. | Includes bibliographical references and index.
Identifiers: LCCN 2022014383 (print) | LCCN 2022014384 (ebook) | ISBN 9781647123239 (hardcover) | ISBN 9781647123246 (ebook)
Subjects: LCSH: Espionage—United States—Equipment and supplies. | Intelligence service—United States—Equipment and supplies. | Electronic surveillance—United States—Equipment and supplies. | Espionage—Technological innovations—United States. | Intelligence service—Technological innovations—United States.
Classification: LCC UB271.U5M27 2023 (print) | LCC UB271.U5 (ebook) | DDC 327.1273—dc23/eng/20221221
LC record available at https://lccn.loc.gov/2022014383
LC ebook record available at https://lccn.loc.gov/2022014384

∞ This paper meets the requirements of ANSI/NISO Z39.48-1992 (Permanence of Paper).

24 23 9 8 7 6 5 4 3 2 First printing
Printed in the United States of America

Cover design by Jeremy John Parker
Interior design by Paul Hotvedt

CONTENTS

ILLUSTRATIONS

ACKNOWLEDGMENTS

I am most grateful to the Woodrow Wilson Center in Washington, DC; Georgia Tech; and Don Jacobs at Georgetown University Press for generously supporting the research and writing of this book. I began the project during a wonderful fellowship year at the Center after receiving a seed grant from Georgia Tech's Small Grants for Research (SGR) Program in the Ivan Allen College, then led by the effective dean, Jackie Royster. Steve Usselman, who was chair of my department at the time, has also been supportive of the book. More recently, the SGR program's Aaron Levine and the current department chair, Hanchao Lu, helped finance the generation of the index. I very much appreciate Don Jacobs's long-standing interest in my research and for soliciting the manuscript. Don was surprisingly knowledgeable about intelligence history and made many valuable suggestions as I was completing the manuscript. I was impressed with the press's efficiency during the pandemic from the reviewer stage to production; a big thank-you to the whole team.

I presented material from several chapters in the book at a variety of venues. I am grateful to the people who invited me and especially to the audiences. In Washington, the incomparable Kathy Olesko asked me to speak at Georgetown University, and knowledgeable colleagues provided helpful feedback on the Cuban Missile Crisis chapter, which I also presented to other audiences. Colleagues at the Society for the History of Technology conferences, at Sigma Xi events, at Georgia Tech, and at a Vienna, Austria, conference provided nice feedback on the chapter "Passing the Global Espionage Torch," including an image-rich version. The Wilson Center hosted several conferences after the year was over where colleagues provided helpful comments. Colleagues in my department either provided feedback at events or read chapters; they include Dan

Amsterdam, Carla Gerona, John Krige, Steve Usselman, and Germán Vergara. Hallie Lieberman provided generous editing and feedback on the New Zealand story told in the preface. Eric Zemmali and Lauren Daniels, two student research assistants at the Wilson Center, cheerfully aided the research, while the librarian Janet Spikes was especially helpful, as was Lindsay Collins at the front desk. Christian Osterman, who directs the History and Public Policy program, was a hospitable colleague. The fellowship cohort at the Center was a wonderful group of friends and colleagues. Not only did many provide feedback on my work, but we also did fun things in Washington and Virginia like visit local restaurants and museums as well as bike and hike. Finally, old and new friends in Washington made the year more enjoyable, including Amy Schwartz, Eric Koenig, Laurie Hart, Nathan Stoltzfus, Gil Pimentel, Ben Fischer, David Charney, Yuval Ravinsky-Gray, and Thomas Berger.

PREFACE

Some people spend their free time embarking on secular pilgrimages to places like Machu Picchu in search of mystery, history, and adventure. While preparing this book, I needed a similar journey to better understand, and get inside, America's secret world of intelligence. My travels took me from the suburbs of Washington, DC, to the far-flung scenes of empire and techno-espionage described in the chapters that follow. The experience was both informative and disturbing. One can read about America's techno-spy empire, one can interview the participants, and one can write about it, but none of these captures the magnitude and audacity of the facilities and technology that girdle the globe.

Machines in the Garden

My first stop was small and close by: the island of Cuba, just ninety miles off the coast of Florida yet still inaccessible because of political restrictions. Like most Americans, my visual image of the 1962 Cuban Missile Crisis was shaped by the U-2 spy plane reconnaissance photos made famous by Adlai Stevenson during his briefing to the United Nations on behalf of President John F. Kennedy. The image, a black-and-white photograph taken from above, was flat and one-dimensional, without any contrast.

I studied such black-and-white U-2 spy plane photographs for hours before visiting former Cuban missile sites in San Cristóbal, Cuba. Accustomed to those images, I was surprised to see the lush terrain in San Cristóbal. By 2018 the hot, humid weather in Cuba had produced a jungle of trees, vines, and weeds covering most remnants of the Soviet missile apparatus.

Cuba might be known for its classic 1950s cars, but in San Cristóbal, the horse-pulled (or ox-pulled) cart remains a popular mode of transportation. And this was the way my casa host, Decter, and our driver, a local farmer, took me to the former missile site in San Cristóbal because the road the Soviets had built for their truck convoys was now a muddy, overgrown pathway. The horse worked hard pulling us past green shrubbery and modest abodes and chicken coops often built from repurposed missile site leftovers like metal from bunkers. Once we reached a ranch-style circular horse training area, we hopped off the cart and walked down to the main missile site. At first there was nothing to see except for the mountains nestled behind the flatlands. The mountains had not been captured in the flat photographic images. Before my very eyes the black-and-white images of missile launchers, tents, and temporary buildings dissolved. There were no visible remnants of the missile apparatus except for a small piece of concrete from a launching pad. The only reminder that this was the location of the Soviet medium-range missiles was a faded illegible marble plaque dated 2007 memorializing the site.

As we left the site and ambled through mango groves, we finally came across ruins that looked like a sculpture in a public garden. Concrete arches were piled up like Picasso figurines overgrown with shrubbery. These were apparently the remnants of concrete missile silos. Decter admired the Soviet welding work on some remaining metal tubes. Behind the garden sculpture we found a pigpen built by farmers out of repurposed concrete forms. These two artifacts were the few visible remnants of this crucial missile site where the United States had identified offensive missiles that could reach America in minutes.

Despite the paucity of visible remnants of missile apparatus at ground zero, museums in Havana housed pieces of artifacts of the most important technical icons of the Cuban Missile Crisis: the U-2 spy plane and Soviet defensive surface-to-air missiles. The most striking artifacts were on display behind the Museum of the Revolution in a park-like exhibit of missiles, planes, and jeeps. The machines were exhibited in the middle of a Caribbean garden. Palms swayed in the front. The Soviet surface-to-air missile next to the engine of Rudolf Anderson's U-2 spy plane looked like a surgical instrument with its thin fishtailed body and red needle front ready to pierce an enemy spy plane violating Cuban airspace. While Anderson's remains were returned to America after he was shot down, debris from his plane is littered across Cuba. This was truly a view from the other side of

Figure P.1 Concrete arches at the San Cristóbal Soviet missile site in Cuba. *Author's Collection*

the conflict. The technologies looked like invaders frozen in the past and discordant against the green garden.

I found replicas of missiles in the most unlikely places. Next to my Airbnb casa in Soroa, there was a sign that read "La Rosa," designating a military base for agriculture. As I strolled down the road, I passed a chicken farm, goats, horses, and a walled military base with a bus parked in front. Farther along I encountered a billboard in the forest with the image of Ché Guevara and another bearded man wearing a typical Cuban sombrero. At the billboard I turned up a curved road and entered a compound, where I found an organic farm and a sign on the other side of the courtyard with a miniature reproduction of an R-12 (NATO SS-4, a medium-range missile also called Sandal). The sign displays the Cuban people's solidarity with the revolution and socialism. The plaque commemorates the site as a medium-range missile installation during the crisis of October–November 1962. The missile model is far from realistic, as its miniature size does not capture the terror of a missile 67 feet long and 5.4 feet in circumference pointed at the United States.

Figure P.2 A Soviet SA-2 missile and U-2 debris on display in the garden behind the Museum of the Revolution in Havana, Cuba. *Author's Collection*

A Cathedral of Intelligence

It was one of those perfect summer days—blue skies, low humidity, comfortable temperature—and I was finally in Springfield, Virginia. I had spent hours poring over Google Maps images of the mysterious National Geospatial-Intelligence Agency (NGA) buildings located at 7500 Geoint Drive. The map featured an odd steel cone that resembled a bunker encasement that bridged two large, crescent-shaped buildings. The address alone reflected the creation of a new street for a new suburban subdivision—actually, a secure campus—in the national security landscape. Before driving through the security gates, a big fuel truck with an American flag emblazoned on its side and "mission critical" pasted underneath passed me on Highway 286. There are plenty of spy agencies in this corner of northern Virginia that need mission-critical fuel, including the National Reconnaissance Office (NRO), about twenty-five miles north in Chantilly. But the NGA building was something different. When it was completed in 2011, it was said to be the third largest federal building in the greater Washington, DC, area, following on the heels of the Pentagon and the

Figure P.3 A Soviet R-12 model in an organic garden in Soroa, Cuba. *Author's Collection*

Ronald Reagan Building. Northern Virginia is what the historian Andrew Friedman called the "covert capital" of US empire, though he focused on the CIA and not the NRO or NGA.[1]

The landscaping, with its freshly planted young trees and neatly manicured grass, and the recently paved roads snaking through the 130-acre campus connecting the parking lots accentuated the newness. The Visitor Center entrance is adorned with an elongated sign identifying the National Geospatial-Intelligence Agency, its address, and the NGA logo, which is a moon shining on Earth at off-center left. The sign is bookended by two big boulders.

All guests have to park in the visitors' parking lot before entering the self-standing glass visitor's control center, where two guards flanked by two flags—one the US flag, the other the NGA's global logo flag—greet guests at the entrance, usually contractors. The NGA probably doesn't get many visiting historians.

A sign on the wall, "No classified conversations allowed at the Visitor Center," greets guests in the sitting area. This would become a theme of the building architecture and visit—an open, glass encrusted space with

Figure P.4 The Visitor Center sign at the US National Geospatial-Intelligence Agency. *Author's Collection*

lots of light—but there are continual reminders of the secret nature of the work of the inhabitants of the building. All the buildings and the campus itself are a metaphor for US national security agencies coexisting with an American ethos of openness.

After my escort picked me up—let's call him Jim—we ambled past some historical poster boards along the outdoor path to the main building, adorned with striking trapezoid windows—reportedly over seventeen hundred of them—a far cry from the National Imagery and Mapping Agency's (NIMA's) former windowless brick building in Bethesda. Ordered chronologically from World War I to the present, the posters chronicled some of the numerous predecessor agencies' greatest hits, from the Cuban Missile Crisis to the Gulf War to the Global War on Terror. Since the NGA is an amalgam of predecessor organizations like the National Photographic Interpretation Center (NPIC) and NIMA, its history is a bewildering alphabet soup of acronyms. With the merging of the US government's mapping and photographic interpretation capabilities, the NGA houses the largest number of employees in one building: some nine thousand in Springfield alone and another five thousand in its St. Louis facility.

Our first stop before going to the museum was a chat over coffee at the in-house Starbucks whose baristas have security clearance. As we entered the atrium that houses the shops, it's hard not to look up and around. The space is the size of the Grand Central Station atrium. It turned out that the bunker-like material was the atrium roof. It looked like a modern cathedral of intelligence because of its opulence and the priorities of our society. And, as Tom Engelhardt quips, national security has become a bit of a religion with its holy warriors and its sacred (classified) texts, dogma, and warrior priests.[2]

My escort plopped his gym bag on the floor and enthusiastically described the state-of-the-art health club facilities. In addition to enjoying the health club, employees can get a haircut at the atrium salon, drop their clothes off at the dry cleaner, bank at the credit union, get a health checkup at the clinic, and dine at several dining rooms and fast-food places. In this respect it resembled the Pentagon's model, which combines the ordinary accoutrements of American life with top-secret rooms and state-of-the-art facilities to secure our nation.

After finishing our coffee, we walked past the Arthur Lundahl Auditorium, named in honor of the father of photointerpretation at the CIA and known internationally as the man who presented John F. Kennedy with spy plane imagery of missiles in Cuba. The museum around the corner housed the common light tables used to view the images. But the picture window in the back revealed a pond with a park bench. The water wasn't there for recreation, however; it was a pool to cool the mega-machines that run the 24,000-square-foot building and its high-tech towers, chillers, and other necessities for a state-of-the-art spy facility. This self-contained-city feature of the NGA resembled the situation at other large intelligence agencies. Lesser known than the CIA, the National Security Agency (NSA), and the NRO, the NGA became a member of the club when it succeeded NIMA in 2003. It is now a full-fledged intelligence agency whose budget is on par with the other heavy hitters in the intelligence landscape.

As we headed to Jim's office to chat about the history of photointerpretation and geospatial intelligence, we took one of thirty-six elevators to his corner of the building. When we walked past the open seating areas with comfortable chairs and benches, Jim called out my non-security-clearance status, "uncleared," in case a classified conversation floated to our ears.

The post-9/11 period was marked by unbridled growth and nearly unrestricted funding for US national security and intelligence. This led to what the journalists Dana Priest and William M. Arkin called "supersize.gov," an expansion of top-secret domestic America. This included "thirty-three large complexes for top secret intelligence work."[3] I never imagined supersize.gov would include a cathedral of intelligence and the jaw-dropping mega-structures at the new NGA building, which was built after Priest and Arkin published their *Washington Post* series in 2010 and book in 2011.

Another enormous national security repository, the Utah Data Center, was completed by the NSA in 2013 to store the vast amount of data hauled in by the NSA's installations around the world. The "heavily fortified" $2 billion complex can store yottabytes of data. NSA chronicler James Bamford said the center was built "to intercept, decipher, analyze, and store vast swaths of the world's communications as they zap down from satellites and zip through the underground and undersea cables of international, foreign and domestic networks."[4] I like to tell my students to imagine what a Martian landing in the United States would say upon encountering such a complex. What would the Martian think about the priorities of our society that we would build a billion-dollar, one-million-square-foot facility to store the world's emails, cellphone calls, Google searches, and digital pocket litter?

It is hard to imagine how this hypertrophied global security state will ever shrink. It is improbable of course that the buildings would be repurposed for other domestic needs like health, infrastructure improvements, and education. Although the intelligence community has been downsized in the past budgetarily, the mega-structures are a new phenomenon.

New Zealand: Radomes in the Vineyard

I was excited when I had the opportunity to teach in New Zealand in January 2020, shortly before the pandemic hit, because I had become fascinated with a spy base built with American technology and located in the heart of Marlborough wine country. Although the intercept station was funded by New Zealand's Government Communication Security Bureau (GCSB), it was part of the UKUSA consortium of the United States, the United Kingdom, Canada, Australia, and New Zealand and part of the Anglo-American signals intelligence (SIGINT) empire. As I had found for Cuba and Springfield, Virginia, Google Maps offered a bird's-eye but somewhat flat view of the facility. I began imagining combining a wine tasting cycling tour with a visit to a spy base in New Zealand's wine country—a spy base visit for wine lovers.

A small group of us from my university's study abroad program was sitting around a brown Formica, rectangular cafeteria table eating chicken curry together on our third day in Wellington, New Zealand's capital, when I broached the topic of doing a bike tour of wine country in Marlborough along with a spy base visit. Two colleagues jumped at the chance: an outspoken Iranian engineer, now a US citizen, Arash, and our forever smiling bear of a man, an American physiologist, Adam. Together we prepared for our adventure. We booked ferry tickets, rented a car, and reserved a motel apartment in Blenheim.

Upon arriving at the motel and depositing our luggage, Adam drove us to the site since he was experienced driving on the left side of the road. As we headed toward Waihopai Valley Road on State Highway 6 we passed miles of verdant vineyards nestled at the bottom of distant mountains. After turning onto Waihopai Valley Road, we saw a sign written in Art Deco style announcing Spy Valley Wines. Curious, we got out of the car to stroll around the vineyard. The site offered a superb view of the green vines set against a golden mountain backdrop. What a fitting entrance to the Waihopai spy base down the road. And, of course, the location inspired its moniker; it became the gateway to our spy base tour. The winemakers had affixed a message in Morse code on the wine's label. When decoded it read, "For Wine Lovers."

As we drove down Waihopai Valley Road, a cascade of lush green vineyards unfolded against the late afternoon sun. When we got closer to the intercept station, an enormous hedge of planted evergreens created a natural wall some fifty feet high, blocking the view. After we passed the hedge wall, suddenly a large moon appeared to rise on the horizon. But it wasn't a moon; it was one of the two white radomes nestled in a vineyard. The radomes protected giant satellite dishes. The view was totally different from what I had imagined. Instead of an arid, cookie cutter layout of vineyards as displayed in the Google Earth satellite view, a luxuriant green landscape framed by blue-tinted mountains whisked by us on both sides of the road.

Adam blurted, "It looks like Epcot in Orlando," referring to the huge geodetic sphere that greets guests as they enter the theme park at Walt Disney World in Florida. The analogy turned out to be more telling than just the golf ball–like structure. Epcot features a dark ride into the past of human communications, from the alphabet to modern telecommunications. It was an easy slippery slope to harness modern global satellites for spy purposes.

Before arriving at the spy base, we saw a road next to the government property. I thought it would be a good vantage point to take some more photographs. We pulled up past a ranch-style house and I took out my camera and started shooting. Within minutes, Adam beckoned me over, "Hey, Kristie, this lady wants to talk to you." I heard a woman screaming from the open front door. Implacable Adam calmly pointed his finger at me and said, "Talk to her."

As I turned toward the door, I saw the woman's contorted face. I tried to tell her it would be great to talk to her about what it's like living next to a spy base, but she was so agitated, yelling at us to leave the property, that she didn't hear me. A young boy peered out of the picture window. Arash, who was more concerned about her reaction, firmly said, "Kristie, you better get in the car." As we sped off the woman shouted, "You are rude. This is private property." We looked around and didn't see a sign or any barrier blocking our entrance down the driveway. "Kristie, you realize I'm Iranian, right?" exclaimed Arash, in his slight Iranian accent. I playfully replied, "Yes, you're a double agent." Of course, if we were stopped by police Arash could be accused of being an Iranian spy, but this deterred only my companions.

As we approached the spy base, the two white domes got larger. On the opposite side of the road I saw a sign for Nobilo Hay Block Vineyard, Nobilo being one of the most ubiquitous Sauvignon Blanc wines in the United States. At the spy station sheep grazed in the fields. Grapevines filled the property in steady rows. Shedding bark trees lined the street. It could be a normal farm except for the high-tech spy apparatus plopped squarely in the middle. The exterior fence looked primitive; it was the kind used to prevent animals from leaving the property. There were no visible guards. I zoomed in with the camera and saw a heftier barbed-wire fence near the buildings. As we got closer to the property, yellow signs warned, "Defence Area: No Admission Except on Business."

Unfortunately, I couldn't think of a reason to gain access to the building, but I wondered how the New Zealand peace movement was effortlessly able to march on defense property. Some had even breached the inner fence. There was a road leading to the entrance, and I urged Adam

Figure P.5 Radomes of a satellite communications intercept station surrounded by vineyards, Waihopai Valley, Marlborough, New Zealand. *Author's Collection*

to drive down it, but spooked by the screaming lady encounter, he floored the accelerator and zoomed off.

The next day as we biked along paths, stopping to sample Sauvignon Blanc at open wine cellar doors, the spy base never came into view. Tourists are kept busy sampling wines at over a dozen wineries north of Route 6. During our lunch stop at a vineyard's outdoor patio, the spy base in the vineyard faded from our thoughts, and we relaxed over food and wine as birds pecked at leftovers on abandoned plates.

On our way back to the motel from the bike shop in its courtesy van, the driver, an older white-haired man, who identified himself as "Mac," said he had worked at the New Zealand Air Force base we passed on the road. He was very amenable to sharing information about Waihopai Station and said it offered good transmission because of the clear and open skies. The US military base had closed, and even with New Zealand's antinuclear stance, New Zealand had a good relationship with the United States. When I asked him how locals felt about the station, he said they didn't mind it.

To learn more about the spy base, I contacted an investigative journalist, Nicky Hager, for a lunch appointment after returning to Wellington. I had read Hager's extraordinary book on the GCSB and its place in the international alliance weeks before, *Secret Power*. We met at the Bucket Fountain, a kinetic sculpture that dumps water in buckets as it moves. It is Wellington's popular outdoor meeting place on funky Cuba Street.

Over fish pie and salad, Hager mentioned that he had been asked to testify before the German Parliament about the global Echelon eavesdropping system in early 2001, before the 9/11 attacks on the United States. After 9/11, the exposed Echelon system receded from the news but grew in secret. Hager reflected on the difference between Echelon, which used a targeted dictionary system of key words to organize information, and the systems revealed in the Snowden documents; the NSA and its SIGINT allies had developed a "full-take" system that hauled in *all* information, not just targeted information. As we finished our lunch, I emphasized that the important story behind Waihopai was really the global aspect that reflected America's hegemony.

While in Wellington, I took a stroll downtown one sunny afternoon to view the shiny new GCSB headquarters built in 2011, now housed in a nine-story glass structure with security shades. It is called Pipitea House and is near the New Zealand Archives and Library and a stone's throw from the Beehive parliament building. I did not contact the GCSB for a visit or enter the building, where I would have been subject to a biometric fingerprint scan. Instead I watched as people walked in and out of the building guarded by a Kohatu, or guard stone; the security shades were drawn.

I found a café nearby, hoping that employees on their breaks would be chatting and drinking coffee there. I was lucky. As I sat at a table at Café Oviedo sipping a latte, I saw a cherubic, rosy-cheeked young man with a lanyard around his neck and a badge bouncing on his white button-down shirt, presumably from the GCSB, chatting with a young man with a beard, clad in blue jeans, sneakers, and a T-shirt that said, "A Terabyte of data is a terrible thing to waste." His Apple computer had a sticker on it: "Splunk." I couldn't hear what they said because the room was too noisy, but after the cherubic GCSB employee left, I briefly talked to the Splunk vendor, who said the company was based in San Francisco and worked on software to search, monitor, and analyze machine-generated big data. It could be applied to security too, he said.

It wasn't surprising that a contractor was talking to people at the GCSB. The NSA and other omnivorous data-crunching technology spy agencies did the same thing. Why develop your own software when the market is creating it for the rest of the technologized world? These machines were hidden in the glass-clad corporate intelligence building.

But it was the machine in the vineyard that symbolized the way in which the spy tech monolith of the Five Eyes countries—Australia, New Zealand, Canada, the United Kingdom, and the United States—led by the NSA, colonized the world. Its intrusion into these bucolic scenes isn't limited to Blenheim, New Zealand. In Menwith Hill, Great Britain, sheep share their pasture with one of the world's largest NSA installations. In Sugar Grove, West Virginia, the NSA shaved a flourishing forest to plant its radomes and antenna; and Yakima, Washington, cowboy country, was chosen for its remoteness.

But the Waihopai spy base is plopped in the middle of wine country. It's not remote. It's a visible reminder of technological spying in a techno-colonized country. The eerie moonscape scene is mysterious and serious. It's not that it doesn't blend in with scenery; it does in a Jurassic Park–like way. But what it stands for clashes with the carefree bike wine tour along the Wairau River. The spy machine was more than just an intrusion into the garden. For the numerous protesters over the years, the station symbolized aggressive American hegemony using the fruits of the eavesdropping technology for unpopular wars like the American-led war in Iraq. Since my visit, the GCSB decided in late 2021 to dismantle the radomes in favor of newer, invisible technological means of interception.[5]

Origins

This book didn't begin with an exploration of the US global security empire at home and abroad. It started more modestly and grew along with new developments. As a historian of technology and science interested in espionage, I had for many years been teaching a course on technology in the service of espionage, which was primarily focused on US efforts. Simultaneously, I had been working on a book on science and technology at the East German Ministry for State Security focusing on its foreign intelligence arm, the HVA (Hauptverwaltung Aufklärung). Unsurprisingly, each of the countries had quite a different approach to spying and the tools to use to acquire secret information. When I interviewed someone like Markus Wolf, the legendary spy chief of East German foreign intelligence, he taught me the fine art of manipulating humans to get them to do your bidding by playing on their weaknesses, whether it was greed, ideology, sex, ego, or some other human frailty. When I taught my course, I saw the way in which the United States emphasized and worshipped technology to acquire secret information. These observations then led to an article titled "Technophilic Hubris and Espionage Styles," and later I launched the writing of this book during my tenure at the Woodrow Wilson International Center for Scholars in Washington, DC. I hope readers enjoy the journey as we unearth the scale and magnitude of the techno-spy empire and the accompanying ethos, "nothing is beyond our reach," from the early days of the 1950s to the present. One more thing I want to mention: most of the protagonists in this story are men. And it would take another project to explore why this was the case and if the techno-spy empire epitomized masculine technology.

Notes

1. See Andrew Friedman, *Covert Capital: Landscapes of Denial and the Making of U.S. Empire in the Suburbs of Northern Virginia* (Berkeley: University of California Press, 2013).

2. Tom Engelhardt, *Shadow Government: Surveillance, Secret Wars, and a Global Security State in a Single-Superpower World* (Chicago: Haymarket Books, 2014), chap. 1.

3. Dana Priest and William M. Arkin, *Top Secret America: The Rise of the New American Security State* (New York: Little, Brown, 2011), 69.

4. James Bamford, "The NSA Is Building the Country's Biggest Spy Center (Watch What You Say)," *Wired*, March 15, 2012, www.wired.com/2012/03/ff-nsadatacenter.

5. David Fisher, "Waihopai Valley Spy Domes 'Iconic' Yet 'Obsolete'—Will Come Down as GCSB Moves to New Technology," *New Zealand Herald*, November 10, 2021, www.nzherald.co.nz/nz/waihopai-valley-spy-domes-iconic-yet-obsolete-will-come-down-as-gcsb-moves-to-new-technology/HZMLR5T2E6UM47NI2CXZZHAE6E/.

INTRODUCTION

At the height of imperialism in the late nineteenth century, cartoonists around the world depicted Great Britain as an octopus grabbing land from adversaries in order to expand her empire. In the twentieth century, several James Bond novels featured the criminal organization SPECTRE, whose logo was an octopus, presumably to symbolize that the organization had a hand in everything. Often the octopus symbol is used by an adversary to depict a malignant enemy whose tentacles reach out to clutch and envelop objects, land, or the globe.

Therefore, it was surprising when the US National Reconnaissance Office created a logo for its public December 2013 satellite launch depicting an angry octopus latching its tentacles around the globe. The caption read, "Nothing Is beyond Our Reach." Obviously, the NRO found nothing offensive about the patch, which was created by an in-house graphic designer. Unlike earlier octopus cartoons, this one was created by an agency that saw the image of a globe-straddling octopus as a mark of global achievement. US technical capabilities allowed its spy agencies to cover every nook and cranny of the world.

Usually satellite launches and the emblems affixed to the satellite's boosters trigger little public commentary. This one was different. Unsurprisingly, the NRO's patch provoked public outrage. After all, it was 2013. Just six months earlier Edward Snowden had surfaced in Hong Kong publicizing previously secret all-encompassing surveillance. Although Snowden's revelations, and the accompanying newspaper articles, primarily focused on domestic spying against Americans, the majority of the files seized by Snowden reveal a global eavesdropping system of staggering capabilities. But this global communication intercept program was just one component of a larger empire of spy technology. *Nothing Is Beyond*

Figure I.1 Late nineteenth-century American cartoon of John Bull (England) depicted as an imperial octopus with its tentacles stretching into various regions of the globe. *Wikimedia Commons*

Our Reach tells the full story of the way in which American technophiles unintentionally helped create a global espionage empire. Intelligence agencies planted spies in the sky, spies in the ether, spies underground, spies in the water, and spies in the mind. In fact, the United States had, and has, the entire planet covered with planes, satellites, unmanned aerial vehicles (UAVs), radios, electronics, tunnels, and submarines. It also used codes, and even pharmaceuticals, in the service of espionage. It is no wonder that by 2013 nothing was beyond the reach of the United States.

But this globe-girding technology produced political and social conse-

Figure I.2 Patch for the NROL-39 spy satellite launch of the US National Reconnaissance Office, 2013. *Wikimedia Commons, National Reconnaissance Office*

quences that either damaged US standing in the world or its image abroad. Each time one of America's major technological intelligence operations or ongoing programs was exposed, it created a political backlash, whether it was the revelations about the Berlin Tunnel in 1956, the U-2 spy plane shoot-down in 1962, the navy or satellite secrets sold to the Soviet Union by traitors during the 1970s, the use of armed drones in the so-called Global War on Terror, or the communications and signals intelligence capabilities.

On Empire

The techno-spy empire was, and is, part and parcel of America's empire and an empire unto itself. The notion that America is an empire is less controversial now than it used to be. Even so, because the United States came into existence as a result of an "anticolonial struggle" and espoused freedom and democracy abroad, many Americans do not feel comfortable with the word *empire* or the claim that the United States is an empire.[1] Since the word *colonies* was discarded in favor of *territories* at the beginning of the twentieth century, anything that resembled an empire was either hidden or disparaged publicly. During the early years of territorial expansion, the land controlled by the United States, such as the Philippines, Guam, Puerto Rico, and a slew of other islands, became invisible. America became associated with the so-called logo map—the iconic map of the continental United States alone surrounded by the Atlantic and Pacific Oceans and Canada and Mexico.[2] Because of this and because America never possessed the same landmass as Great Britain's empire, a truly colonial empire, or even the same level of control over the people of another country, the term *empire* was not commonly used. But this soon changed.

Historians and political scientists added qualifiers. Arthur Schlesinger dubbed the United States an "informal empire" because he thought it was not colonial but still possessed the imperial apparatus of empire, like troops, planes, bases, and even American retail shops "spread around the luckless planet." Other commentators dubbed it a "reluctant empire" or an "empire by invitation." More recently, historians like Daniel Immerwahr have brought attention to the hidden empire of the "territories."[3] Although the United States did not mimic the Roman, British, and French Empires in controlling other nations or possessing large overseas landmasses, it had its own unique form of empire, colonizing other countries with American companies and American consumerism, from IBM to McDonald's fast-food chains to cinemas stocked with American movies to military bases. As the empire historian Niall Ferguson writes, Americans lack an "imperial cast of mind. They would rather consume than conquer."[4]

Just as the ubiquitous US military bases constitute "a new form of empire," as Chalmers Johnson suggests,[5] so too did US spy technology—in the sky, under the ocean, in the ether, and underground—constitute a new type of empire, one that was both visible and invisible, one whose defining characteristic was not vast colonial territories. The visible empire dotted the globe with eavesdropping installations, radar stations, antennas, and submarines. The invisible empire substituted technology for territory. With powerful globe-crawling technology or hidden technology like underground cables, the United States did not need the land former empires held to be defined as an empire. It was a technology-spanning empire rather than a territorial one.

The growth of the techno-spy empire chronicled in this book was not necessarily a conscious development by spy agencies until after the terrorist attacks of September 11, 2001. During the early years, intelligence officers did not sit around a table and plot global dominion using spy technology, like Ernst Stavro Blofeld in the James Bond movies. As I show, satellite capabilities were initially targeted at denied areas like the Soviet

Union, despite their global capabilities. But other countries increasingly became the focus of the satellites' gaze. It was a gradual process but then metastasized as threats proliferated.[6] As technological capabilities increased, targets expanded. Often the spy technology tracked with US foreign policy and military interventions. It was only after 9/11 that spy agencies like the National Reconnaissance Office and the National Security Agency (NSA) became consciously global and made grandiose pronouncements about global information dominance.

Technophilic Hubris

During the Cold War, the United States developed an espionage style that reflected its love affair with technology, or technophilia, whereas the Soviet Union and the Eastern Bloc continued the tradition of using humans to collect intelligence. America has a long tradition of "technological enthusiasm," a phrase used by the eminent historian of technology Thomas Hughes.[7] Though Hughes was referring primarily to the era of great inventors like Thomas Edison, and most historians would agree that enthusiasm has turned into a full-blown love affair with technology, a love affair that has often morphed into technophilic hubris and a new religion. In fact, by the Cold War, technology had become a cure-all, a fix for numerous problems. Therefore, it should be no surprise that technological solutions were also applied to the intelligence problem of a closed society. The rise of the military-industrial-academic complex and growing technical capabilities during the 1950s facilitated this development. Because of the propensity of the United States to use technical solutions to solve problems, it developed a dizzying array of technological wonders to serve as mechanical eyes and ears abroad.[8]

Within intelligence circles, a latent debate exists on the relative merits of human and technical intelligence. In the bafflegab of the intelligence community, *hum*an *int*elligence gathering is called HUMINT and *tech*nical *int*elligence gathering is called TECHINT, among a long list of other INTs (from *int*elligence). As should be apparent, the United States favors and favored technical means to collect intelligence more than other countries like the Soviet Union, especially during the Cold War. This doesn't mean that the United States eschewed human intelligence gathering or that the Soviet Union didn't have satellites or eavesdropping capabilities. The United States, for instance, had its share of volunteers and recruits.

It's a tendency. When the Central Intelligence Agency (CIA) was founded in 1947, it was charged with the human clandestine collection of intelligence, but by the early 1950s, it sought technical means of collection. Many early directors of central intelligence, like Allen Dulles and Richard Helms, were not happy with the increased use of technical means, but they were painfully aware that in the 1950s their attempts to plant humans in the closed society of the Soviet Union had failed. It wasn't just that those directors thought humans were a better collection method; Dulles, who relished the old-fashioned cloak-and-dagger world, quipped that technical intelligence took "the fun out of intelligence" while digging deep into the pockets of taxpayers to pay the exorbitant price tag.[9]

The use of technical intelligence and the use of human intelligence shouldn't be seen as an either-or dichotomy. Common sense suggests spy agencies should use both in conducting the collection of information. After all, a tip from a human source can better direct technology to its target, as will become clear in the chapters that follow.

That being said, there was often a cat-and-mouse spy game involving technical and human intelligence between the United States and the Soviet Union. This is one of the themes of this book. In fact, the Soviet cats of human intelligence often caught the US mice of technical intelligence during the Cold War. It became very common for the United States to develop new and expensive technology only to have it betrayed by a Soviet human agent within a year or two.

Instead of dwelling on the debate over the relative merits of human or technical intelligence, this book argues that the emphasis on technical intelligence and America's technophilia had the unintended consequence of catapulting the United States into becoming a global espionage superpower. While both the Soviet Union and the United States dominated the global landscape during the Cold War,[10] it was technical intelligence that expanded the reach of the United States. It was technical intelligence that transformed the national security state into a global security state. And it was the power of technical intelligence that led to the hubris of the motto "Nothing Is beyond Our Reach" emblazoned on an octopus-girdling-the-globe patch for the National Reconnaissance Office satellite launch.[11]

The mind-set that "nothing is beyond our reach" is not limited to the NRO. It permeates the whole intelligence community and the US government. The Snowden archive also contained information about data-mining

Figure I.3 Special Source Operations unit emblem depicting an eagle's claws clutching the cables around the globe. *Vector Images*

programs with names like "Boundless Informant" that echoed the limitless nature of US intelligence's capabilities. In addition to the telling program names, the NSA created emblems featuring a globe and the NSA technology used to cover it. Most striking is the emblem for the Special Source Operations program, responsible for the secret relationship with companies like AT&T and Verizon that contributed to fiber optic capabilities around the world. The emblem depicts an American eagle clutching fiber optic cables that envelop the globe.

For the US intelligence community there are, apparently, no limits. What are the implications of the staggering global capabilities and hubris of the United States? Will American technology be like the artificial wax wings and feathers given to the mythical Icarus so that he could have superhuman capabilities, only to have his wings melt when he flew too close to the sun? Does global technological collection really help?

There was already a backlash when the Snowden documents revealed that the NSA was spying on friends and foes alike, including tapping the German chancellor's phone. But the NSA's activities were only the tip of the iceberg. The newer National Geospatial-Intelligence Agency and the NRO extended those capabilities to add visual surveillance to the NSA's ears.

The militarization of intelligence by means of partnerships between the CIA and the military to create missile-carrying drones caused greater and blowback (to use Chalmers Johnson's word) internationally ;trikes killed innocent people abroad. It will not be surprising ıtional outrage from such events contributes to the decline of Will our technological wings melt like Icarus's by flying too : edge of human decency?

But another aspect of US technological intelligence capabilities has been largely ignored: the question of whether this overwhelming collection of information helps or hinders intelligence efforts. Is bigger better? Will intelligence consumers drown in the tidal wave of information or be able to harness it effectively?

The Organization of This Book

This book tells a three-act story about the ascent of the US intelligence community from its nascent period in the early 1950s using traditional human espionage methods to a behemoth spanning the globe with powerful technology during the post-9/11 war on terror. The first act focuses on the foundations of a technological espionage style developed in the 1950s by highlighting a group of technophiles who had President Dwight D. Eisenhower's ear and who were respected by the CIA. Why was it that a civilian agency like the CIA began to sprout technological wings by developing the U-2 spy plane and spy satellites, technologies that would traditionally belong to the military? The early chapters also showcase several iconic scientific and technological projects like the Berlin Tunnel and the CIA's mind control experiments. While the latter two projects are well known, this book offers a new perspective and unearths new documents to tell the story from the vantage point of the CIA's emerging focus on using science and technology for collecting intelligence information.

The second act opens with the story of the U-2 spy plane and how US intelligence agencies found missiles on Cuba. Traditional accounts of the Cuban Missile Crisis focus on the role of the U-2 spy plane or aerial reconnaissance in finding the missile and the crisis following the discovery. Chapter 4 showcases the role of human spies in discovering the missiles and the time leading up to the crisis. It also reveals the name of the crucial agent who passed on the tip about long-range missiles on Cuba.

As we move into the 1970s, the CIA increased its technological focus and launched projects in the ocean. Stansfield Turner decreased the cadre of human spies in favor of technology at the CIA, an agency tasked with human intelligence gathering. Spy satellites were no longer the exception but the norm. Both the NSA and the NRO continued to expand. These efforts increased America's global coverage.

Even though spy satellites are world-circling machines, during the early years they were primarily used to target so-called denied areas like the Soviet Union and China within the global war between communism and capitalism. It was indeed a surprise to learn that the CIA and the air force did not build spy satellites with the intention of covering the globe. Once those technological capabilities were understood, however, the intelligence community harnessed the capabilities to expand their reach and power.

The third part of the book, or act 3—the most original contribution in terms of uncovering new archival sources as well as its argument—opens with the story of the evolution of the NSA and its global expansion. Because of its historic ties to the British and their Government Communications Headquarters (GCHQ) during World War II, the United States had close ties to British communications intelligence institutions. When the British passed the global espionage torch to the NSA, they remained very active in global operations by trading British territory for American technology. Unlike the United States in the early Cold War, Great Britain retained a colonial outlook and subtly became part of US intelligence operations abroad, especially through the cooperative sharing agreements like the UKUSA, which later morphed into a strong alliance and even consortium, consisting of New Zealand, Australia, Canada, the United Kingdom, and the United States.

The chapter following the NSA story is a bit of a coda because it showcases the newly revealed story of how the CIA and the West German Federal Intelligence Service (BND) bought the Swiss encryption firm Crypto AG and rigged machines destined for countries in the global south in order to read their messages.[12]

While some of the NSA's operations became more widely known because of Snowden's 2013 revelations, two other globe-spanning agencies are lesser known but are the visual complements of the NSA's ears: the global eyes of the NRO and the colossal NGA. The ultra-secret NRO was responsible for building the satellites that hauled in an overwhelming amount of material, while the NGA analyzed the haul. They were equal in importance to the NSA.

The final chapter of the fully global section focuses on drones as part of the global empire and the militarization of intelligence as their surveillance capabilities were transformed into missile-carrying machines used to target terrorists. While satellites offered a panoramic view, drones could hover over the target both for surveillance and for killing.

By the denouement of the story, with the expansion of spy agencies in the post-9/11 era and the new focus on fighting terrorism, US intelligence had become truly global—its machines pulsating the world with spy planes, spy satellites, eavesdropping technology, submarines, and drones. At this point, the surveillance technology took a dark turn, when missiles were attached to drones, turning them into killing machines. Drone bases also began to dot the globe, complementing or adding to the existing US military bases as sources of American power projection abroad.

The conclusion pulls together the various examples from the book to assess the intelligence consequences of the global espionage technology: information overload.

Each part of the book can be read separately, though each chapter builds the story and argument. For example, if a reader wants to jump right into the fully global part of the book without learning about the foundations that led to it, this can easily be done.

Notes

1. Michael Cox, “Still the American Empire,” *Political Studies Review* 5 (2007): 4.

2. Daniel Immerwahr, *How to Hide an Empire: A History of the Greater United States* (New York: Farrar, Straus and Giroux, 2019), 7–8.

3. Arthur M. Schlesinger, *The Cycles of American History* (Boston: Houghton Mifflin, 1999), 141; Arthur Schlesinger Jr., “The American Empire? Not So Fast,” *World Policy Journal* 22, no. 1 (Spring 2005): 43–46; Ruth Oldenziel, “Islands: The United States as a Networked Empire,” in *Entangled Geographies: Empire and Technopolitics in the Global Cold War*, ed. Gabrielle Hecht (Cambridge, MA: MIT Press, 2011), 13–41. For an agnostic analysis comparing America to earlier empires like the Roman Empire, see Charles S. Maier, *Among Empires: American Ascendancy and Its Predecessors* (Cambridge, MA: Harvard University Press, 2006).

4. Niall Ferguson, *Colossus: The Rise and Fall of the American Empire* (New York: Penguin, 2004), 29.

5. Chalmers Johnson, *The Sorrows of Empire: Militarism, Secrecy, and the End of the Republic* (New York: Henry Holt, 2004), 1.

6. I would like to thank my colleague Dan Amsterdam for calling my attention to the metastatic expansion of the technology.

7. Thomas P. Hughes, *American Genesis: A Century of Technological Enthusiasm, 1870–1970* (Chicago: University of Chicago Press, [1989] 2004).

8. See Kristie Macrakis, "Technophilic Hubris and Espionage Styles during the Cold War," *Isis* 10 (2010): 378–85.

9. Memorandum, "Proposed Topics for Unclassified Histories," September 12, 1973, 11, www.cia.gov/library/readingroom/docs/CIA-RDP76B00734R000100070010-3.pdf.

10. See Michael Warner, *The Rise and Fall of Intelligence: An International Security History* (Washington, DC: Georgetown University Press, 2014), 131.

11. See Engelhardt, *Shadow Government*, 10–12.

12. Robert Dover and Richard J. Aldrich, "Cryptography and the Global South: Secrecy, Signals and Information Imperialism," *Third World Quarterly* 41, no. 1 (2020): 1900–1917.

I

FOUNDATIONS

1

THE DAYS OF MATA HARI ARE OVER (AN ORIGIN STORY)

On the moonlit night of September 5, 1949, two Ukrainians squatted in the main body of an unmarked CIA C-47 transport plane ready to jump; each of them had a parachute pack and a small suitcase strapped to his waist. They had received extensive training in Morse code, weaponry, ciphers, and radio operations. During the flight they sang the Ukrainian partisan refrain

> Belt after belt, on into battle
> Ukrainian insurgents never retreat.

The plane had taken off from the US Air Force base in Wiesbaden, West Germany, in the American zone of occupation, and flew east toward western Ukraine. As it approached L'vov (Lviv), Ukraine, the two jumped out, one after another, and parachuted safely into a field near the city.[1] Their goal was to make contact with the Supreme Council for the Liberation of Ukraine and the Ukrainian Insurgent Army. The CIA never found out if they met with anyone from the Ukrainian resistance movement; the team never contacted their CIA handlers in West Germany using clandestine radios as instructed. The CIA history on the Ukrainian nationalist allies reported laconically, "The Soviets quickly eliminated the agents."[2]

But instead of halting plans because of the deaths, the operation sparked considerable interest at headquarters and even led to a joint program with the British, who were also parachuting agents into Soviet territory.

The CIA had high hopes for the Ukrainian nationalists, although many of them had unsavory pasts and had collaborated with Nazi Germany during World War II. The agency also sent agents to Lithuania in the same unmarked C-47 and had plans for six or more drops a year. The Ukrainian jump marked the beginning of the CIA's attempt to send Russian émigrés equipped with radios behind enemy lines in order to have eyes and ears behind the Iron Curtain. The CIA desperately sought early warning of a surprise Soviet military attack.

After the first failed mission, the CIA sent dozens of Ukrainian agents into Ukraine by air or land. Most of them were captured and killed. If the agents stayed alive, the KGB usually turned them to work as double agents feeding back disinformation. Between 1949 and 1954, when the program ended, the CIA, Great Britain's MI6, and the West German Gehlen Organization parachuted about 150 agents into Ukraine, Belorussia, and Moldavia.[3]

Harry Rositzke, a spy, linguist, author, and cattle farmer, knew a lot about the Ukrainian operations. In fact, he ran the parachute jumps from 1949 to 1954. Born in 1911 as Heinrich August Rositzke in Brooklyn, New York, to German immigrants, he was typical of the scholar-turned-spy generation that joined the Office of Strategic Services (OSS) during the war. After earning a PhD at Harvard in German philology, he started teaching and wrote on the arcane subject of Anglo-Saxon grammar and vowel duration in High German, only to abandon that career for the life of a spy in the OSS. Like others in the OSS, he joined the CIA when it was founded; he then became the first Soviet Division chief.

He later told the *Washington Post*, "We were sending people into the Ukraine—people forget there was an active resistance movement there. . . . We'd fly them in and parachute them from C-47's." "We never lost a plane," he added, without mentioning they had lost a lot of human lives.[4]

After Rositzke retired from the CIA, he started to tend the 350 acres he had bought in the Virginia countryside. He also penned five books about the CIA and the KGB. According to Rositzke, the Department of Defense was the actual player of the CIA marionette. The "Department of Defense dictated almost exclusively" the "CIA's intelligence targets" for fifteen years after World War II. In fact, during the first five years, "the CIA operated almost solely as an instrument of the Department of Defense." Their first request in 1948 was for the CIA to send agents into Eastern Europe to ferret out any inklings of a Soviet invasion of Western Europe.

During a heated Pentagon conference session, "an Army colonel" banged "his fist on the table" and shouted, "I want an agent with a radio on every goddamn airfield between Berlin and the Urals."[5]

The task was not an easy one. Agents could not simply walk across the border into the Soviet Bloc. CIA chroniclers referred to the closed Soviet society as a "denied area": journalists, Western diplomats, tourists, and even foreign Communists were not allowed into the country. The CIA could not use such people to take photographs, conduct visual observations, or talk to citizens.[6] As result, Western intelligence agencies had to resort to sneaking in agents by air, land, and sea.

The Ukrainian nationalists who died after the parachute jump had escaped to the West from their Carpathian mountain hideaway about a year before the failed mission. The Ukrainian resistance movement leadership had sent them to the West to find American support and to promote their cause against the Soviet reoccupation of Ukraine.[7]

Mykola Lebed, a balding and serious-looking man and a "fervent" nationalist, was the key Ukrainian leader of the liberation movement who aided the CIA in its effort to recruit from Ukrainian émigrés. He served as the group's foreign minister while based in Munich and provided the CIA with Ukrainian partisans for CIA-sponsored "missions against Moscow."[8] But there was one problem.

Lebed was a war criminal who had killed Ukrainians, Poles, and Jews during World War II. He also took part in the assassination of the Polish minister of the interior in 1934, for which he had gone to prison only to escape five years later when Germany attacked Poland. But the CIA brought him to America because he was "rendering valuable assistance" in Europe, according to the head of the CIA's Office of Special Operations, Willard G. Wyman. The CIA initially smuggled him into the country under an assumed identity. After a few years, agency officials brought him in legally under a clause in the Central Intelligence Agency Act of 1949 that allowed it to bring in one hundred foreigners a year "in the name of national security," bypassing immigration laws.[9]

Lebed was just one of hundreds of émigrés or refugees with unsavory pasts; many of them had collaborated with the Nazis or were Nazi war criminals. It was a devil's pact, but the CIA needed sources and the Ukrainian nationalists, with their fervent hatred of the Soviet Union and paramilitary experience, were prime recruiting ground.

Both the British and the Americans attempted to enter the Soviet Union and its satellite states by air, land, and sea, sending partisans and émigrés by parachute drops, with fake papers, or on submarines or E-boats (a fast-attack German World War II boat). And both the CIA and the British Secret Intelligence Service (SIS) used former Nazis or Nazi collaborators to do so. Favorite target countries were the Baltic states of Estonia, Latvia, and Lithuania for sea operations; Albania for overland ones; and Ukraine for parachute agents. The operations extended from the northern Baltic states to the Turkish frontier in the south.[10]

Ultimately, the Ukrainian parachuting operation was seen as a major failure, along with all the other American and British efforts. The 1998 CIA history of the Ukrainian episode, which was declassified in 2005, concluded, "In the long run, the Agency's efforts to penetrate the Iron Curtain using Ukrainian agents was ill-fated and tragic."[11] Hundreds of lives were lost. The CIA director asked the US Army general Lucian Truscott to fly to Europe to report on the parachute operation; he was not impressed. During a meeting with a local CIA chief, his aide quipped, "The only thing you're proving is the law of gravity."[12]

At first, the explanation for the agent penetration failure was the Soviet Union's suffocating security system. A 1955 report to the president is typical in the way it describes the scene in the Soviet Union and other Soviet Bloc countries: "The security zones at the border, the general restrictions in the interior, the thousands of security police, and the innumerable informers among the population are brutally effective in limiting the infiltration, exfiltration, and usefulness of agents."[13]

Recently declassified materials from Eastern Bloc and Soviet archives document in telling detail the nature of the counterintelligence operations against the British and American Ukrainian operations. In an operation code-named Spiders, the Polish Secret Service collaborated with the Soviet security services in wide-ranging deception operations against the West. While Western intelligence thought the Ukrainian underground resistance movements were under their control, in fact, the Poles and Soviets created fictitious underground organizations to dangle in front of Western intelligence. The Eastern Bloc successfully lured agents into many traps. The files also document what the CIA feared: many agents were killed or turned to work for the other side.[14]

The scale of Soviet operations against the Organization of Ukrainian Nationalists (OUN) was even larger than the Americans imagined. By January 1947 the Ministry of State Security (MGB, later called the KGB) had

"680 residents, 1,920 agents, and 15,345 informants" in western Ukraine alone.[15]

Hunting and killing Ukrainian nationalists crossed borders. By the late 1950s, when these nationalists had become agents for Western intelligence agencies, the KGB started assassinating them. Stepan Bandera, considered the most important Ukrainian nationalist by the CIA, was found dead on the steps of his Munich apartment building on October 15, 1959. Surprisingly, the assassin, Bogdan Stashinsky, confessed to the CIA because he decided to defect after he suspected that the KGB wanted to kill him since it thought assassins were too dangerous to keep alive. At first, the CIA doubted his story because of inconsistencies in his description of the hit, which involved a gun that shot poisonous material into the suspect's face, emitting a vapor that would kill the target without leaving a trace. But after corroborating information from other defectors, they believed him. To Stashinsky, the hit wasn't a murder but rather the patriotic duty of someone employed by the state. The German state thought otherwise at its trial.[16]

But the CIA would soon find out that it was not just the Soviet security state that doomed their agent operations. The Soviet Union had a much more powerful secret weapon in its seasoned human intelligence apparatus: a mole in the United Kingdom, Harold Adrian Russell "Kim" Philby, who was a high-ranking official in the SIS. Philby was just one of hundreds of British and American agents the KGB had recruited in the West but one of the few who worked for British intelligence.

Philby obtained most of his information from James Jesus Angleton, the CIA's chief counterintelligence man. Philby had met Angleton in London when he traveled there to learn about intelligence from the more experienced British. Soon after cultivating Angleton in his home country, Philby received a post as the British liaison to American intelligence in Washington, DC, from 1940 to 1951. During Philby's time in Washington, the two met once a week for boozy lunches at Harvey's on Connecticut Avenue, the most famous and exclusive restaurant in the capital. They also talked on the phone every other day.

They started their lunches with bourbon on the rocks, progressed to lobster and wine, and ended with brandy and a cigar. Once tipsy, Angleton, peering through his heavy, black-framed glasses, and Philby, the ebullient bon vivant, pumped each other for information. Both dutifully reported on their meetings to their respective masters, the CIA and MI6.

But Philby also penned reports to the KGB about operations, which it quickly sabotaged. And while Philby cultivated many friendships, Angleton had few close friends, and Philby was one of them.[17]

Their discussions about intelligence were wide-ranging, but the various covert operations against the Soviet Union were at the top of the list since they were ongoing. Philby even tried to persuade the CIA to take over the British Ukrainian network. He also recommended that the State Department take over other émigré groups because of his service's lack of funds.[18]

Aside from the blown Ukrainian parachute operation, Philby was heavily involved in an Albanian operation involving émigrés. After describing a joint CIA-SIS parachute drop in Cyprus, for which he had "precise information about the timing and geographical co-ordinates of their operations," he cryptically commented, "I do not know what happened to the parties concerned. But I can make an informed guess."[19]

The CIA's collaboration with former Nazis was not limited to individuals. Leaders at the CIA created and collaborated with the predecessor to the West German Federal Intelligence Service (Bundesnachrichtendienst [BND]), the Gehlen Organization, led by Reinhard Gehlen, a former head of the Nazis' Foreign Army East, which worked against the Soviet Union. Gehlen's expertise on the Soviet Union, and the wartime files about it he secreted in a cave, made him very attractive to the CIA. Philby also learned about the CIA's takeover of the anti-Soviet section of the German army and reported in his memoirs, "Many of Harvey's lobsters went to provoke Angleton into defending, with chapter and verse, the past record and current activities of the von Gehlen organization."[20]

Even if Angleton defended the Gehlen Organization, many at the CIA felt ambivalent about it, and later some officers claimed "revulsion" over working with "personnel with known Nazi records." Others felt that "American intelligence is a rich blind man using the Abwehr as a seeing-eye dog." In 1949, the same year the parachute operations launched, the CIA took over the Gehlen group.[21] But later, with the arrest of Heinz Felfe in 1961, the CIA learned that the Gehlen Organization had been riddled with Soviet moles and double agents.

By October 27, 1952, a joint US-UK "Murder Board" had been set up to kill off the most unsuccessful covert operations. The "jury" consisted of twenty-six senior officers. They concluded, "Our operations have failed and there is no alternative to offer."[22]

As a result of their admission of failure, the CIA halted its agent penetration operations against the Soviet Union and its satellite states by 1954. Allen Dulles, the avuncular pipe-smoking OSS chief, who became director of Central Intelligence (DCI) in 1953, commented that "the possibility of recruiting and running any such sources was as improbable as placing resident spies on the planet Mars."[23]

The Technophiles Go to Washington, DC

As the CIA was closing down its attempts to penetrate the Soviet Union using secret agents, President Dwight D. Eisenhower was obsessing over a possible future surprise nuclear attack. He was already knowledgeable about intelligence because of his World War II experience as the Supreme Allied Commander in Europe and valued both SIGINT and photographs taken from aerial reconnaissance. He learned about Ultra, the British term for their success at breaking the German Enigma machine code, firsthand from Winston Churchill. And while he knew about the value of aerial reconnaissance from his experience with the US military, he recalled after the war that he did not realize "what a science it had become" until after visiting the British Air Ministry's Photographic Interpretation Unit, which was mainly staffed with women because the men thought women possessed a greater capacity for detail work ("a group of girls," noted Eisenhower).[24]

One of Eisenhower's favorite wartime intelligence stories was about FORTITUDE, an Allied web of deception woven to fool the Germans into thinking the Allies were going to land in Pas-de-Calais instead of Normandy. Recalling the event to his biographer, Stephen Ambrose, long after the war, he would look up to the sky and frown, then flash his trademark grin, slap his thigh, and exclaim, "By God, we really fooled them, didn't we!"[25]

Although Eisenhower could laugh at the Allies' surprise attack in Normandy, he was shocked by the Japanese surprise attack at Pearl Harbor for many years. He was "haunted" by the fear of another "devastating surprise attack" against the United States.[26]

His first step in examining the state of human intelligence was to ask World War II combat hero and retired US Air Force lieutenant general "Jimmy" Doolittle to investigate the CIA and report back to him.[27] Doolittle chaired a panel to examine the CIA's covert action and intelligence activities and to provide recommendations on improving US intelligence. The resulting Doolittle Report acknowledged that US intelligence was still in its infancy, but the panel members worried about the resulting shortfall of information from "an implacable enemy whose avowed objective is world domination." The committee found that the information obtained by parachuting agents into the denied territories was "negligible and the cost in effort, dollars and human lives prohibitive." Like others, they referred to the "tight security controls" in the Soviet Union and its satellite states that made "the problem of infiltration by human agents . . . extremely difficult." This led them to the "conviction that much more effort should be expended in exploring every possible scientific and technical avenue of approach to the intelligence problem." Specifically, Doolittle and his committee recommended an all-encompassing scientific-technical approach using "communications and electronic surveillance, high altitude visual, photographic and radar reconnaissance with manned or unmanned vehicles, upper atmosphere and oceanographic studies, physical and chemical research etc."[28]

Despite the CIA's failings, Eisenhower decided to keep Allen Dulles, who admitted there were shortcomings in Soviet collection and that the CIA had no important agent networks on the ground in Russia. To solve this problem, Dulles, with the support of his brother, Foster Dulles, and the president, took steps to open the CIA's first Moscow Station.

The first head of station, Edward Ellis Smith, arrived in Moscow in spring 1954. To support his cover, he resigned from the CIA and became an official employee of the State Department's Office of Security. Smith, a thirty-four-year-old divorcé, was also a failure. He slept with his maid, who turned out to be a KGB colonel. The KGB filmed the couple in action and then tried to blackmail Smith; as a result, he decided to tell the ambassador to Russia, Charles Bohlen. When the ambassador returned to Washington, DC, in spring 1956 he went golfing with President Eisenhower and complained that the "CIA placed a man in my embassy without telling me, and he got involved with a Russian girl and they took pictures of them in the nude." Smith left Moscow in July 1956. But he was not the only one who had been seduced by KGB swallows and blackmailed with sex photographs; twelve embassy personnel confessed to Bohlen that they had also been victims of KGB-sponsored seduction.[29]

The Doolittle panel was just one committee among a blizzard of government-convened groups that recommended using science and technology in intelligence since efforts at human intelligence had faltered. But around the same time that Eisenhower asked for a review of US intelligence, he had become deeply concerned about Soviet technological capabilities.

Eisenhower's fear of surprise attack increased in spring 1953 when a US military attaché observed a new Soviet intercontinental bomber, the Bison, a jet engine plane like the US B-52 bomber, at Ramenskoye, south of Moscow. The Bison was also on display at the 1954 air show in Moscow. This stunned the intelligence community and Eisenhower, who wanted to know the size of the fleet. After the air show the Bison bomber made headlines in the United States, and the American public also became concerned about Soviet military might.[30]

Eisenhower was not the only one concerned about a surprise military attack. It was actually Trevor N. Gardner, a special assistant to the secretary of the air force, who prodded the Eisenhower administration into action. Gardner, an engineer and Welshman who immigrated to California as a child, was only thirty-nine in 1954 and an "evangelical champion of new technologies." Three-star generals put up with this brash, well-tailored young man who advocated for more missile development, even if they called him a "bastard" and "son-of-a-bitch" in the hallways at the Pentagon.[31]

Gardner had become alarmed when a RAND Corporation report declared that a Soviet surprise attack could destroy 85 percent of the Strategic Air Command's (SAC's) bombers. With a "cocktail in hand," he told Lee DuBridge, head of the Defense Scientific Advisory Board, that his panel was a waste of time and that the committee sat on their "dead asses in fancy offices in Washington" squandering taxpayers' dollars "going through a lot of goddamn motions on a lot of low-level shitty exercises—all in the name of science." He told DuBridge the committee should conduct a study on surprise attack and America's ability to meet it. He thought that was "the true story, not" the "shit Washington" was "feeding the American people."[32]

The members of the Defense Scientific Advisory Board traveled to see Eisenhower at the White House in March 1954. DuBridge then suggested that Eisenhower should invite one of the most prominent members of his committee, MIT president James R. Killian, to the White House for breakfast to ask him to chair a secret committee on technological, military, and intelligence methods to prevent a surprise attack.[33]

Killian was no stranger to Eisenhower. The two had met when Ike was president of Columbia University (1948–53) and became close friends. Killian even attended two "intimate stag dinners at the White House." Eisenhower liked and had complete confidence in the "genial South Carolinian," who had a "cherubic countenance" and was "as disarmingly pleasant as a successful hotel manager," according to a 1957 *New York Times* profile written when Killian became America's first science adviser to the president. The political journalist Theodore H. White later characterized Killian as "a brisk, incisive man with the manner and dispatch of a brilliant surgeon" when he entered the Washington, DC, scene in the 1950s.[34]

It was not surprising, therefore, that Eisenhower chose Killian to organize leading scientists and engineers to formulate ways to keep the United States competitive in innovative technology. Killian formed three big groups consisting of forty-two scientists to look into offensive technology, defensive technology, and intelligence. The committee became known as the "Surprise Attack Panel" because its final report was titled "Meeting the Threat of Surprise Attack," but its official name was the Technological Capabilities Panel (TCP).

Also formed in 1954, it echoed the Doolittle recommendation (Doolittle was also on the TCP): "We obtain little significant information from classical covert operations inside Russia. . . . The scale of the Soviet security and control activity is enormous. We cannot hope to circumvent these elaborate measures in an easy way. But we can use the ultimate in science and technology to improve our intelligence take."[35]

While a retired air force general led the Doolittle panel, a science administrator and MIT president led the Surprise Attack Panel. Killian was not a scientist; he majored in business and engineering administration at MIT and became managing editor of the MIT-published *Technology Review* in 1930. Karl T. Compton, who was MIT's president at that time, recruited Killian to become his executive assistant, and Killian rose through the ranks at Compton's side while assisting in organizing MIT's wartime research. He then succeeded Compton as president in 1949 and served until 1959.[36]

Killian contacted a close friend, neighbor, and colleague from Cambridge, Edwin "Din" C. Land, best known as the president of the Polaroid Corporation, and a millionaire and inventor, to head the ultra-secret intelligence section. Although he was often seen in public as a showman for the Polaroid Instant Camera, Land usually retreated into the lab for days at a time and was good at keeping secrets. The public did not know of his classified government work until others reported on it many years later. Killian considered him an "authentic genius" whose "eloquence and lucid exposition incited" presidents' imaginations. At the time, the forty-five-year-old Land was in Hollywood, California, providing advice to Alfred Hitchcock on three-dimensional technology for movies. He quickly dropped that project and traveled back to the East Coast to serve as chair of the intelligence section of the technology panel. Land also became one of the most influential members of the Surprise Attack Panel and an evangelist for science and technology at the CIA.[37]

Since Land did not like big committees and thought any such group should be able to fit into a taxicab, his was the smallest of the three subcommittees. It consisted of six people, including Harvard's James G. Baker, a leading designer of aerial lenses; the Nobel Prize–winning physicist Edward Purcell, also from Harvard; and Allen Latham Jr., an engineer from Arthur D. Little and a former treasurer of the Polaroid Corporation. In preparation for the report, Land and his committee visited Washington, DC, for numerous briefings, field trips, and conferences with every major US defense and intelligence organization. According to Richard L. Garwin, a physicist colleague, "for their frequent trips around Washington in radio-dispatched CIA automobiles, the panelists were prudently assigned code names."[38]

The panel was not impressed with the Central Intelligence Agency. Land commented later, "We would go in and interview generals and admirals in charge of intelligence and come away worried. Here we were, five or six young men, asking questions that the high-ranking officers couldn't answer."[39]

The Killian committee recommended adopting "a vigorous program for the extensive use, in many intelligence procedures, of the most advanced knowledge in science and technology," using techniques from the physical and biological sciences. This approach, they thought, might expand a "very limited core of hard facts" about Soviet capabilities and intentions.[40]

Specifically, the intelligence group made two recommendations: build a high-flying airplane, later dubbed the U-2, to photograph the Soviet Union and develop a missile-firing submarine, later called the Polaris. These reports were so secret that they were not included in the general TCP intelligence section report but rather were sent directly to the appropriate offices and shredded later.[41]

When Killian and Land met with Eisenhower to make their recommendations, Land "told the President we were confident this aircraft could and would find and photograph the Soviet Union's Bison bomber fleet." Eisenhower approved the U-2 but "stipulated that it should be handled in an unconventional way so that it would not become entangled in the bureaucracy of the Defense Department or troubled by rivalries among the services."[42]

It was indeed an unusual arrangement, as photoreconnaissance had always been the bailiwick of the military and such flights usually took place only during wartime. By the early 1950s, the air force and navy had been conducting peripheral reconnaissance, but like the parachute program, the reconnaissance flights were unsuccessful, and many servicemen died. As a result, the air force began to do research on building planes that could fly at a higher altitude in order to evade Russian radar.[43]

But Eisenhower and his scientific advisers worried that an air force high-altitude plane could lead to war. Alternatively, Eisenhower's scientific advisers, led by Edwin Land, came up with the idea of having the CIA sponsor a nonmilitary airplane with the support of the air force. Of course, the air force was not happy ceding the lead to the CIA and tried to wrestle the plane away from the CIA. Eisenhower had to intervene in this quarrel. He made his position clear: "I want this whole thing to be a civilian operation. If uniformed personnel of the armed forces of the United States fly over Russia, it is an act of war—legally—and I don't want any part of it."[44]

The U-2 spy plane had already been rejected by the air force when Clarence "Kelly" Johnson, an engineer and designer for Lockheed, shopped it around as the CL-282, in essence a glider with an engine. Although it could fly higher than any plane the air force had designed, it had just one engine and limited landing gear. Gen. Curtis E. LeMay from SAC took a cigar out of his mouth at a briefing and told the group that if he wanted high-altitude photographs, he would put cameras on his B-36 bombers: "He was not interested in a plane that had no wheels or guns." He left the room and said it was a waste of time.[45]

Despite the air force's pooh-poohing of the unusual design, Trevor Gardner and Edwin Land liked the idea, as did other civilians. Gardner thought the plane was most suitable for the Soviet target and for strategic intelligence.[46]

This was not the first time Land, James Baker, and Edward Purcell advocated for aerial reconnaissance. They had already been advising the air force on aerial reconnaissance since early 1952. Their offices were located on Beacon Hill in Boston over a secretarial school, and that is where they produced the landmark Beacon Hill report on air force aerial reconnaissance.[47]

Meanwhile Gardner had approached the CIA about the unique aerial reconnaissance plane. Allen Dulles was initially skeptical of technological espionage because he favored the old-fashioned kind, which depended on agents, not technology. He also did not want to get involved with projects belonging to the military.

Land would have to persuade Dulles to support the plane; he underlined again the way in which science and technology could enhance intelligence collection. He thought there were many reasons the CIA, with the "appropriate assistance of the Air Force," was the right place for overflights. The committee thought it was the "kind of action and technique that is right for the contemporary version of CIA; a modern and scientific way for an Agency that is always supposed to be looking. . . . [W]e feel that you must always assert your first right to pioneer in scientific techniques for collecting intelligence—and choosing such partners to assist you as may be needed."[48]

After Dulles approved the president-endorsed project, he appointed Richard M. Bissell, the CIA's deputy director of plans, to serve as manager of the U-2 project. Bissell, whom Killian knew from his time as an MIT economics professor, was a respected economist who wore trademark horn-rimmed glasses. He did not know anything about airplanes, but he did know how to create a super-secret government bureaucracy to shield the U-2 program from public scrutiny. He was also a "leading advocate of technical rather than human means of intelligence collection," a predilection that came after he penned a study in 1953 and concluded that very little could be done against the Soviet Union using secret agents to prevent future uprisings like the 1953 East Berlin revolt.[49]

Bissell was actually more than just an advocate of technology; he disdained traditional espionage using spies and battled with intelligence leaders and officers in the agency who thought the job of the CIA was to use humans to gather intelligence. Later he became an enemy of Richard Helms, DCI from 1966 to 1973. As Tim Weiner notes, "They personified the battle between spies and gadgets" that began with the launch of the U-2 spy plane.[50]

Bissell and Land were not the only ones advocating for technology.

William Baker, president of Bell Labs, was also active on a variety of presidential advisory boards. He served on the President's Foreign Intelligence Advisory Board (PFIAB) for thirty years, until 1990, an unprecedented tenure. During this time, he "campaigned with single-minded determination" to make sure that American technology was at the forefront, especially in the fields of satellite and electronic technology, as Cliff Clifford, an adviser to four Democratic presidents, noted in his memoirs, *Counsel to the President.* He describes how Land and Baker gave him a "graduate course in modern technology" and introduced him to the "brave new world of modern technology." In short, the "tutelage of Drs. Baker and Land turned us all into missionaries for intelligence collection by 'technical means'": that is, electronic, photographic, and satellite espionage.[51]

In fact, it was Baker's and Land's missionary zeal to promote science and technology in espionage that animated Eisenhower to change the course of US intelligence by shifting the emphasis to technology. Eisenhower is often touted as the president who advocated and supported the new technological espionage, but it was really his scientific advisers who whispered in his ear. As the story of the U-2 spy plane shows, Eisenhower began to have doubts about the new technology.

Eisenhower's Soul-Searching

Although Eisenhower had become enthusiastic about the U-2 spy plane after Land's frequent White House visits, he continued to have deep reservations about reconnaissance over the Soviet Union because he thought it could start a war. This led him to propose the "Open Skies" initiative to Khrushchev at the Geneva summit conference in summer 1955 while the U-2 was still under construction. The proposal would allow each side to provide airfields and to conduct aerial photography in the United States and the Soviet Union. Unsurprisingly, Khrushchev rejected the proposal. But while it was under consideration, Eisenhower told his advisers, "I'll give it one shot. Then if they don't accept it, we'll fly the U-2."[52]

By early 1956, as the U-2 spy plane was undergoing final safety tests for deployment, Richard Bissell was cooking up a cover story in case the plane was detected or shot down on an overseas mission. Bissell decided that the most plausible cover story was that the plane was conducting high-altitude weather research for the National Advisory Committee on Aeronautics

(NACA) (precursor to NASA). After obtaining their approval, along with the approval of a long list of other governmental agencies, the plane was almost ready to fly to Europe.[53]

Meanwhile, Eisenhower's anxiety about the U-2 increased as the launch date approached. To mollify these concerns, the CIA assured him that Soviet radar would not be able to detect the plane, and even if it did, the Soviet fighter planes could not fly higher than 55,000 feet and would not be able to attack the U-2 spy plane at 72,000 feet. The CIA also assured him that in the unlikely event a plane crashed or was shot down, the "pilot would not survive" and the "plane would disintegrate."[54]

But the president understood the urgent need for intelligence on the Soviet Union's military capacity. There had been an increase in Bison bomber sightings, and there was national anxiety about the Soviet Union surpassing the United States in guided missile development. On June 21, 1956, Eisenhower met with Bissell, Killian, and Land and approved a ten-day overflight schedule in the Soviet Union starting in July. But the CIA had already initiated U-2 flights over East Germany and Poland in June.[55]

As soon as Dulles briefed Eisenhower on the first U-2 flights over Eastern Europe he asked whether radar had tracked the planes. Although radar did track the planes, it picked them up at only 42,000 feet, not at 72,000 feet. It still was not clear how well the Soviets could track high-altitude planes over the Soviet Union when the first flight left Wiesbaden on July 4, 1956.[56]

Eisenhower wanted to know how the July flight went. He told Andrew J. Goodpaster, his staff secretary responsible for intelligence matters, "to advise Mr. Allen Dulles that if we obtain any information or warning that any of these flights has been discovered or tracked, the operation should be suspended."[57] Eisenhower's worst fears were realized when the Soviet Union handed a protest note about these intelligence flights over the Soviet Union to the US embassy in Moscow. As soon as Eisenhower read the note, he asked Goodpaster to call Bissell to stop all U-2 overflights until approval was granted again.[58]

Eisenhower was very disappointed in the CIA because they told him that the flights would not be tracked or detected. After Dulles discussed deploying U-2s in the Far East, Eisenhower told him he had "lost enthusiasm" for the U-2 missions. He pointed out that if the Soviet Union flew a reconnaissance aircraft over the United States "the reaction would be drastic": it would be shot down. And if Americans learned about these flights over the Soviet Union, they would be shocked because the United States had violated international law.[59]

By fall 1956 Eisenhower had become "discouraged" that most if not all of the U-2 flights had been tracked. The CIA had not considered "world opinion," although great efforts had been made to show that the United States was "not truculent" and did not want war.[60]

Eisenhower's concerns about the U-2 flights continued, and by the end of 1958 he expressed his doubts about the continuation of the U-2 overflights to his Board of Consultants on Foreign Intelligence. He questioned whether the intelligence gathered was "worth the exacerbation of international tensions." In Eisenhower's mind the "detection of surprise attack is the important thing." The U-2, he thought, did not "solve the problem of detection of surprise attack."[61]

The intelligence board disagreed and continued to push for overhead reconnaissance, this time with satellites. They were at loggerheads with the president, who said this was one of the "most 'soul-searching' questions to come before a president." General Hull tried to appease Eisenhower and highlight the merits of the program by noting that U-2 photography had discovered that the feared Bison bomber plane was not being produced in the quantities originally thought, which saved money that would have gone to building more US bombers to close the gap. Even so, approving the flights over the Soviet Union that could cause war and damage his reputation for "honesty" were "agonizing" decisions for Eisenhower.[62]

The Corona Spy Satellite

The U-2 spy plane was not the first proposal for overhead reconnaissance during the early years of the Cold War. The US Air Force, Army, and Navy had long been interested in the possibility of unmanned satellites. As early as 1946, RAND produced a report, "Preliminary Design of an Experimental World-Circling Spaceship." By the early 1950s, Richard Leghorn, "a compact, dashing man with dark hair and a mustache" and Boston native and MIT-trained physicist, became a strong advocate for the strategic use of satellite reconnaissance. He had served in World War II as an aerial tactical reconnaissance pilot. Leghorn thought, just as the United States had monitored the enemy's military installations during the war, reconnaissance of the Soviet Union's installations could prevent a nuclear war.

Once an atomic attack was already launched, there was very little one could do, but with prior knowledge it would be easier to prepare. Leghorn also thought the shooting down of a reconnaissance airplane was an act of war and therefore promoted working on a device that would fly so high it could not be shot down.[63]

It should be remembered that there was a pronounced climate of fear surrounding a surprise nuclear attack during the mid-1950s. Half of all American adults apparently felt that they were more likely to die in a Soviet nuclear attack than from diseases caused by old age, according to a poll. People even began to dig fallout shelters in their backyards stocked with Geiger counters and oxygen tanks.[64]

While the military conducted early work on a satellite called WS-117 L ("WS" stood for "Weapons System"), high-altitude balloon reconnaissance was being used and produced much of the technology that was later used in overhead reconnaissance. Despite early interest and small steps, satellite reconnaissance did not take off until it received a major stimulus from the Soviet Union.

On October 4, 1957, the Soviet Union launched Sputnik, an earth satellite, into space; this technological achievement stunned the American public and the press. Recently released top-secret CIA files, however, reveal that the CIA and the US policy community were not surprised and already knew of the Sputnik research. Even so, this event pushed the US government into a frenzy of action. President Eisenhower ordered intensive research on space satellites and asked the military to spin off part of the weapons system satellite into a reconnaissance satellite. By early 1958 Eisenhower made a US reconnaissance satellite a "national security objective of the highest order." Again, he asked the CIA to partner with the air force.[65]

Like the U-2 spy plane project, the CIA and the air force orchestrated a huge cooperative project between the government and industry. While the CIA did not work on the actual building of the satellite, Bissell hired ITEK to work on the camera component, and the final photographic product was analyzed by the photointerpretation center headed by Arthur Lundahl.[66] The project's code name was Corona, but the public knew it as the US Air Force's Discoverer program.

In August 1960, after thirteen failed attempts, the Corona spy satellite launched into the sky; it was the first successful flight. It was good timing because the Soviet Union had shot down Gary Powers's U-2 spy plane in May. Satellite imagery of missile launch sites and military installations quickly replaced photographs from the U-2.

The CIA saw the U-2 spy plane and the Corona reconnaissance satellite as a "triumph of American ingenuity and technology." It was seen as the "Cold War equivalent of the Manhattan Project."[67] In fact, it became very common to refer to any proposed large-scale and expensive technical intelligence project as a Manhattan Project for national security. Just as the US government had turned to scientists and engineers to build a bomb to fight in World War II, so did the government turn to science and technology during the early Cold War to fight the intelligence battle against the Soviet Union.

Bissell proclaimed that both technical projects—the U-2 spy plane and spy satellites—produced "a revolution in intelligence collection."[68] The CIA and other intelligence agencies now had the capability to collect more information in a day than an army of spies would collect in a decade. The amount of information collected, of course, strained the ability of any human to analyze it; analysts were deluged with data. As a result, powerful computers were built later to sift through and sort the material.

It also became common to invoke the death of Mata Hari, who epitomized human intelligence, while proselytizing for the shift to technical intelligence. Arthur Lundahl referred to aerial reconnaissance and photography as the "Mata Hari with glass eyes" in his historical overview of aerial photography. He also proclaimed, "We had gone from Mata Hari to the U-2 and we were in the space age, and the results were coming in as we watched."[69]

George Kistiakowsky, Killian's successor as the president's science adviser and a physical chemist who worked on the Manhattan Project, referred to the CIA's efforts to recruit and handle agents in this way: "[It] . . . was a total failure. They were usually intercepted and liquidated. And the defectors, who came over by the thousands, were a decidedly mixed bag. Generally, it was pitiful. It was clear that the time of Mata Hari had passed."[70]

Some version of the phrase "Mata Hari with glass eyes" seems to have been coursing around military circles at least since World War II as aerial reconnaissance apparently supplied about "80% of military information" from which military strategy was decided, according to Lt. Derryfield N. Smith, an army air corps intelligence officer, who penned an article for the *Air Forces Newsletter* titled "Mata Hari with a Glass Eye," published in 1941. Lundahl's reference should not be surprising as he had served in World War II and focused on aerial reconnaissance. But it is astonishing to see that Smith's use of the phrase predated Lundahl's. Did Lundahl steal it from Derryfield, or was it just a phrase he heard in the community?

In any case, Derryfield was more pessimistic about the advent of this new technology, a "one-eyed Mata Hari," and thought it led to unemployment for human spies. The cartoon at the beginning of the article, which is available online, depicts a disheveled man with a beard holding a sign that reads, "Unemployed~~~~1st Class Spy." But he also saw the merits of an aerial camera: "Without passport, false whiskers or invisible ink, the aerial camera . . . can make an instantaneous record" of a single area in one picture that led to many victories.[71]

The Sputnik launch also created great concern about the quality of US technology, in particular, the state of the US ballistic missile program, among scientists and the public. One of the CIA's scientific consultant panels proclaimed the United States was in "a period of grave national emergency." The panel, which included George Kistiakowsky, thought that US ballistic missile research lagged behind that of the Soviet Union by two to three years. They advocated for interweaving "guided missile intelligence" with US research and development. The panel told Allen Dulles that "the technical competence of CIA should be expanded without delay" and that the CIA should make "direct connections with US missile contractors."[72] This move was just one more step in technologizing the CIA.

And this is the story of how the CIA, a civilian agency whose emphasis at first had been on the collection of intelligence using human spies, had become involved in technical collection projects usually housed in military intelligence agencies. By 1960, it had become clear that overhead reconnaissance needed its own institutional structure. The National Reconnaissance Office opened in 1961, the first step in the US trajectory toward becoming a global espionage power. And by the time armed drone technology emerged in the 2000s, the CIA could launch missiles from an unmanned aerial vehicle from its Langley, Virginia, headquarters that could hit targets in Afghanistan, halfway across the world.

Launching an Eavesdropping Empire

While the CIA did not seem like the appropriate place to house technical reconnaissance intelligence, it was not surprising when President Harry

S. Truman approved the creation of the National Security Agency in 1952. The US Army and Navy had already developed strong signals capabilities during World War II, and in their place the United States had created the Army Security Agency in 1946. This is what morphed into the NSA, a hybrid military-civilian institution.[73]

Signals intelligence had long been a successful way to collect intelligence. The British, in particular, had successfully used SIGINT to intercept and decipher German messages transmitted by the Enigma machine during World War II, in the Ultra program. But the British went way beyond simply using technology. Their most successful achievement during the war was the marriage of technical and human intelligence. In addition to the Ultra decrypts, the British developed the Double-Cross System. When the British MI5 captured German agents, instead of jailing or killing them, they doubled them to work against Nazi Germany.[74]

Because the United States had difficulty conducting human intelligence against the Soviet Union during the postwar and early Cold War periods, it relied on SIGINT. And unlike the situation with aerial reconnaissance, technical devices were already in place.

The United States had already partnered with the British during World War II in signals intelligence but renewed their vows in the early postwar period to target the Soviet Union. The Five Eyes (FVEY) alliance in the agreement was composed of the United States, Britain, Canada, Australia, and New Zealand.[75]

The new Anglo-American SIGINT cooperation came at a time when the British Empire was in decline and US global power was on the ascent. As the intelligence historian Richard Aldrich notes, "These two countries were closest because they alone shared the experience of managing a system of world power, albeit one in decline and one in the ascendant."[76] Although the British Empire was in decline, it still had close ties to Australia and New Zealand, where strong SIGINT capabilities emerged. By the end of the Cold War, the two countries, along with former or existing colonies, maintained facilities pulsating the globe with their all-hearing ears.

At the beginning, the United States profited from Britain's colonial empire. As Calder Walton writes, "On the basis of the UKUSA Agreement, Britain's outposts of empire thus became as important for Washington for SIGINT collection as they had been for the British government itself."[77] Given the enormous size of the Soviet Bloc countries, the United States alone could not target them. But with the remnants of the British

Empire—its colonies and former colonies—as well as Britain itself, the two countries were able to surround the Soviet Union with relay stations and listening posts. Before the creation of the NSA, the United States relied on Britain for a substantial amount of signals intelligence from the Soviet Union and "shared or operated as many as seven Sigint sites on UK domestic or foreign territory."[78]

While the Anglo-American signals intelligence partnership led to many successes during the Cold War, the sharing of information between the two intelligence agencies also had its problems, especially against the Soviet Union's formidable human intelligence operations. One of the first fiascos was the Berlin Tunnel operation. By summer 1955, Allen Dulles went to the White House and reported to Eisenhower on both the progress of the U-2 and the Berlin Tunnel: "I've come to tell you about two acquisition projects—one very high and one very low."[79]

Notes

1. Harry Rositzke, *The CIA's Secret Operations: Espionage, Counterespionage and Covert Action* (New York: Reader's Digest, 1977), 18–19; and Tim Weiner, *Legacy of Ashes: The History of the CIA* (New York: Doubleday, 2007), 43–45. For moon phases, see www.calendar-12.com/moon_calendar/1949/september.

2. Kevin C. Ruffner, "Cold War Allies: The Origins of CIA's Relationship with Ukrainian Nationalists," *Studies in Intelligence*, 1998, 39. Rositzke claims they radioed back after four days (*CIA's Secret Operations*, 19). See also Matthew M. Aid, ed., *Cold War Intelligence Online*, Brill Online Primary Sources, 2013.

3. Matthew M. Aid, "The National Security Agency and the Cold War," *Intelligence and National Security* 16, no. 1 (2001): 30–31.

4. Paul Lewis, "Harry Rositzke, 91, Linguist and American Spymaster," *New York Times*, November 8, 2002; Bart Barnes, "Harry Rositzke Dies," *Washington Post*, November 7, 2002, www.washingtonpost.com/archive/local/2002/11/07/harry-rositzke-dies/955c40af-92e7-495b-8264-3ba89c50e90f.

5. Rositzke, *CIA's Secret Operations*, xxii, 4.

6. Rositzke, 20.

7. Rositzke, 19.

8. Ruffner, "Cold War Allies," 23, 26–27; and Weiner, *Legacy of Ashes*, 41.

9. Weiner, *Legacy of Ashes*, 41.

10. Christopher Andrew and Oleg Gordievsky, *KGB: The Inside Story* (New York: Harper, 1991), 388–89.

11. Ruffner, "Cold War Allies," 43.

12. Tom Bower, *The Red Web: MI6 and the KGB Master Coup* (London: Aurum Press, 1989), 204–5.

13. Foreign Relations of the United States (FRUS), "Intelligence Community, 1950–55," 695n3, https://history.state.gov/historicaldocuments/frus1950-55Intel.

14. Jan Bury, "Operation Spiders: Fighting an Early Cold War Ukrainian Subversion behind the Iron Curtain," *International Journal of Intelligence and Counterintelligence* 30 (2017): 241–68.

15. State Archive of the Russian Federation (GARF), fol. R-9478, o 1d. 1285, II, 267–81. Jeffrey Burds found this document and refers to it in his article, "The Early Cold War in Soviet West Ukraine, 1944–1948," *Carl Beck Papers in Russian and European Studies*, no. 1505 (January 2001): 37.

16. For the CIA's description of Bandera and his assassination, see February 4, 1948, Subject: Stefan BANDERA, https://www.cia.gov/readingroom/docs/BANDERA%2C%20STEFAN_0010.pdf; and Memorandum for the Record, Assassination of Stefan Bandera, April 22, 1976, https://www.cia.gov/readingroom/docs/BANDERA%2C%20STEFAN_0081.pdf. A new book documents the career of Stashinsky: Serhii Plokhy, *The Man with the Poison Gun: A Cold War Spy Story* (New York: Basic Books, 2016).

17. Ben Macintyre, *A Spy among Friends: Kim Philby and the Great Betrayal* (London: Bloomsbury, 2014), 132–33.

18. Stephen Dorril, *MI6: Inside the Covert World of Her Majesty's Secret Intelligence Service* (New York: Simon & Schuster, 2002), 239.

19. Kim Philby, *My Silent War: The Autobiography of a Spy* (New York: Modern Library, [1968] 2002), 159.

20. Philby, 152.

21. Weiner, *Legacy of Ashes*, 42.

22. Bower, *Red Web*, 205, 213.

23. Richard Helms with William Hood, *A Look over My Shoulder: A Life in the Central Intelligence Agency* (New York: Ballantine Books, 2003; rev. ed., n.p.: Presidio Press, 2004), 124.

24. Christopher Andrew, *For the President's Eyes Only: Secret Intelligence and the American Presidency from Washington to Bush* (New York: HarperCollins, 1996), 200–201.

25. Stephen Ambrose, *Ike's Spies: Eisenhower and the Espionage Establishment* (New York: Random House, 1981), 319.

26. James R. Killian, *Sputnik, Scientists, and Eisenhower: A Memoir of the First Assistant to the President for Science and Technology* (Cambridge, MA: MIT Press, 1967), 68.

27. Richard V. Damms, "James Killian, the Technological Capabilities Panel, and the Emergence of President Eisenhower's 'Scientific-Technological Elite,'" *Diplomatic History* 24, no. 1 (Winter 2000): 65.

28. J. H. Doolittle, Chair, William B. Franke, Morris Hadley, and William D. Pawley, "Report on the Covert Activities of the Central Intelligence Agency" (1954); available at https://www.cia.gov/library/readingroom/docs/CIA-RDP86B00269R000100040001-5.pdf, introd. and p. 4.

29. Richard Harris Smith, "The First Moscow Station: An Espionage Footnote to Cold War History," *International Journal of Intelligence and Counterintelligence* 3, no. 3 (1989): 342–43; and Charles E. Bohlen, *Witness to History, 1919–1969* (London: Weidenfeld & Nicolson, 1973), 456.

30. Donald E. Welzenbach, "Science and Technology: Origins of a Directorate," *Studies in Intelligence* 30, no. 2 (1986): 14. See also Philip Taubman, *Secret Empire: Eisenhower, the CIA, and the Hidden Story of American's Space Espionage* (New York: Simon & Schuster, 2003), 30.

31. Taubman, *Secret Empire*, 11–12.

32. Michael Beschloss, *Mayday: Eisenhower, Khrushchev, and the U-2 Affair* (New York: Harper & Row, 1986), 73–74.

33. Gregory W. Pedlow and Donald E. Welzenbach, "The CIA and the U-2 Program, 1954–1974," Central Intelligence Agency, History Staff, Center for the Study of Intelligence, 1998. This report has been published as a book with a foreword by Chris Pocock: Gregory W. Pedlow and Donald E. Welzenbach, *The Central Intelligence Agency and Overhead Reconnaissance: The U-2 and OXCART Programs, 1954–1974* (New York: Skyhorse Publishing, 2016), 32.

34. "Science Expediter, James Rhyne Killian, Jr.," *New York Times*, November 8, 1957, 10; Eric Pace, "James Killian, 83, Science Adviser, Dies," *New York Times*, January 31, 1988, 38; Welzenbach, "Science and Technology," 15; and Beschloss, *Mayday*, 74, for stag dinners.

35. "Report of the Technological Capabilities Panel of the Science Advisory Committee: Meeting the Threat of Surprise Attack, February 14, 1955," vol. 2, 145 [hereafter TCP Report]. Available at the Dwight D. Eisenhower Library, Abilene, Kansas, Records of the White House Staff Sections, Box 16, Killian Report: Technological Capabilities Panel. Also available online: https://link.gale.com/apps/doc/CK2349020051/USDD?u=gainstoftech&sid=bookmark-USDD&xid=049ece09&pg=1.

36. Pace, "James Killian, 83, Science Adviser, Dies."

37. Killian, *Sputnik, Scientists, and Eisenhower*, 87; Welzenbach, "Science and Technology," 18.

38. Richard L. Garwin, "Edwin H. Land: Science, and Public Policy," *Journal of the Irish Colleges of Physicians and Surgeons*, 1993. Originally a paper presented at Light and Life, a Symposium in Honor of Edwin Land, November 9, 1991, https://fas.org/rlg/land.htm.

39. Garwin, 18; Land, quoted in Pedlow and Welzenbach, *Central Intelligence Agency and Overhead Reconnaissance*, 35.

40. TCP Report, 44, 136–37.

41. Welzenbach, "Science and Technology," 19.

42. Killian, *Sputnik, Scientists, and Eisenhower*, 82.

43. Pedlow and Welzenbach, "CIA and the U-2 Program, 1954–1974," preface; see also Pedlow and Welzenbach, *Central Intelligence Agency and Overhead Reconnaissance.*

44. Beschloss, *Mayday*, 105–7.

45. Welzenbach, "Science and Technology," 12.

46. Welzenbach, 14.

47. Welzenbach, 17–18.

48. Edwin H. Land to Allen W. Dulles, November 5, 1954, Memorandum and Report, CIA, CREST.

49. Richard M. Bissell, *Reflections on a Cold Warrior, from Yalta to the Bay of Pigs* (New Haven, CT: Yale University Press, 1996), 92–96; Thomas Powers, *The Man Who Kept the Secrets: Richard Helms and the CIA* (New York: Knopf, 1979), 79; Pedlow and Welzenbach, "The CIA and the U-2 Program, 1954–1974"; and Pedlow and Welzenbach, *Central Intelligence Agency and Overhead Reconnaissance*. See also Weiner, *Legacy of Ashes*, 113.

50. Weiner, *Legacy of Ashes*, 113.

51. Clark Clifford with Richard Holbrooke, *Counsel to the President* (New York: Random House, 1991), 352.

52. Beschloss, *Mayday*, 105; and Dwight D. Eisenhower Library [hereafter DDEL].

53. Pedlow and Welzenbach, *Central Intelligence Agency and Overhead Reconnaissance*, 96–97.

54. Beschloss, *Mayday*, 118; and DDEL.

55. Pedlow and Welzenbach, *Central Intelligence Agency and Overhead Reconnaissance*, 106–7.

56. Pedlow and Welzenbach, 108–9.

57. A. J. Goodpaster, Memorandum for the Record, July 5, 1956, DDEL.

58. A. J. Goodpaster, Memorandum for the Record, July 11, 1956, DDEL.

59. A. J. Goodpaster, Memorandum for the Record, July 19, 1956, DDEL.

60. A. J. Goodpaster, Memorandum for the Record, October 3, 1956, DDEL.

61. John S. D. Eisenhower, Memorandum of Conference with the President, December 22, 1958, DDEL.

62. A. J. Goodpaster, Memorandum for the Record, February 8, 1960, DDEL.

63. Curtis Peebles, *The Corona Project: America's First Spy Satellites* (Annapolis, MD: Naval Institute Press, 1997), 5–7; and Taubman, *Secret Empire*, 43, for "compact" man.

64. Ben R. Rich and Leo Janos, *Skunk Works: A Personal Memoir of My Years at Lockheed* (New York: Little, Brown, 1994), 121–22.

65. Bissell, *Reflections on a Cold Warrior*. For newly released documents, see www.cia.gov/news-information/press-releases-statements/2017-press-releases-statements/sputnik-60-years-later-cia-releases-declassified-documents.html.

66. Jonathan E. Lewis, *Spy Capitalism: ITEK and the CIA* (New Haven, CT: Yale University Press, 2002).

67. Taubman, *Secret Empire*, 33.

68. Bissell, *Reflections on a Cold Warrior*, 93.

69. Arthur C. Lundahl, "Consider the Mata Hari with Glass Eyes," "rough draft" of speech, 25 pp. I would like to thank Gary E. Weir, chief historian at the NGA, for sending me a copy of this speech, contained in the papers of the National

Photographic Interpretation Center (NPIC) now housed at the NGA. The second quotation in this paragraph is from Bissell, *Reflections on a Cold Warrior*, 134.

70. William E. Burrows, *Deep Black: Space Espionage and National Security* (New York: Random House, 1986), 54.

71. Derryfield N. Smith, "Mata Hari with a Glass Eye," *Air Forces News Letter* 24, no. 15 (September 1941): 1–4; available at https://books.google.com.

72. Letter to Allen Dulles from Robert R. McMath, Lawrence A. Hyland, George B. Kistiakowsky, and Francis H. Clauser, October 23, 1957, www.cia.gov/library/readingroom/docs/DOC_0003030512.pdf.

73. Aid, "National Security Agency and the Cold War," 32–33.

74. J. C. Masterman, *The Double-Cross System in the War of 1939 to 1945* (New Haven, CT: Yale University Press, 1972).

75. Aid, *Secret Empire*, 33.

76. Richard J. Aldrich, *The Hidden Hand: Britain, America and Cold War Secret Intelligence* (Woodstock, NY: Overlook Press, 2002), 9.

77. Calder Walton, *Empire of Secrets: British Intelligence, the Cold War and the Twilight of Empire* (London: Harper Press, 2013), 154.

78. David Vincent Gioe, "The Anglo-American Special Intelligence Relationship: Wartime Causes and Cold War Consequences, 1940–63" (PhD diss., University of Cambridge, 2014), 119; and James Bamford, *Body of Secrets: Anatomy of the Ultra-Secret National Security Agency from the Cold War through the Dawn of a New Century* (New York: Doubleday, 2001), 403.

79. Beschloss, *Mayday*, 94, for Dulles quote.

2

CAN A TUNNEL BECOME A DOUBLE AGENT?

I was riding the Washington, DC, metro home one day after a hike in the Shenandoahs when a lawyer from the hiking group, curious about a project I was working on about US intelligence, asked me if a tunnel can become a double agent. His question was prompted by the discussion we were having about the relative risks of human versus technical intelligence. The very bright lawyer thought he had the right answer when he posed the question. It was pretty clear to him that only humans can betray other people and become double agents; technology is an inanimate object, not a person. Imagine his surprise when I very quickly said, yes, a tunnel can become a double agent. For the lawyer had forgotten one major thing about technology: it is human built and created and run by humans.

The story about the tunnel takes place in Berlin, Germany, during the early 1950s. Although the wall had not been erected yet, the city was divided into four sectors, with the Western powers, Britain, France, and the United States, occupying the western side and the Soviet Union the eastern side. Although there was still vehicle and foot traffic among the sectors and between the halves of the city, people had to present identification at a checkpoint before proceeding into another sector. Because of this easy access and the frontline proximity, Berlin became a hub for the major spy agencies—the CIA, the KGB, the SIS, those of the French, and more—doing brisk business in the spy trade. Some newspapers claimed there were "27 separate agencies of Western intelligence known to be at work in Berlin."[1] Because of its status as a spy city with the enemy at close proximity, it should not come as a surprise that a spy agency would want to build a tunnel to spy on enemy communications. But the need for such a tunnel arose from a series of events that began after the end of World War II in 1945.

Black Friday

In late 1946, William Weisband, a heavyset linguist, was wandering around the offices at the US Army Secret Intelligence Service's highly secretive installation and headquarters in Arlington Hall, a former girls' school in Arlington, Virginia. Weisband was considered "very gregarious and very nosy" when he worked there. Cecil Phillips, a cryptanalyst, recalls,

> He would come around and ask questions about what you were doing. . . . He was never aggressive. If you said, as I often did, "Nothing important" or "I'm doing something as dull as hell," he would wander off. . . . I never heard him offer a political thought. He was around everywhere all the time. He cultivated the senior officers.[2]

At one point, he leaned over Meredith Gardner's shoulder just as the brilliant cryptanalyst and linguist was decrypting a telegram from the New York residency to Moscow, dated December 1944. Despite Weisband's nonchalant demeanor, he must have been startled when he read the telegram listing some of the scientists who worked on the US atomic bomb.

Along with Meredith Gardner and Cecil Phillips, Weisband worked on a project code-named Venona, which had broken Soviet codes. Gardner and Phillips did not know one thing at the time, however: Weisband was in fact a mole for Moscow and was eager to immediately tell his masters about the explosive telegram. But there was one problem. He had just been ordered to break off contact with Moscow because Elizabeth Bentley, a former KGB spy, switched sides and spilled the beans to the FBI. So despite the explosive news for the KGB, it took over a year for information about the telegram to reach Moscow.[3]

Because Weisband had warned the Russians that the United States had broken many of their codes (not just Venona), they changed codes and ciphers and started using the one-time pad (a secure encryption system in which a key is generated and used once) on October 29, 1948, a Friday. In addition, they switched communication from wireless to landlines. All of a sudden, US signals intelligence lost its ears. These events later became known as "Black Friday" and were considered one of the "most significant losses in US intelligence history."[4] At that point, no one suspected that Weisband's treacherous act would not only accelerate plans to open the National Security Agency in 1952 but also lead to one of the most audacious espionage operations of the twentieth century.

While American intelligence was reeling from its recent losses, British intelligence had been hatching a plan to tap into Russian landlines in the divided city and spy capital, Vienna, Austria. Peter Lunn, a champion competitive skier, became chief of station in 1948 even though he was only in his midthirties. A soft-spoken, trim, small man with "piercing blue eyes," he oversaw the development of the Vienna spy tunnel, from recruiting a source at the post office to digging under a house to supervising the take.[5]

The story goes that Lunn and his team had the ingenious idea of placing the head of the tunnel under a Harris Tweed shop. The only problem was that the floor started to buckle because the shop got so much business.[6]

Lunn and his team, consisting of eavesdroppers and tunnel diggers, built several tunnels in Vienna. The project was destined to become a dress rehearsal for the Berlin Tunnel. The most noteworthy tunnel was in the British sector of Vienna under a short cobblestoned street, the Aspangstrasse. Amid the rubble of postwar Vienna, the British had found a boarded-up old shop opposite the railroad freight station. Ostensibly abandoned, the shop had many visitors who made their way to the steel-reinforced backdoor, descended a rickety wooden staircase, and encountered yet another door leading to a short tunnel where the British tapped Soviet landlines.[7]

According to the CIA, it did not take long before they heard about the Vienna tunnel operations, and SIS agreed to share the intelligence take from the buried cables. In the meantime, the CIA began to investigate the possibility of tapping buried cables in divided Berlin, the spy capital of Germany. The American sector, in particular, offered a good contiguous location to the Soviet sector.[8]

The CIA's early idea to tap landlines in East Berlin did not include digging a tunnel but rather concentrated on recruiting a spy ring at the East German Post Office. The decade of the 1950s was a challenging one for using human sources in espionage; penetrating Soviet and East German communications was no exception. One of the most significant agents was code-named the Nummermädchen, the Numbers Girl. Unlike in the United States, the Post Office in Germany was also responsible for telephones. No one ever found out the real identity of the Numbers Girl, but she worked in the switching office and could determine Soviet and East

German users of the cables. Through another source in the East German Ministry of Post and Telecommunications, the CIA obtained a map and was able to locate a good line to tap. The only problem was reaching it. Later, and the CIA's clandestine history makes it clear that they did not know exactly when, they decided to build a tunnel.[9]

Certainly, the World War II code breaker extraordinaire, Frank Rowlett, played a part in stimulating the idea for a tunnel to tap lines. A "fastidious Virginian" who drawled his words with his pipe clamped between his teeth, Rowlett was part of a US team that broke the notorious Japanese cipher machine "Purple" during World War II.[10] Like the British success from Ultra (the take from the Enigma machine intercepts), "Magic"—the code name for the intercepts from the Japanese machine—made clear the importance of code breaking in war, whether hot or cold.

Like Weisband, Rowlett worked at Arlington Hall, but before that he had been chief of intelligence in the US Army's Security Agency and ended up at the National Security Agency when it was founded in 1952. In the meantime, though, he had become frustrated when Soviet wireless traffic stopped. One day he was talking to William (Bill) Harvey, a friend at the CIA, in the hope they would launch a clandestine mission to penetrate the Soviet landlines in order to read the Soviets' mind like they had read the Japanese mind during World War II.[11]

He found receptive ears in Harvey, a man who created his own legend by acting like a cowboy in Berlin. According to Robert Lamphere, an FBI official who worked closely with him, "Harvey was odd-looking[,] . . . with protruding eyes and a pear-shaped body. His voice was like a bullfrog." (His nickname was "Pear.") Unfortunately, Harvey had to leave the FBI under a cloud after a few years because he crashed his car in Washington's Rock Creek Parkway after drinking too much at a party. But the CIA's Office of Special Operations took him, and he continued his womanizing and "three martini lunch[es]" there. He also always made sure to carry a gun, either leaving it on his desk or strapping it in his armpit.[12]

In any event, Harvey liked Rowlett's idea, and the CIA quickly ordered a study of Soviet landlines in Europe. Harvey moved to Berlin in 1952 to become chief of base (until 1960), and Rowlett moved his office from the NSA to the CIA. Harvey was put in charge of the tunnel, and Rowlett reported to CIA chief Allen Dulles with the results.[13]

From the British perspective, however, it was their idea to build another tunnel, this time jointly with the United States. For British Intelligence, as

Ian Fleming quipped in *From Russia with Love*, America was primarily a rich source of funding. The British did not think much of US operational capabilities. According to George Blake, Peter Lunn told the story of the Berlin Tunnel from beginning to end when they were at the Berlin Station together: "He made it quite clear that this had been essentially an SIS idea and his own to boot. American participation had been limited to providing most of the money and facilities."[14]

This time, America contributed its engineering know-how using the Army Corps of Engineers, that builder of empires. Since the CIA did not have the manpower to build a tunnel, Allen Dulles simply contacted senior army commanders who were sympathetic to the tunnel project. In particular, Maj. Gen. Arthur Trudeau, the new chief of army intelligence who had been trained as an engineer, became an enthusiastic supporter.[15]

The Army Corps of Engineers was the same group responsible for constructing large-scale American projects like the Manhattan Project, the Panama Canal, and the Pentagon among many other buildings, dams, and bridges around the world. They also built several top-secret intelligence installations and buildings (including the National Geospatial-Intelligence Agency building in Springfield, Virginia, discussed in chap. 9). Walter Schaaf, an American civilian, was the chief of engineering and construction for the Army Corps of Engineers in Berlin, where he supervised the building of hospitals, schools, housing, and commissaries for the large number of US military personnel in Berlin and their families. He also oversaw the Berlin Tunnel.[16]

Before building the tunnel in Berlin, the celebrated engineers, consisting of three officers and fifteen enlisted men, tested a model in the New Mexico desert, digging holes, hauling dirt, and measuring cylinders. But the engineers were not told where this tunnel was to be located until later. When they were ready, the team sent steel tubes and other supplies in crates on boxcars on a train from Sandia, New Mexico, to Fort Lee, Virginia. From there the two hundred tons of packed crates traveled on a freighter to Bremerhaven, Germany, arriving in August 1954. When the goods arrived in Germany, the cover story was that it was radar intercept equipment. From Bremerhaven the crates were loaded onto the boxcars of a US military train traveling to Berlin at night through Communist East Germany. But the real problem was how to hide the digging of a tunnel under the noses of the East German border guards and what to do with the dirt.[17]

The tunnel was not just an engineering marvel. Harvey and his team had to find a good place along the border to dig the hole and find a way to disguise the operation. They settled on Rudow, a locality within the southwestern Berlin borough of Neukölln and part of the American sector. This bordered Alt-Glienicke in the Eastern Sector where the cables were located. To disguise the operation, they built a unique warehouse with a large basement (it was unusual for a warehouse to have a basement, especially such a big one) in plain sight of East German border guards. The basement was used to hide the dirt, enough to fill the equivalent of twenty American living rooms.[18]

By May 1953 plans for the tunnel began to take shape. The CIA's code name for the joint operation with the British was PBJOINTLY. The division of labor was decided at a conference in late 1953. The tasks were divided pretty evenly, with the United States providing the material and building the tunnel, recording all the signals, and processing all the telegraphic material in Washington, DC; it also provided most of the money. The British built the vertical shaft to the cable to be tapped, delivered the signal for recording, and jointly manned a US-UK Center in London to process the voice recordings. The tunnel was completed on February 28, 1955, and the tap chamber was done by March 28. According to the CIA's clandestine history, the "bilateral [arrangement] caused few, if any problems."[19]

The 1,476-foot tunnel—as long as the Lincoln Memorial reflecting pool in Washington, DC, and the same height as the Empire State Building in New York City if turned vertically—was now operational and disguised. But how long would that last?

Enter George Blake

Meanwhile, George Blake (born Behar), a British SIS officer, returned to the United Kingdom from his captivity in Korea in spring 1953. Slightly built and swarthy, with hazel eyes, Blake was born in Rotterdam to a British mother and a Turkish Jewish father who was a trader and naturalized Englishman. After joining the Dutch resistance against the Nazis, Blake moved to the United Kingdom and served in the Royal Navy before the SIS recruited him in 1947. Soon after, he was sent to Korea where his cover was British vice-consul in Seoul, but he was captured and imprisoned early in the Korean War, in 1950. Though some people say he was brainwashed during this time, Blake claims his conversion to communism was based on his strongly held beliefs. He therefore volunteered to work for the KGB by becoming a mole.[20]

When Blake returned to the United Kingdom, he started his job with SIS in the fall, joining a new unit, Section Y, responsible for technical operations against the Soviet Union, as second in command. Specifically, the section analyzed the take from the Vienna Tunnel operation, along with the take from other telephone tapping. Since most of the information was in Russian, Blake's Russian-language skills were valued. Section Y was housed at 2 Carlton Gardens, a townhouse with a chandeliered marble entrance and a monumental staircase leading up to Blake's office in a converted bedroom.[21]

Within weeks of starting the new job, Blake was making copies of reports about operations against the Soviet Union. And the copies went right into the hands of his case officer, Sergei Kondrashev. Since the KGB was worried that British counterintelligence surveillance teams might recognize the seasoned first case officer, Nikolai Rodin, they chose the thirty-year-old Kondrashev, who had never served in London before, to work with Blake. With his cover as first secretary for cultural affairs, he organized tours or got people tickets for events. But at night he met with his agents.

On one foggy evening in late October, Kondrashev walked out of the underground station at Belsize Park and took a brief stroll. Then Blake emerged from the station, and as he walked away he saw a man in a "grey, soft felt hat and smart grey raincoat" who almost seemed "part of the fog" walk toward him carrying a newspaper in his left hand, in a scene reminiscent of a spy film. Kondrashev greeted him warmly, and together they walked up the street a bit before Blake handed over the first secrets from his new job. The folded piece of paper contained a list of all the SIS's telephone tapping operations in the Vienna Tunnel operation as well as information about microphones planted in Soviet and Eastern Bloc embassies in Western Europe. At this meeting they also discussed the need for a camera to photograph all the documents. Within three weeks he received a Minox spy camera.[22]

This first act of betrayal was the hardest for Blake. In his memoirs, he describes that an hour after the meeting, he was back at his mother's apartment enjoying a glass of wine and a late dinner. The dinner remained in his memory primarily because the "room seemed particularly cozy and secure after the damp foggy night outside and the dangers of the clandestine meeting" he "had just lived through."[23] He was in from the cold. The meets, however, soon became routine; thereafter Blake met with Kondrashev every three or four weeks.

Blake was valued by the KGB; his code name in the files was "Diomid" (sometimes erroneously translated as "Diamond"). Blake did not just betray the Berlin Tunnel operation. During his time in Berlin, he passed on extensive material on Western agent networks in the Eastern Bloc. According to a KGB report, George Blake, along with Kim Philby and Heinz Felfe, helped eliminate "the adversary's agent network in East Germany."[24]

Not only was he a prized mole in the SIS, but he was secretary for meetings in the Y Section and passed on every scrap of information to his case officer. One of the most significant minutes from an SIS meeting came from a joint CIA-SIS conference about the Berlin Tunnel held in London on December 15–18, 1953. Kondrashev immediately sent a coded cable to Moscow about this meeting, but the photographed reports were only sent later in February. In other words, the Berlin Tunnel was betrayed from the moment it was approved. Kondrashev commented dryly on the material, "The information on a planned intercept operation against internal telephone lines on GDR territory to a radar station is of interest."[25]

After receiving Blake's explosive material about the Berlin Tunnel and other audio surveillance, the KGB did everything to protect their source. Only three people in the First Chief Directorate knew the agent existed at all. No one else knew his real name.[26] Therefore, they had to watch and wait for an opportunity to come up to reveal that they knew about the tunnel without compromising Blake. That opportunity was the rainy spring of 1956. But the life of a double agent is usually brief. And Blake's luck ran out in 1961. He was betrayed by a spy code-named Sniper who wanted to defect to the West from Poland.

Although "Sniper," who was later identified as Col. Michal Goleniewski, deputy chief of Polish counterintelligence, did not know Blake's real name, he provided enough information for SIS and MI5 to identify him. After several days of interrogation and a stay in a country cottage, where Blake cooked the pancakes, he confessed.

The "Discovery" of a Tunnel

It was not until the night of April 21–22, 1956, at the height of the Cold War, that Soviet and East German signals officers "discovered," in dramatic fashion, the jointly built tunnel beneath the streets of Berlin.

April 1956 had been an unusually wet month in Berlin, and after heavy rains many telephone and telegraph cables were flooded and began to short-circuit on the Eastern side near KGB headquarters in Karlshorst and Wünsdorf. Soviet signal troops and East German Post and Telegraph technicians worked hard to reestablish service. In particular, a crucial cable used by the Soviets as an early warning system between Moscow and Wünsdorf was down but was repaired and then replaced. These developments were, of course, worrisome to the Western spies, who checked their tap on April 19 and noted it was in good condition, with no faults. They reported back to CIA headquarters that "available precautions [had been] taken including the primary one of crossing fingers."[27]

But the CIA's luck was not going to last long. By April 22, shortly after midnight, CIA and SIS observers saw around fifty men digging, about three to five feet apart, on the east side of Schönefelder Allee in the Alt-Glienicke borough of East Berlin. They had started digging directly over the cable and the tap. By 2:00 a.m., they had discovered the top of the tap chamber.

In addition to tapping the cables for eavesdropping, the CIA and SIS had installed a microphone near the tap and could overhear the Soviets and East Germans during their journey of discovery. At 2:10 a.m., the eavesdroppers concluded, "First fragments of speech indicated the tap chamber aroused no suspicion." The Russians and Germans seemed to agree that the discovery was a manhole covering a repeater point.[28]

As the workers enlarged the hole, they saw cables and a trapdoor they assumed to be "some sort of box." At first, the Russians thought the chamber was related to sewage work or a wartime high frequency transmission cable. By 3:30 the Soviets left the site in a truck, and no sounds were recorded from the tap microphone until 5:00 a.m. However, the Western eavesdroppers still listened in on office telephone conversations between the chiefs of the Soviet signal services who had reported their discovery of the chamber. When they returned to the site, a member of the crew entered the chamber and the eavesdroppers heard the statement, "The cable is tapped."[29]

By 7:00 a.m., many more Russians and East Germans began to arrive at the site, including the KGB's Signals Regiment. They continued to enlarge the hole and started making movies to document the find. There was also a lot of discussion about the trapdoor. The Russians referred to it as a box and thought it might be booby-trapped. In fact, it was the entrance to the tunnel.

When German cable splicers examined the cables, they determined they were tapped and noted that "everyone must have been quite drunk" not to see that they were cut and tapped. At this point, the eavesdroppers overheard the Russians say that there must be some way to enter the place but that it was unlikely they constructed a passage. Finally, someone from the party saw the microphone but said, "That is not a microphone"; another person described it as a "black ball."[30]

By 11:45, a German exclaimed, "The box is an entry to a shaft." The team started by boring a hole near the trapdoor and then decided to simply take off the door hinges; then they lowered themselves into the tap chamber while identifying the padlock as "of English origin." Although they opened the trapdoor, they could not get into the door separating the tap chamber from the equipment chamber, so they broke a hole through the wall, saw the equipment chamber, and described "a completed installation—a telephone exchange[—] . . . an installation for listening in."[31]

At this point, they made more movies of the site and "frequent exclamations of wonder and admiration were heard." They heard a German cry out, "It must have cost a pretty penny," and a Russian-speaking German added, "How neatly and tidily they have done it." But another German thought it was a "filthy trick."[32]

By 3:30 in the afternoon, the Germans cut the tap wires and fifteen minutes later started focusing on the microphone, which had been picking up all the conversations for the CIA-SIS eavesdroppers to hear. One of the Germans assumed it was an "alarm device—probably a microphone," but a few minutes later they started to take the microphone apart. According to the CIA's official history, "Shortly afterward the microphone went dead and, after 11 months and 11 days, the operational phase of PBJOINTLY was completed."[33]

As a result of the overheard conversations, the cable traffic, and the binocular observations of the site, the British and American spies concluded, "Soviet discovery of PBJOINTLY was purely fortuitous and was not the result of penetration of the US or UK agencies concerned."[34] They were wrong.

Much to the surprise of the tunnel planners, who assumed that the Soviets would remain quiet about the discovery, Moscow quickly turned it into a propaganda tool. Within forty-eight hours, the Soviets staged an elaborate evening press conference. Berlin journalists assembled at the Red Army officers' club cinema in Karlshorst for the briefing.[35]

When the journalists arrived at Karlshorst, Col. Ivan Kotsiuba, the Soviet military commandant in the city, greeted them. After announcing the discovery of the spy tunnel, Kotsiuba escorted them to the tunnel with Soviet military police on motorcycles, the convoy only arriving in Alt-Glienicke at twilight. Floodlights illuminated the scene. "Come, gentlemen, follow me," said Kotsiuba. "Look, almost German workmanship—but not done by Germans." The journalists were allowed to walk in the tunnel and reached Harvey's handwritten notice in German and Russian: "You are now in the American Sector."[36]

The Soviet "discovery" of the Berlin Tunnel received widespread media attention in the East and in the West. In the West, the tunnel was celebrated as representing "Yankee ingenuity"; it was seen as a real technological marvel. The *Washington Post* wrote, "Yankee resourcefulness and ingenuity is not a myth after all."[37] After praising the "500-yard tunnel" as "a venture of extraordinary audacity—the stuff of which thriller films are made," the *New York Herald Tribune* went on to detail the remarkable equipment discovered in the tunnel: the temperature and humidity control equipment, tapping boosters, power-control units, and the ultrasensitive microphone that picked up the discovery of the tunnel. The paper was in awe, reporting that it couldn't have been done without "the great experts in the field" who "did a remarkably tidy piece of work."[38]

West Germans saw the tunnel as "an astounding feat, which has greatly enhanced American prestige." It also captured their imaginations as they marveled at the "boldness of burrowing under the Russian noses, and its technical accomplishment."[39]

In the East, the tunnel became a propaganda coup. Although newspapers there respected the technical achievement and recognized the large amount of money that had been invested in the design and construction, they trumpeted that the tunnel represented an "international scandal" and was a "breach of the norms of international law." Editorials addressed to the West Berlin Senate suggested that Berlin was kept divided to offer Western spy agencies a "base for launching provocations against the GDR."[40]

Neues Deutschland (New Germany) the major East German newspaper and mouthpiece of the Socialist Unity Party of Germany (Sozialistische

ZEFYS Zeitungsportal / DDR-Presse • Neues Deutschland, Mi. 25. April 1956, Jahrgang 11 / Ausgabe 100 / Seite 6

‹ 24.04.1956 • 26.04.1956 › • ND • BZ • NZ

gehe zu Seite 6

Zoom

- Startseite DDR-Presse
- Kalenderfunktion
- Volltextsuche
- Weitere Funktionen

BERLIN

NEUES DEUTSCHLAND
25. April 1956 / Nr. 100 / Seite 6

Nicht in fremden Gärten wühlen! *Zeichnung: Berg*

Gebrüder Saß auf amerikanisch

Bei den Berlinern fiel gestern eine Klappe — wie man so sagt. „Genau wie damals die Gebrüder Saß!" — So riefen uns mehrere an, als die Spionageaffäre Altglienicke bekannt wurde. Nun muß man wissen, daß vor etwa 30 Jahren diese beiden Brüder ein berüchtigtes Geldschrankknacker - Paar war, das seinen, wenn auch traurigen Weltruf damit bekundete, daß es durch einen 280 Meter langen Stollen unterm Wittenbergplatz einen tolldreisten Einbruch verübte. Ist es nicht bezeichnend, daß bei den Berlinern automatisch diese Gedankenverbindung zustande kam, als das neue, bisher in der Tat unübertroffene Gangsterstück des US-Geheimdienstes bekannt wurde? Automatisch setzt man diese neuen uniformierten Spione gleich jenen alten Berufsverbrechern, Bankräubern und asozialen Elementen, und genauso sind diese Gangster auch einzuschätzen, die draußen in Altglienicke ein Stück lieferten, wie es unter zivilisierten Staaten bisher wohl einmalig ist.

lich, so umfangreich und auch so kostbar wie an der Schönefelder Chaussee ist uns noch keiner in die Hände gefallen. Hier wurde manche Million der sagenhaften Marshallplanhilfe investiert, wie der Augenschein ergibt.

Wieder Westberlin sagten wir. Hat Westberlin aber nicht einen Senat, der verantwortlich ist für das, was auf seinem Territorium geschieht? Wußte er das, was sich da draußen an der Schönefelder Chaussee abspielte? Das wäre doch eine Angelegenheit, die Franz Neumann, den Vorsitzenden des westberliner Polizeiausschusses, brennend interessieren müßte.

„Nicht nur der Schutz der Berliner, sondern auch das Recht in Berlin muß gewährleistet sein", heißt es in einer Erklärung, die der westberliner Senat erst gestern wegen irgendeiner Räuberpistole von sich gab. Hier, in diesem in der Geschichte des Völkerrechts unerhörten Fall „Spionagetunnel Altglienicke" hat der westberliner Senat die beste Möglichkeit, diese seine Worte in die Tat umzusetzen.

Elfenbein. Seide u

Indische

Pressegeschichte (1)

Das Internationale Ausstellungszentrum der Gesellschaft für kulturelle Verbindung mit dem Ausland an der Weidendammbrücke, das sich unter den Berlinern und auswärtigen Besuchern schon viele Freunde erwarb, verspricht in den nächsten vier bis sechs Wochen ein Anziehungspunkt besonderer Art zu werden. Eine in Deutschland erstmalig veranstaltete Schau indischer Volkskunst mit gleichzeitigem Verkauf wird dort am Donnerstag eröffnet. Um es vorwegzunehmen: Sie wird kein Nachbild der den Berliner Messebesuchern schon bekannten Leipziger Ausstellung indischer Volkskunst sein. Sollte jene vor allem einen Eindruck ausschließlich der indischen Volkskunst vermitteln, so wird diese darüber hinaus einen allgemeinen Überblick über das heutige Indien, seine Menschen, seine Industrie und Landwirtschaft geben. Wandgemälde, Bilder, Fotos und grafische Darstellungen, Aussprüche von Gandhi und Nehru und schließlich die durch stilisierte indische Architekturelemente betonte Inneneinrichtung bilden den äußeren Rahmen der eigentlichen Volkskunstausstellung.

Die etwa 2000 ver
Ausstellungsstücke, von
tere 34 000 im Lager
sind, werden in Vitrinen
Teil in die Wände eingel
und auf großen, zehn Me
Tischen gezeigt. Durch d
Arrangements erhält de
ein anschauliches Bild v
kunstschaffen in den ver
Staaten und Provinzen
ßen südostasiatischen L

So erfährt man, daß
malereien und Basterzeu
Heimat in Orissa haben,
len, Kannen und Zierg
aus getriebenem und
Kupfer dagegen im G
Neu Delhi. Die Holz- u
beinschnitzereien, meiste
aus dem religiösen und d
leben darstellend, stan
allem aus Bengalen. D
handwerker im gebirgig
mir schickten wunder
Türkis-Mosaik besetzte
Gegenstände aus ziselier
Schmuckkästchen aus
Sandelholz kommen aus
Ledergürtel und -taschen
bay, Messingarbeiten
gegenstände aus Silberfi
Haidarabad.

8-Millionen-Defizit z

200 000 DM Einsparungen noch in diesem Jahr / Erste Ü

Rund 200 000 DM wollen die Werktätigen des Betriebsteiles Omnibus der BVG noch in diesem Jahr einsparen. Dies beschlossen sie auf ihrer gestrigen ersten Ökonomischen Konferenz im Kulturhaus der BVG in Niederschönhausen. Sie wollen damit die Planrückstände in der Selbstkostensenkung wettmachen, die aus der erhöhten Beanspruchung der Fahrzeuge während der strengen Frostperiode des vergangenen Winters entstanden sind.

Mit verbesserten Reparaturmethoden in den Omnibushöfen werden die BVGer dem Defizit
ihres Betriebes v
das ausschließl
Betriebsteil en
Leibe rücken.
Wartung der Rei

zeit der Pneus um zeh
erhöhen. Rund 23 000 D
mit diesem Vorschlag d
mischen Konferenz einge
den. Während des Som
die BVG ab S-Bahnhof
Omnibusse zu einem
nach dem Freibad Müg
von den einzelnen Sta
Berlins Sonderomnibusse
liner Tierpark nach Frie
verkehren lassen, um die
tät zu erhöhen.

In der Diskussion teilt
diente Aktivist und Ko
des „DO 54" Goltz mit, d
Jahre 1960 durch Erne

Personen (5)

Wikipedia, GND (21)

Figure 2.1 Cartoon from the East German newspaper *Neues Deutschland* satirizing the exposure of the Berlin Tunnel. *CIA Reading Room*

Einheitspartei Deutschland [SED]) produced a caricature captioned, "Do Not Burrow in Other People's Yards." The cartoon depicted a divided garden. On the right (the East) it was full of flowers with the sign "Democratic Sector," and on the left (the West) it was a barren piece of land with a molehill with a dollar-sign flag on the top; an arm is pulling a mole out of the hole wearing US-marked earphones, army pants with pliers and plugs hanging out the pocket, and a US Army cap stenciled with the word *Espionage.* The paper described it as a "gangster act."[41]

Propaganda against the Western "imperialists" was not limited to newspapers. The tunnel became the leading tourist attraction in Berlin, drawing some ninety thousand East Berliners to well-publicized tours of the expensive underground listening post of the "capitalistic warmongers." There was even a mobile snack bar doing brisk business located on the Eastern side where factory workers were brought to witness the American act of imperialism.[42]

Curiously, there were no tours available on the Western side. This led a broadcaster to quip, "Why don't we open a tourist entrance at our end of the tunnel and cash in on the publicity. Step up, one and all. Only a quarter. See modern espionage in electronic form and all underground."[43]

Human Betrayal of Technology

Immediately after the Soviets discovered the tunnel, the CIA and the SIS launched a thorough investigation into whether the tunnel had been betrayed by a penetration agent, but they found no such evidence. They spent three months analyzing the cable traffic, the microphone conversations in the tap chamber, and visual surveillance from the Rudow warehouse. Hugh Montgomery, a member of the Berlin Tunnel team, recalled many years later, "We didn't dream it had been betrayed. . . . All the evidence suggested it was random. There'd been flooding and short-circuiting on the lines and they'd dug at several points along the way. Also, the Soviets took care to send in the East Germans. So far as we were concerned, it was all an accident."[44]

This was not the first time the Soviets fooled the West with their disinformation, their cover stories and legend tactics. Nor was it going to be the only time the Soviets found out about high-grade expensive Western spy technology through a human source. In the case of the tunnel project, the human source was George Blake, which takes us back to the lawyer's question about whether a tunnel can become a double agent.

But there is more. In fact, there had been a chain reaction of betrayals: the story did not start with George Blake but rather with William Weisband, who had informed the Soviets of the technical interception project Venona, which led to the idea to build a tunnel to eavesdrop on landlines in the first place. Then Blake betrayed the tunnel project, and another human, Michal Goleniewski, betrayed him. Technology is not only built by humans but run and installed by humans. Human foibles and duplicity became part of the technological projects.

In this case from the 1950s, the joint British-US project got caught in the enormous web of ideological spies the Soviet Union had recruited from the 1930s through the 1950s. In fact, while Blake was taking part in meetings about the tunnel and passing on the secrets to his handlers, two other high-profile Soviet agents, Donald Maclean and Guy Burgess, fled to the Soviet Union because they were under investigation. There was a lot of talk about traitors in the office as Blake was passing on the tunnel secrets to his handler. It rattled him for a few weeks; then he got over it.

Torrents of Material

Even though the Berlin Tunnel was betrayed by Blake and discovered, the CIA felt it hauled in useful information on the Soviets' Order of Battle and other military information, along with gossip that could be used against Soviet officers. But the agency was also overwhelmed with the amount of information the AMPEX recorders taped and the amount of information that needed to be transcribed. The CIA's Richard Helms was astonished by the "torrent" of information reaching Washington, DC, from the tunnel operation and defended the short-lived operation by referring to the 600 tape recorders, the 800 rolls of tape, and the 1,200 hours of recording every day. To add to Helms's statistics, the CIA's history notes that the project used 50,000 reels of magnetic tape weighing 250 tons; 317 employees at the voice processing center, transcribing 368,000 conversations of 20,000 Soviet two-hour voice reels; and 350 people at the teletype center, also transcribing five-digit amounts of information. Finally, this all led to 1,750 reports and 90,000 translated messages or conversations.[45] And the project lasted less than a year. Imagine the flood of data if it had continued.

Allen Dulles thought the take was "a highly valuable flow of raw intelligence" but was concerned about processing it, even with 50 full-time translators in DC and the on-site teams, in addition to 250 Russian émigré translators in the United Kingdom. Finally, Richard Bissell, then a CIA program manager, thought the tunnel was a success but was concerned about the amount of information it hauled in and was tempted to issue a "ration" on how many words the German station was allowed to transmit per month. He thought that the flow of information to Washington was "counter-productive."[46]

The Berlin Tunnel story was one of the first major technological projects the Soviets found out about because of a mole or double agent or defector. Many more would follow during the Cold War. The US projects only grew in size and global scope. After the tunnel fiasco, the U-2 spy plane was put in commission, followed by spy satellites, and the United States was on a trajectory to becoming a global espionage power.

Notes

1. "Wonderful Tunnel," *Time*, May 7, 1956.

2. Christopher Andrew, *The Defence of the Realm: The Authorized History of MI5* (London: Allen Lane, 2009), 377–78.

3. Ken G. Robertson and Michael R. D. Foot, *War, Resistance and Intelligence: Essays in Honour of M. R. D. Foot* (Barnsley: Cooper, 1999), 213.

4. David Stafford, *Spies beneath Berlin* (Woodstock, NY: Overlook Press, 2002), 47.

5. Stafford, 14.

6. Stafford, 35.

7. Stafford, 20.

8. David E. Murphy, Sergei A. Kondrashev, and George Bailey, *Battleground Berlin: CIA vs. KGB in the Cold War* (New Haven, CT: Yale University Press, 1997), 205–37.

9. Murphy, Kondrashev, and Bailey, 211, for Nummermädchen; see also CIA, "Clandestine Services History: The Berlin Tunnel Operation, 1952–1956," www.cia.gov/library/readingroom/docs/CIA-RDP07X00001R000100010001-9.pdf.

10. Stafford, *Spies beneath Berlin*, 49–50.

11. Stafford, 51.

12. Robert J. Lamphere and Tom Shachtman, *The FBI-KGB War: A Special Agent's Story* (New York: Random House, 1986), 61; and Stafford, *Spies beneath Berlin*, 51–52.

13. Stafford, *Spies beneath Berlin*, 53.

14. George Blake, *No Other Choice: An Autobiography* (New York: Simon & Schuster, 1990), 180.

15. Steve Vogel, *Betrayal in Berlin: The True Story of the Cold War's Most Audacious Espionage Operation* (New York: Custom House, 2019), 136.

16. For the US Army Corps of Engineers in Europe, see Robert Grathwol and Donita M. Moorhus, *Building for Peace: U.S. Army Engineers in Europe, 1945–1991* (Washington, DC: Center of Military and History and Corps of Engineers United States Army, 2005).

17. Murphy, Kondrashev, and Bailey, *Battleground Berlin*, 214. For the crate travel from Sandia, New Mexico, to Berlin, see Vogel, *Betrayal in Berlin*, 142, 146–49.

18. G., "Turning a Cold War Scheme into Reality: Engineering the Berlin Tunnel," *Studies in Intelligence* 48, no. 2 (2004) (original version); extracts, *Studies in Intelligence* 52, no. 1 (2008), https://www.cia.gov/static/bc24245a1a548b8e0dfab3aa976cb06d/Engineering-the-Berlin-Tunnel.pdf.

19. CIA, "Clandestine Services History."

20. Roger Hermiston, *The Greatest Traitor: The Secret Lives of Agent George Blake* (London: Aurum, 2013), 2–6; and Blake, *No Other Choice.*

21. Hermiston, *Greatest Traitor.*

22. Hermiston, 155–56.

23. Blake, *No Other Choice*, 18.

24. Christopher Andrew and Vasili Mitrokhin, *The Sword and the Shield: The Mitrokhin Archive and the Secret History of the KGB* (New York: Basic Books, 1999), 438.

25. Murphy, Kondrashev, and Bailey, *Battleground Berlin*, 216.

26. Murphy, Kondrashev, and Bailey, 217–18.

27. CIA, "Clandestine Services History," appendix A, "Discovery by the Soviets of PBJOINTLY."

28. CIA.

29. CIA.

30. CIA.

31. CIA.

32. CIA.

33. CIA, 15.

34. CIA, 2.

35. Stafford, *Spies beneath Berlin*, 155.

36. CIA, "Clandestine Services History."

37. "The Tunnel of Love," *Washington Post*, May 1, 1956.

38. "Berlin Reds Flock to See 'U.S. Wire-Tap Tunnel,'" *New York Herald Tribune*, May 27, 1956.

39. "Reds Man Guns at 'Spy Tunnel' outside Berlin," *Chicago Tribune*, May 29, 1956.

40. CIA, "Clandestine Services History," appendix D, 2.

41. *Neues Deutschland*, April 25, 1956, in CIA, "Clandestine Services History," appendix D, 6.

42. "Berlin Reds Flock to See 'U.S. Wire-Tap Tunnel.'"

43. NBC, "CIA May Have Ordered Wiretap Tunnel-Dreier," May 17, 1956, in CIA, "Clandestine Services History," appendix C.

44. Hugh Montgomery, interview by David Stafford, Washington, DC, April 2001; quote in Stafford, *Spies beneath Berlin*, 172.

45. Helms and Hood, *Look over My Shoulder*, 137–38; and Donald P. Steury, *On the Front Lines of the Cold War: Documents on the Intelligence War in Berlin, 1946 to 1961* (Washington, DC: CIA History Staff, Center for the Study of Intelligence, 1999).

46. Beschloss, *Mayday*, 437. For Bissell comment, see Thomas Huntington, "The Berlin Spy Tunnel Affair," *Invention and Technology* 10, no. 4 (Spring 1995), www.inventionandtech.com/content/berlin-spy-tunnel-affair-1.

3

IN THE MIND

On November 28, 1953, around 2:00 a.m., Frank R. Olson, a forty-three-year-old government scientist, crashed through a closed window on the tenth floor of the Statler Hotel in New York City and plunged to his death. The night manager, Armand Pastore, rushed out of the front door of the hotel to find Olson lying on the sidewalk flat on his back with his legs bent and broken. When Pastore looked up he saw a shade pushed through the empty window frame.[1]

Pastore called the police, and together they went up to Olson's room, no. 1018A, where they saw another man, Robert V. Lashbrook, sitting on the toilet holding his head in his hands. Lashbrook told the police that he had awakened to the sound of crashing glass, saw a broken window and an empty bed, and came to the conclusion that Olson had committed suicide. Later, Olson's wife claimed Lashbrook told her that he had seen Olson charging for the window.[2]

What Alice Olson did not know at the time was that both Olson and Lashbrook worked for the CIA on an experimental LSD project to assess its suitability for mind control in an interrogation program code-named MKULTRA. Lashbrook was the CIA liaison for the Fort Detrick program on biological warfare, and Olson ostensibly worked at the Army Chemical Corps' Special Operations Division (SOD) at Fort Detrick as a biological warfare research scientist. It was not until 1975 that Olson's apparent suicide and the CIA's pioneering use of LSD made headline news as a result of the Rockefeller Commission's investigation into the CIA's illegal domestic spying operations.[3]

I opened this chapter with the Olson death to highlight that this sensational case made headline news in the 1970s and became embedded in the consciousness of many Americans as a shocking case of the CIA's abuse of power. The story is well known. It has been depicted in popular culture. The death and the MKULTRA program were also subjects of intense scrutiny by the Senate Select Committee on Intelligence, chaired by Frank Church, as well as later hearings conducted by the committee and the Subcommittee on Health and Scientific Research. In fact, given the attention it received, one would have thought that the tragic case would have led to more caution in the future. Instead, some forty years after the death became public, unsavory methods of interrogation in the aftermath of 9/11 surfaced, highlighting the recurrent use of pseudoscientific methods in pursuit of the enemy of the day and an extraordinary case of historical amnesia.

Interrogation Methods

It may seem counterintuitive that a hallucinogenic drug like LSD would be used by an intelligence agency to control a human being; the counterculture image of a person on an "acid trip" is that of someone out of control. But when the CIA began experimenting with the drug in 1951, its effects were still untested.

A recently declassified document from 1953 describes some of the hoped-for effects: "It creates serious mental confusion and makes the human mind temporarily susceptible to suggestions. . . . LSD-25 could be used in the interrogation of unwilling subjects for the purpose of getting them to 'confess' as the material stimulates subjects to talk more freely."[4]

Although some of the joint research between SOD and the CIA investigated harnessing LSD for biological and chemical warfare, another area of research focused on effective methods for interrogating defectors, refugees, prisoners, and other willing or unwilling subjects using a number of different methods like hypnotism, the polygraph, and drugs besides LSD.

The CIA was apparently impressed by the Soviet Bloc's ability to coerce people to confess to crimes they had not committed. One very well-known case was that of the Hungarian Josef Cardinal Mindszenty, who was put on trial in 1949 and confessed to treason he did not commit "with a glazed look in his eyes." The CIA speculated that Mindszenty and other Eastern Bloc defendants became "zombielike" through hypnosis.[5]

But the experience of Robert Vogeler, a thirty-nine-year-old American vice president at International Telephone and Telegraph (ITT) based in Communist Hungary who had close ties to US intelligence, was an even bigger stimulus for the CIA to reverse engineer Eastern Bloc methods. Vogeler had been abducted from a car by two gun-wielding Hungarian border guards in November 1949, arrested, charged with espionage, imprisoned, and tortured. Although he was sentenced to fifteen years in prison, he was released after seventeen months.[6]

The director of the CIA at the time, Roscoe Hillenkoetter, advised CIA agents in the field, as well as naval intelligence, to move Vogeler quickly to the United States before interrogating him if he were to be released. The CIA and the navy were interested in the "implications in terms of medical research and interrogation techniques."[7]

These observations, along with navy explorations of using drugs in operations, led to an ultra-secret CIA project code-named Bluebird undertaken by the Office of Security and the Office of Scientific Intelligence. Col. Sheffield Edwards (1902–75), an earnest man who had been in the US Army during World War II, managed the program, and Morse Allen, another security man, officially headed it. Allen had served in naval intelligence during the war and also had experience rooting out Communists in the 1930s and again after the war in the State Department. Although Allen had no academic training in the behavioral sciences, he took CIA short courses in hypnotism and the polygraph. Both techniques were pillars of the Bluebird program, but the polygraph, or lie detector, became synonymous with the CIA. It used the machine to vet foreign agents and later its own personnel; it became the cornerstone of counterintelligence methods. The machine measured blood pressure, heart rate and heartbeat, perspiration, and other physiological changes to determine honesty. It was also a psychological tool: it instilled fear in subjects or challenged liars to "beat the polygraph." It wasn't foolproof, but the CIA still placed a lot of faith in the machine, despite Office of Security reports that it worked only seven out of eight times.[8]

The security office's interrogation program set up teams to vet agents and defectors for the CIA in West Germany, France, South Korea, and Japan. Each team usually consisted of a medical officer, an interrogator, a hypnotist, and a security technician. Edwards selected the code name after a member of the group opined that Bluebird should create methods to make people being interrogated "sing like birds."[9] The goal of the program was to develop "any method" to "get information from a person against his will and without his knowledge." The CIA sought to control "an individual to the point where he will do our bidding against his will and even against such fundamental laws of nature such as self-preservation."[10]

In 1953, Morse Allen produced a short training film called *The Black Art* with colleagues in his department. The film opens with an American agent having a drink with an "Oriental" person; the agent surreptitiously spikes the drink, and the man falls asleep and is hypnotized. The "Oriental" removes a document from the opposition's office safe and hands it to the American. The film ends by encapsulating the CIA's new mantra: "Could what you have just seen be accomplished without the individual's knowledge? Yes! Against an individual's will? Yes! How: Through the powers of suggestion and hypnosis."[11]

In fact, the name of the game for a case officer who recruits and runs agents is to manipulate spies to do their "bidding." Eastern Bloc spy agencies relied on other methods like ideology and exploited human weaknesses such as sex, fear, or ego to manipulate people, but the CIA, characteristically for a US intelligence agency, aspired to use science and technology to solve pesky intelligence problems like recruitment. (And, of course, the CIA is known for using money and ego as recruitment tools too.)

The interrogation programs used a number of different scientific methods and experiments to control people and a cascade of code names: MKCHATTER, Bluebird, Artichoke, MKNAOMI, MKSEARCH, and MKULTRA. The CIA programs had emerged from World War II OSS efforts with so-called truth drugs, like scopolamine, sodium amytal, pentothal sodium, and marijuana as well as knockout drugs. By the time Artichoke, the new name for Bluebird adopted in 1951, became operational, the CIA combined the polygraph with hypnosis and drugs to elicit information from victims. The CIA consulted with a New York hypnotist and even contracted a magician, John Mulholland, to assist in tips on deceiving people to do things like surreptitiously spike drinks with drugs.

The Bluebird/Artichoke staff planned to experiment domestically and abroad. Defectors, refugees, and POWs served as unwitting guinea pigs abroad, while students were witting guinea pigs at home. The United States had a rich source of prisoners in occupied West Germany. In fact, in 1946 the US Army had taken over a Nazi transit camp for captured US and British pilots in a quiet German town north of Frankfurt called Oberusal and dubbed it Camp King. With its already outfitted prison cells it became an ideal place for the US Army and US intelligence to interrogate prisoners. It was officially called the 7707th European Command Intelligence Center but quickly gained a reputation as Camp King, a base for the Counterintelligence Corps officers known as the "rough boys." The CIA also had a number of secluded safe houses in the area and even a gabled villa a few miles from Camp King, called Villa Schuster.[12]

With this prime real estate in occupied Germany, the CIA was immune from legal prosecution and worked under strict secrecy. As a result, they began to send teams of Bluebird interrogators to West Germany. At a Frankfurt meeting discussing how to experiment on three defectors, one double agent and one suspected double agent, with the drug researcher and University of Rochester professor G. Richard Wendt, a CIA officer stated that "disposal of the body would be no problem."[13]

It should be noted that despite the connotation of "disposal" as "kill," the CIA issued several memos titled "Disposal of Maximum Custody Defectors," describing that disposal meant providing a facility to keep "disposed" persons in security until their knowledge of operations was no longer valuable to the enemy. The CIA was also obsessed with discovering drugs that would cause amnesia, erasing any memory of a victim's ordeal: "It remains the dream of the interested agencies that a drug is forthcoming that can be given to a person orally, without his knowledge, that will result in his revealing anything the interested party would like to know, and the person would have complete amnesia for the event."[14]

But the journalist and author Gordon Thomas claims that "expendables"—"individuals of dubious loyalty or suspected Soviet double agents"—were brought to safe houses near refugee camps in Munich, Germany, and pumped with massive doses of drugs, some of which had been prepared by Frank Olson at Fort Detrick. The rest got electroshock therapy. According to Thomas, "The 'expendables' were killed and their bodies burned," although no documentary evidence exists to substantiate this murder spree.[15]

There is documentary evidence, however, that shows "subjects" were deceived into thinking they were undergoing a medical exam before the team applied the so-called Artichoke treatment—the triad of drugs, hypnosis, and the lie detector test. The CIA left behind telling reports of several cases of this kind in West Germany.

Case #1, as the victim is identified, was between thirty and forty years old and in good health, fairly robust, but he was considered unreliable and irresponsible by his CIA case officers. He liked to get drunk and brag about his numerous conquests.[16]

On June 6, 1952, the Artichoke team transported "Case #1" from a prison to a large heavily guarded safe house (likely Villa Schuster but unnamed) in a small town. The victim was blindfolded and wore sunglasses as he was transported through the village so he was unaware of his location and bystanders would not see his blindfolded eyes. On arrival, the victim was allowed to relax before he was told he would be undergoing a complete physical and psychiatric exam. The team liked this "medical-type cover" story. Not only would it serve to gain the trust of the victim and establish rapport with the Artichoke team, but it would also provide them with an assessment of the victim's physical capability and mental status. A team member drew blood and took a urine sample as part of the ruse.[17]

The next day, one of the team members with a fictitious name and posing as a doctor explained to the victim that "certain medical injections" were necessary to bring his health back to normal. The "subject" allegedly remained agreeable, and the team concluded that they had succeeded in gaining his trust while "establishing a remarkable screen for the Artichoke work." They injected the victim with a light dose of sodium pentothal before starting to hypnotize him. He was hypnotized in twenty minutes. But this was only a "dry run," and the team asked no questions of the man who they thought might be lying to them.

The next day, the team tried a real interrogation. At noon the victim was given a "heavy dosage of sodium pentothal intravenously." The report documents that he became drowsy and went into a full coma. The Artichoke team began to stimulate him by shaking him and sharply slapping his face. Then they gave him a stimulant. They wanted him in what they frequently referred to as a "twilight state." After the stimulant started working, he became talkative and regressed. They were pleased with results as the victim talked to one of the team members as though he was a schoolboy friend. He staggered back to his bedroom next to the exam room accompanied by team members and was heavily guarded.[18]

The Bluebird/Artichoke program was run by Office of Security men like Morse Allen and Sheffield Edwards. CIA leaders were painfully aware that Bluebird/Artichoke personnel had no scientific background. In an anonymized report to the chief of the CIA's medical staff, the author suggested that one of the reasons Artichoke "failed to produce positive results" was a "failure to get scientifically trained personnel in key positions." Therefore, he recommended recruiting scientifically trained personnel.[19] By the time of the infamous MKULTRA, the much larger program based in the more elite and academic Technical Services Division (later Office Technical Services), the behavioral sciences program was run by a PhD scientist, Sidney Gottlieb. It also included topics like personality assessment, brainwashing, and electroshock depatterning treatments. LSD and other drugs were just one part of the behavior control programs.

Enter Sidney Gottlieb, the Real Dr. Strangelove

The man chosen to head the CIA's behavior control experiment emerged as a real-life Dr. Strangelove, a chemist with a stutter and club foot, characteristics that amplified his image as a mad scientist. His name was Sidney Gottlieb; he received a PhD in chemistry in 1943 from the California Institute of Technology, where he worked on a topic on plants, "Studies on a growth inhibitor in guayule." Gottlieb has always been described as a chemist, but it is not widely known that his research was on plants and that the program also experimented with botanicals. Gottlieb traveled to South America to collect plants to test their suitability as pharmaceuticals and poisons.[20]

Gottlieb worked with Olson and was present at Deep Creek Lodge, a secluded cabin in Maryland, nine days before Olson's death, where SOD and CIA scientists gathered for a retreat. After dinner, the army and CIA scientists were offered a glass of Cointreau. Unbeknownst to the group, Robert Lashbrook had spiked the bottle of Cointreau with LSD. The victims, including Olson, were only told twenty minutes after the fact.[21]

Although the evening started off with hilarity and fun, Olson's mood quickly changed, and he became paranoid and schizophrenic. He told his wife he was going to quit his job and acted in such an alarming fashion that CIA scientists sent him to see Dr. Abramson, the CIA psychiatrist who had experimented with LSD together with Gottlieb in New York City. That was why Olson was staying at the hotel from which he plunged to his death.

After the Church Committee report in 1975, Olson became a poster child for CIA abuses. His son, Eric Olson, who is convinced the CIA murdered his father because he was about to blow the whistle on Project Artichoke, has kept the story alive. In 2017 Netflix released a docudrama miniseries combining interviews (including with Eric Olson) and archival footage with live reenactments from Frank Olson's life and death titled *Wormwood*.[22]

Lesser known and literally only a footnote in the Church Committee report is the death of yet another man, Harold Blauer, a professional tennis player who sought psychiatric help after a divorce. Blauer died of heart failure when his circulation collapsed after he was injected with a synthetic mescaline derivative at the New York Psychiatric Institute. Although this was an experiment under contract from the US Army Chemical Corps and not the CIA, it illustrates that the use of unwitting subjects and disregard for human life took place in other parts of the government under the cloak of secrecy during the 1950s.[23]

The CIA's flirtation with drugs, mind control, and use of unwitting subjects was so controversial and horrifying that it was intensely scrutinized by the media, the Rockefeller Commission, and the Senate Select Committee on Intelligence. Although Gottlieb ordered the files destroyed in 1973, enough financial files remained to piece together the story, especially the CIA's contracts with eighty-six universities, hospitals, prisons, and research institutes. Also, after the Olson episode, the CIA began experiments with unwitting subjects such as prostitutes, criminals, and state prisoners in safe houses and prisons. Over the years, more files emerged that escaped the shredder. Even more telling are the recently released files relating to Bluebird and Artichoke since they document the origins of the program as a tool for interrogation.

Surprisingly, the mind control program also received scrutiny and censure internally at the CIA, but it was not until 1963 that the Inspector General issued an order. The extract from the 1957 Inspector General report on the operations of the Technical Services Division merely has a section on "influencing human behavior" that is descriptive, not proscriptive, though it does note that the program needed to be reviewed to determine if it should be continued.[24]

The 1957 report does not condemn experimentation on unwitting subjects or even mention the Olson death. It recommends continuing the program as long as it is done economically. The Inspector General considers some of its objectives, including the main one of improving interrogation techniques. He points out that there are different methods of breaking down an "individual's resistance to interrogation," but the "classical methods of pressure, duress or torture" often led to unreliable knowledge. He saw the Chemical Division's approach as using psychedelics "to create within the individual a mental and emotional situation which will release him from restraint of self-control and induce him to reveal information willingly under adroit manipulation" neutrally. By 1957 drugs like LSD had apparently been used in "six different operations on a total of 33 subjects." No details are supplied about how LSD was actually used in real-life situations on six occasions.[25]

The MKULTRA program, so called because it was "ultra-sensitive work" ("MK" is the code name prefix, and the code name may have been inspired by the World War II Ultra project to decode Enigma machine messages), did not have to undergo ordinary financial audit processes even though it used 20 percent of the Technical Services Division budget. In fact, the Inspector General's Office knew very little about the program. It was not until 1963 that the new Inspector General, John S. Earman, learned more about the program. He wrote his report in the context of new public knowledge about LSD and the emerging counterculture movement of the 1960s and a new CIA director, even if it is not mentioned in the report itself. Despite the lack of material, it was clear to Earman that manipulating human behavior both within and outside the agency was "distasteful and unethical." He further found that "the lack of consistent records precluded use of routine inspection procedures and raised a variety of questions concerning management and fiscal controls."[26]

As a result, the Inspector General report completed in 1963 recommended the "termination of MKULTRA on unwitting subjects."[27] Earman also had reservations about the effectiveness of using drugs in interrogation.

> As of 1960 no effective knockout pill, truth serum, aphrodisiac, or recruitment pill was known to exist. . . . Three years later . . . [the] situation is unchanged with the exception that real progress has been made in the use of drugs in support of interrogation. . . . Ironically, however, the progress here has occurred in the development of a total psychological theory of interrogation, in which the use of drugs has been relegated to a support role.[28]

As was the case in other operational areas like the Berlin Tunnel and spy planes and satellites, many at the CIA seemed to think the quick fix or magic bullet of science or technology instead of old-fashioned espionage would solve their interrogation problems. As Earman noted, any of the drugs used alone would not solve the interrogation problem but rather helped in supporting roles using "a total theory of interrogation." Interestingly, he also pointed out that there was a "tendency toward over-reliance on and misuse of drugs in lieu of perfecting classic espionage techniques."[29]

"You Can't Be Less Ruthless than the Opposition"

Pulling a dictum out of the real world of intelligence, John le Carré, in his classic Cold War espionage novel, *The Spy Who Came in from the Cold,* had Control (head of the British intelligence agency) tell the protagonist, Alec Leamas, "You can't be less ruthless than the opposition."[30] The CIA certainly heeded this call for ruthless methods when it developed the mind control program and justified it as a countermeasure to what they saw as the Communist enemy's success in interrogation.

In addition, they erroneously claimed that Communist interrogators used drugs to produce their stunning results, a paradigmatic example of what is called "mirror imaging" in intelligence circles or "projection" among laypeople, where one intelligence service thinks the enemy is practicing what the other one is doing or admires. In this case, the CIA assumed that the Soviet Bloc and other Communist countries had the same faith in science and technology to solve problems as the United States did. But they did not. The CIA soon found out that the Communist agencies did not use drugs during interrogations. Instead, they used old-fashioned techniques.

When CIA officials testified at the Church Committee hearings in 1975, they claimed that the "CIA had received reports that the Soviet Union was engaged in intensive efforts to produce LSD; and that the Soviet Union had attempted to purchase the world's supply of the chemical." They further claimed that "the Communists were utilizing drugs, physical duress, electric shock, and possibly hypnosis against their enemies."[31]

Interestingly, the CIA director, Allen Dulles, had hired two distinguished academics to work on brainwashing and Communist interrogation techniques in 1953. Harold Wolff, a neurologist at Cornell's Medical School, was then treating Dulles's son because he had suffered brain damage from a head injury during the Korean War. Wolff then asked his colleague at Cornell, Lawrence Hinkle, to work with him on the CIA-sponsored project. In addition, they formed the Human Ecology Society, 1953–54, with rich CIA funding.[32]

The results were far from what the CIA claimed. In fact, the study, first a classified version completed in April 1956, called "Communist Control Methods," a recently declassified appendix to that, and then an unclassified version published in the *AMA Archives of Neurology and Psychiatry,* made clear that the Communists did not use science and technology in their interrogation and indoctrination of captured enemies.

The published paper, "Communist Interrogation and Indoctrination of 'Enemies of the State,'" is a detailed, fifty-nine-page scholarly "Analysis of Methods Used by the Communist State Police," according to the subtitle. The medical journal was a curious place to publish the piece, as it is a comparison of KGB interrogation methods with those of Communist China. After a lengthy history of the Cheka, the Soviet secret police, and details of the arrest, detention, isolation, interrogation, and "trial" and the "confession" of the victim, the paper turns to the same topics in China. While China favored group incarceration and interactions, the Soviets conducted intensive isolation practices and the development of the relationship between the interrogator and the prisoner. The main conclusion of the paper was that the secret police conducted these interrogations with no use of "esoteric methods" or drugs and the practice went back many years. They noted that the secret police had unlimited power and that their actions were "swift" and "arbitrary." The main ingredient in their success was the "total isolation" of the prisoner, and their success rested on the human need for companionship.[33]

To underline the lack of scientific hocus-pocus using drugs, electroshock, or other pulp fiction–type machines, the classified version included an appendix stating that there was a lack of "scientific design and guidance, drugs and hypnosis in communist interrogation and indoctrination procedures." The appendix even pooh-poohed the CIA's notion that "Pavlovian conditioning" was used to control human behavior. Instead, the authors stated emphatically, "The findings of this investigation are that scientists have *not* participated." The methods were organized and developed "by the police officials themselves."[34]

These emphatic conclusions by eminent scientists in 1956 must have been forgotten by the time CIA officials testified to Congress in 1975 that the Soviet Union and the KGB used drugs on subjects. Also, it seems that experiments on unwitting subjects using LSD and other psychoactive drugs continued at least until 1963, the year the CIA's Inspector General officially banned them.

Of course, these experiments took place in the context of 1950s America, a time of conformity, a time of new drugs and experimentation, a time of great faith in the positive effects of science and technology, and, most important, a time of great fear of communism. This was not the first time that the US government took extraordinary measures in times of fear of the enemy. Nor was it to be the last.

In the context of 1950s America, CIA leadership harbored global aspirations as well. Allen Dulles, who served as CIA director from 1953 to 1961 and who had been deputy director of the CIA a few days after Artichoke launched, felt that mind control "could be the decisive weapon" of the age. He believed that any nation that discovered how to manipulate people's minds could "rule the world." This was all part of the CIA's faith in science and global aspirations. If there was a way to control the human mind, "the prize" would "be nothing less than global mastery."[35]

KUBARK

After the Inspector General's recommendation to end MKULTRA, Gottlieb and his colleagues continued a similar operational program called MKSEARCH, which did not use unwitting subjects. But the major development for interrogation techniques was the production of the so-called KUBARK Counterintelligence Interrogation Manual, written in July 1963 and not declassified until 2014. KUBARK was a code name for the CIA, and the manual was intended to "provide guidelines" for CIA interrogators, especially for the counterintelligence interrogation of "resistant sources."[36]

The CIA found members of Eastern Bloc and other Communist intelligence or security services particularly recalcitrant when it came to interrogation. While they recognized that the interrogator is at an advantage, they still faced challenges from the "training, experience, patience and toughness of the interrogatee." For these cases, the CIA found "a principal source of aid" from "scientific findings." The author of the manual thought that an intelligence agency that used "modern knowledge" to solve its problems enjoyed "huge advantages" over services that conducted their business "in eighteenth century fashion."[37]

Nevertheless, KUBARK's new interrogation methods were remarkably similar to those of the Eastern Bloc, even with the nod to using science and technology. The methods included isolation, solitary confinement, stress positions, and self-inflicted pain. The CIA then added its holy triad—polygraph, hypnosis, and psychiatry—to the Communists' old-fashioned interrogation methods as outlined by Hinkle and Wolff.

Oversight and Memory

America's intelligence organizations undergo more internal and external review and oversight than any other intelligence agency in the world. The CIA's Inspector General had reviewed the mind control program in the late 1950s and early 1960s; Congress then reviewed it again in the context of scandal in the mid-1970s. It also received intense scrutiny by the media, perhaps the third watchdog on call in America. Despite these controls, abuses of power and secrecy in the intelligence community persisted once the sunshine of publicity from the televised Church Committee hearings faded into the shadow of forgetfulness.

Part of the rationale for the Senate committee to investigate the mind control episode, it wrote, was "to prevent the recurrence of such abuses in the future." It continued, "The best safeguard against abuses in the future is a complete public accounting of the abuses of the past."[38] But did the 1975 investigations prevent recurrences of abuses thirty years later?

Tortured Human Intelligence

The terrorist attacks of September 11, 2001 led to quick and decisive action by the president of the United States, George W. Bush, and the CIA's Counterterrorism Center (CTC). Within days the CTC sought out potential CIA detention centers abroad to house captured terrorists. And within a week, Bush signed a covert action Memorandum of Authorization (MON) authorizing the director of the CIA to capture and detain potential terrorists, although no mention was made of interrogation. The Geneva Conventions on Torture did not apply to detainees because they were considered "enemy combatants" abroad.[39]

The CIA had developed guidelines for undertaking interrogations in the 1980s, but the Senate Select Committee found no evidence that it consulted them as it prepared to interrogate captured terrorists. Forgotten was the experience with mind control for interrogation or the KUBARK counterintelligence manual. Nor did the CIA consult with other law enforcement agencies or the US military on how to interrogate suspected terrorists. Even though earlier statements by the CIA condemned "physical abuse" and "inhumane physical or psychological techniques" and found that they were "historically proven to be ineffective,"[40] institutional fear and anger took the CIA on another path of unreflective action.

CIA Contract Psychologists

James Elmer Mitchell, an air force psychologist, had provided briefings to the CIA's operational psychologists and officers on a variety of topics between 1998 and 2000, but it was not until May 2001 that he received a mysterious telephone call from the CIA asking him to appear at headquarters for an interview. He had not applied for a job, but he was curious, so he drove to headquarters in Langley for the interview. While at CIA headquarters he mentioned he was retiring from the air force in a couple of months, but he did not want to work for the government and planned to open his own business and do some contracting. He turned down their offer of a job as "chief of a research branch . . . that housed operational psychologists." By August 2001, however, he arranged a "personal services contract with the CIA." On 9/11, he called the CIA and volunteered to work for them.[41]

By December 2001 Mitchell had taken part in a brainstorming session on Islamist extremism at the Philadelphia home of the eminent psychologist Martin E. P. Seligman, who had pioneered the concept of learned helplessness. Also in attendance were several professors, law enforcement officials, and intelligence officers, including the CIA psychologist Kirk M. Hubbard.[42]

When the CIA obtained an al-Qaeda manual that included ways to resist interrogation, its Office of Technical Services hired Mitchell and his partner, Bruce Jessen, to issue a report on the manual. Both psychologists had served in the air force Survival, Evasion, Resistance and Escape (SERE) school and learned about coercive interrogation techniques the enemy might use on US military personnel. In particular, they were influenced by the harsh interrogation techniques used by the Chinese Communists. The idea at the school was to subject US personnel to the same interrogation methods the enemy had used in order to learn how to resist them. This, of course, mirrored the adage, "You can't be less ruthless than the opposition."

Even though both psychologists had extensive experience in mock interrogations, neither had carried out real interrogations. Further, they had no language skills, no expertise on terrorism and al-Qaeda, and no relevant research. Their PhD research was on high blood pressure and family therapy, respectively. They did, however, have contacts in the intelligence and psychology community and an unusual entrepreneurial drive. Mitchell formed the company Mitchell Jessen and Associates, and the CIA reportedly paid them $81 million from 2001 to 2009, when the contract ended under a cloud.[43]

The Death of Gul Rahmen

On October 29, 2002, Gul Rahmen, a suspected Afghan militant, was brought to an abandoned brick factory near the airport in Kabul, Afghanistan. The CIA had converted the factory into a primitive secret prison that became known as the Salt Pit by the CIA, as Cobalt in a Senate Select Committee report, as the Dark Prison by detainees, and as the dungeon by the lead CIA interrogator.[44]

Rahmen proved to be an uncooperative prisoner, refusing even to acknowledge his name. The CIA described him as having a strong "resistance posture." As a result, he was given the "rough treatment;" CIA officers and guards dragged him up and down the dirt prison corridors while he was sleep deprived.

By the time the CIA's contract psychologists, James Mitchell and Bruce Jessen, met Rahmen, CIA employees had concluded their unsuccessful questioning. Mitchell later wrote that he thought it was counterproductive to insist that Rahmen admit his identity as stated on his driver's license because it diverted attention from more important issues. His partner, Jessen, was responsible for questioning him along with "CIA OFFICER I." The interrogation included "48 hours of sleep deprivation, auditory overload, total darkness, isolation, a cold shower, and rough treatment."[45]

According to a CIA report, Rahmen was often seen shivering during his detention. The prison lacked heating or cooling, and he had been shackled to the cell wall while lying on a cold concrete floor. He was naked from the waist down, without even the prison-issued diapers, but had a sweatshirt on. As prison guards made their rounds on the morning of November 20, they found Rahmen dead.

A later autopsy concluded that he had not been beaten to death and did not have remnants of a truth drug in his bloodstream but had probably died of hypothermia.[46] Like the Frank Olson death fifty years earlier, Rahmen's cause of death, however, was unclear to the public. Was it violent torture or hypothermia caused by making him sleep half-naked shackled to a concrete wall in close to freezing temperatures? All these irregularities triggered an investigation into the new practices of detention and interrogation in the new global CIA prisons.

According to the Senate Committee Report on Torture, nudity at the site was the norm and part of a strategy of humiliation, along with wearing diapers. Prisoners were hosed down with cold water while they were shackled naked in cold rooms. Loud music played constantly in the permanently darkened building that had painted-over exterior windows. Guards checked on detainees using headlamps. According to a CIA interrogator, many of the Cobalt Site detainees "literally looked like a dog that had been kenneled." When the doors to the cells were opened, "they cowered."[47]

Once the news of Rahmen's death reached CIA headquarters in Langley, leaders there claimed the interrogation techniques had not been approved. Lawyers like the head of the Inspector General Department, John Rizzo, and leaders like CIA director George Tenet, claimed they did not know the details of the detention site in Afghanistan. The death, however, sparked a thorough review. Despite finding shortcomings and abuse at the site, CIA OFFICER I, a junior officer, with little experience, who ordered Rahmen shackled half-naked to the cell wall in a room with an ambient temperature of 36 degrees, was given a "cash award" of $2,500 for his "consistently superior work" four months after Rahmen's death; he continued to manage the detention site until July 2003.[48]

In April 2002 the CIA's chief of operational psychologists called Mitchell on his cellphone. He had just left a meeting at Langley, but the chief asked him to come back immediately and prepare for a trip abroad. At the CTC meeting, Mitchell learned that the Pakistani government had captured Abu Zubaydah, the highest-ranking al-Qaeda facilitator ever caught, and that the United States had taken him into custody and rendered him to a secret CIA prison in Thailand.[49]

Abu Zubaydah, who was blind in one eye as a result of a botched attempt at plastic surgery before he was captured, had a severe leg wound when he was rendered to a hospital in Thailand. The CIA flew in a doctor from Johns Hopkins University Hospital who successfully saved his life and tended to his leg wound. By the time Mitchell arrived in Thailand, the FBI had already interviewed Abu Zubaydah in the hospital using rapport-building techniques. The FBI obtained a lot of useful information even when Abu Zubaydah was still on a feeding tube. He allegedly told them that "Mukhtar," who was Khalid Sheikh Mohammed (KSM), was the mastermind behind the September terrorist attacks. Later, the CIA claimed that they received this information through enhanced interrogation techniques (EITs), but this was not true.[50]

When Abu Zubaydah was moved to a detention cell, the CIA sedated him and took him to an "all-white room" with four bright halogen lamps and "no amenities." He was subjected to sleep deprivation, loud noise, and limited interaction with a small number of people. He was kept naked. The cell did have air-conditioning, however. The security officers "wore all black uniforms, including boots, gloves, balaclavas, and goggles," to keep Abu Zubaydah from identifying them. At this point, the FBI complained that they were being cut out of the picture even though they had obtained good information from "report [*sic*: rapport] building."[51]

In fact, the FBI claimed Abu Zubaydah spoke of uranium-based explosives and told them about the "Dirty Bomb Plot," devised by an American, José Padilla, nicknamed Abu Amerikani. The CIA later claimed that they elicited this information. Regardless of who elicited what information, the CIA stubbornly pushed for one piece of information, which did not concern the FBI as much: "impending future terrorist plans against the United States."[52]

While Abu Zubaydah did provide valuable information on al-Qaeda operations that led to countless intelligence reports, he did not provide information on possible future attacks. As a result, the CIA claimed he was "uncooperative." He was placed in isolation for forty-seven days while Mitchell and others went home for personal reasons and to plan a future course of action. By July 2002, "novel interrogation techniques" were discussed at a meeting at CIA headquarters. During this meeting, Mitchell provided a list of twelve possible interrogation techniques. By July 24, the attorney general approved ten of them: "attention grasp, walling, the facial hold, the facial/insult slap, cramped confinement, wall standing, stress positions, sleep deprivation, use of diapers, and use of insects." Waterboarding was approved later, in August.[53]

The intensive EITs used on Abu Zubaydah took place for nineteen days in August and accelerated quickly from attention grasp to confinement in a big box and a little box to slaps if he denied having further information.

Finally, the two psychologists started using the waterboard method. This entailed placing him on a gurney with his head tilted downward. A cloth was then placed over his mouth and nose and water poured on the area for seventeen seconds. During his thirty-eight waterboard sessions, he provided "NO useful information." Instead, during one session he was rendered unconscious, "with bubbles rising through his open, full mouth," and another time he vomited the rice and beans from his meal ten hours earlier. He cried, begged, pleaded, and whimpered. He denied having further information.[54]

By the end of the enhanced interrogation sessions, the CIA celebrated success by confirming that Abu Zubaydah did not have further information. They deemed the EITs effective and planned to use "Mitchell's template" for future aggressive interrogation of high-value targets.[55] He had been the first guinea pig, and his case marked the birth of EITs. And future interrogations of high-value targets like KSM did indeed follow the EIT template, especially emphasizing waterboarding.

KSM and Waterboarding

One of the most important terrorists caught and detained by the Pakistanis and the CIA in March 2003 was Khalid Sheikh Mohammed, known as the mastermind of 9/11. The photograph of him that was frequently printed in the newspapers depicted a disheveled man with unruly black hair and mustache along with a protruding potbelly under a white T-shirt.

While KSM was in Pakistani custody, the CIA and the Pakistanis interrogated him using some sleep deprivation but no other coercive techniques. He denied that he possessed any knowledge of future attack plans in the United States or of the whereabouts of Osama bin Laden or al-Zawari. Given his recalcitrance, within days, the CIA moved him to the Cobalt / Salt Pit site in Afghanistan and an interrogator said, "Let's roll with this new guy." Within hours of his arrival, interrogators began to use EITs, including facial and abdominal slaps, facial grabs, stress positions, standing sleep deprivation, nudity, and water dousing. The chief of interrogations ordered rectal rehydration. Apparently, the CIA's EITs caused KSM to "clam up," and CIA interrogators decided to adopt a "softer Mr. Rogers persona."[56]

When the softer Mr. Rogers persona only turned up fabricated information, the CIA transferred KSM to another interrogation site code-named

Blue located in Poland. On his arrival he was stripped and placed in a standing sleep deprivation position. The CIA quickly started using the waterboarding technique, the "big stick" of the EITs.

CIA contract interrogators Mitchell and Jessen used the waterboard method on KSM 183 times on fifteen different occasions. Sometimes there would be more than three sessions in a twenty-four-hour period, thus exceeding the Office of Medical Services guidelines. The first application lasted thirty minutes, exceeding the CIA's Office of Legal Counsel's opinion by ten minutes. At this point he offered some information on a plot against Heathrow Airport and Canary Wharf in Great Britain, but it turned out to be fabricated. Even so, the CIA was interested in learning about future plots against America, not other countries, and pressed KSM on this point during every waterboard session. Finally, CIA headquarters concluded that the waterboard interrogation technique was not working on KSM. The deputy chief of the CIA interrogation program thought it was "ineffective" and had "potential for physical harm" and that it "may poison the well."[57]

Nevertheless, Mitchell stated that he had not seen a "resistor [*sic*] like KSM" and then pulled out all the stops and used all the EITs on him, to no avail. Their interests were narrowly focused: "They only wanted to hear him speak if there was revealing information on the next attack," they told him. They devoted all measures to "the single issue" of the "next attack on America."[58]

Peculiar Human Intelligence

According to the Senate Intelligence Committee Report on Torture, the enhanced interrogation methods were not an effective way to acquire intelligence or to make the detainees more cooperative. While some detainees produced useful intelligence after undergoing enhanced interrogation, those who were given the chance did so before those measures. Many detainees fabricated information, leading to faulty intelligence.[59]

As news of the EITs slowly leaked into the press, the CIA began an influence campaign to provide the press with information to make the agency look good. But the controversial technique was seen in a less than favorable light and was deemed torture by many. Its use tarnished the image of America abroad.

By December 2007, the House Senate Conference for the fiscal year

2008 Intelligence Authorization Act voted to include an amendment banning coercive interrogation methods. In its place they recommended using the Army Field Manual on Human Intelligence Collector Operations as a standard for all US government interrogations. President Bush vetoed the act with the justification that the special coercive techniques worked against vicious terrorists and helped foil plots. He told the American public in a radio speech that the techniques saved American lives, whereas using the Army Field Manual "could cost American lives." But when the constitutional lawyer Barack Obama took office in January 2009, he quickly closed all the detention centers and required all US government officials to abide by the Army Field Manual on Human Intelligence. He banned the coercive techniques and branded them a "mistake."[60]

Historical Amnesia

Earlier in this chapter, I quoted a passage from the 1977 Senate Select Committee Report in which the authors made a nod to history and its role in helping to prevent future abuses. It is striking that the Senate Intelligence Committee Report on Torture of 2014 described one of its goals for producing the reports as preventing abuses in the future by a public accounting of past abuses. The report criticized the CIA's abuse of power and hoped the report would "prevent future coercive interrogation practices"; it did not want "history to be forgotten."[61]

Although the CIA's post-9/11 enhanced interrogation techniques did not use drugs (except when medically required) as a method to elicit information, there are striking similarities between the EIT program and the mind control experiments of the 1950s and 1960s. First, it should be clear by now that both programs sought to create and use novel interrogation methods that promised full control over a human being that would lead to eliciting valuable intelligence information. And they both drew on the behavioral sciences to find this magic bullet. Second, both programs failed in their quest for total control over a human being through unusual methods and received public censure. And third, in both programs, deaths triggered internal and eventually external critical reviews that led to their downfall.

Unlike Olson, of course, Rahmen was a CIA detainee, not an employee. He was the first prisoner to be interrogated in the Salt Pit. And unlike the previous interrogation methods, detainees were not given truth drugs or

LSD. But like Olson, the death sparked an investigation by the CIA and later by the Senate Select Committee for Intelligence that led to a massive, 6,800-page report of which the "summary report" was published, numbering 549 pages with 2,725 footnotes.[62]

These investigations also led to more public knowledge about the new interrogation method, the so-called enhanced interrogation technique, devised by the two CIA contract psychologists, Jessen and Mitchell.

While the legacy of the LSD and drug component of the earlier behavior control experiments remained strong in American culture, the fact that it was at its heart a program to improve interrogation methods has been largely overlooked and forgotten. Perhaps the CIA did not use LSD and truth serums during the second episode because they did indeed learn from the past. But the point is that the same department, the Office for Technical Services, sought other psychological methods to find a magic bullet for behavior control.

In essence, the main lesson of the first episode of abuse behind the cloak of secrecy was never learned. What accounts for this historical amnesia? In a quest to find out why the past was ignored, I interviewed several senators who served on intelligence committees to find out.

During my tenure at the Wilson Center in Washington, DC, I had the opportunity to interview the CEO Jane Harman, who had served on the Senate and House intelligence committees. When I asked her why the Senate Committee on Intelligence did not have a historical memory, her answer was, "Congress isn't graduate school, it's a political arena, more like the Roman Coliseum than Harvard University, tomatoes are thrown, metaphorically, lions cruise around, it's a hard environment."[63]

Notes

1. "Plunge Kills U.S. Defense Aide," *New York Times*, November 29, 1953; "U.S. Employee Visits N.Y. to See Doctor; Plunges Ten Floors," *Chicago Daily Tribune*, November 29, 1953, 30; "Scientist Killed in Hotel Plunge," *New York Herald Tribune*, November 29, 1953; and Michael Ignatieff, "What Did the C.I.A. Do to His Father?," *New York Times Magazine*, April 1, 2001, sec. 6, 56. See also the Frank Olson Project: www.frankolsonproject.org.

2. "Plunge Kills U.S. Defense Aide"; "U.S. Employee Visits N.Y. to See Doctor; Plunges Ten Floors"; "Scientist Killed in Hotel Plunge"; and Ignatieff, "What Did the C.I.A. Do to His Father?" See also the Frank Olson Project: www.frankolsonproject.org.

3. John Marks, *The Search for the "Manchurian Candidate": The CIA and Mind Control* (repr., New York: Norton, 1991), 91.

4. Central Intelligence Agency, Information Report, "Research Data on D-Lysergic Acid Diethylamide (LSD-25)/Potential for BW and CW," September 7, 1953, CIA-RDP80-00809A000500200004-2, CREST, retrieved from FOIA Electronic Reading Room,

5. Marks, *Search for the "Manchurian Candidate,"* 23.

6. For contemporaneous accounts, see Foreign Relations of the United States reports: https://history.state.gov/historicaldocuments/frus1950v04/d532; and https://history.state.gov/historicaldocuments/frus1949v05/pg_451. A number of articles appeared in the *New York Times*, including reports of his "confession." See, e.g., "Avowal of Guilt Made by Vogeler in Budapest Trial," *New York Times*, February 19, 1951, www.nytimes.com/1950/02/19/archives/avowal-of-guilt-made-by-vogeler-in-budapest-trial-itt-executive-on.html. For his book, see Robert Vogeler, *I Was Stalin's Prisoner* (New York: Harcourt, Brace, 1952).

7. CIA-MKULTRA Files, CD, #0000144907, Interrogation of Mr. Robert Vogeler, June 23, 1950.

8. Marks, *Search for the "Manchurian Candidate,"* 23–24.

9. H. Albarelli Jr., *A Terrible Mistake: The Murder of Frank Olson and the CIA's Secret Cold War Experiments* (Walterville, OR: Trine Day, 2019), 28.

10. CIA-MKULTRA Files, January 25, 1952, Memorandum: Mori:0000144686, 1–2.

11. CIA-MKULTRA, I & SO Training Film: Hypnosis, Mori: 0000149585.

12. Stephen Kinzer, *Poisoner in Chief: Sidney Gottlieb and the CIA Search for Mind Control* (New York: Henry Holt, 2019), 40–42.

13. Marks, *Search for the "Manchurian Candidate,"* 41.

14. CIA-MKULTRA files on CDs: Mori nos. 0000184586, 184585 (March 7, 1951), 184588 (May 1, 1951); Memo, January 25, 1952: CIA-MKULTRA files: 0000144585, 4, on amnesia.

15. Gordon Thomas, *Secrets and Lies: A History of CIA Mind Control and Germ Warfare* (Old Saybrook, CT: Octavo Editions, 2007), 66–67.

16. CIA-MKULTRA CD, #0000149441, "Artichoke Cases, June 1952," July 3, 1952.

17. CIA-MKULTRA CD.

18. CIA-MKULTRA CD.

19. CIA-MKULTRA CD, #0000144585, January 25, 1952, memorandum for Chief, Medical Staff.

20. Sidney Gottlieb, "Studies on a Growth Inhibitor in Guayule" (PhD diss., California Institute of Technology, 1943), https://thesis.library.caltech.edu/10023.

21. Senate Report, 74–79.

22. *Wormwood*, www.netflix.com/title/80059446.

23. US Senate, *Foreign and Military Intelligence, Book I, Final Report of the Select Committee to Study Governmental Operations with Respect to Intelligence Activities* (Washington, DC: Government Printing Office, 1976), 386n3a.

24. Excerpt from the IG report, "Operations of TSD," National Security Archive, John Marks materials.

25. Excerpt from the IG report, "Operations of TSD."

26. J. S. Earman, Inspector General, July 26, 1953, Memorandum for Director of Central Intelligence and Report of Inspection of MKULTRA, 38, 2, CIA Electronic Reading Room.

27. Earman, Inspector General, July 26, 1953, Memorandum.

28. Earman, 17.

29. Earman.

30. John le Carré, *The Spy Who Came in from the Cold* (New York: Pocket Books, [1963] 2001), 15.

31. US Senate, *Foreign and Military Intelligence, Book I*, 392–93.

32. Marks, *Search for the "Manchurian Candidate,"* 135.

33. Lawrence E. Hinkle and Harold G. Wolff, "Communist Interrogation and Indoctrination of 'Enemies of the State': Analysis of Methods Used by the Communist Secret Police (A Special Report)," *AMA Archives of Neurology and Psychiatry* 76 (August 1956): 115–74.

34. CIA, "Communist Control Methods, Appendix I: The Use of Scientific Design and Guidance, Drugs and Hypnosis in Communist Interrogation and Indoctrination Procedures," FOIA Electronic Reading Room, CIA-RDP65-00756R000400020007-9; emphasis in original.

35. Kinzer, *Poisoner in Chief*, 50, 58.

36. CIA, "KUBARK Counterintelligence Interrogation, July 1963," FOIA Electronic Reading Room. This manual was declassified in 2014.

37. CIA, "KUBARK Counterintelligence Interrogation, July 1963," 2.

38. US Senate, "Project MKULTRA, the CIA's Programs of Research in Behavioral Modification," in *Joint Hearing before the Select Committee on Intelligence and the Subcommittee on Health and Scientific Research of the Committee on Human Resources, United States Senate*, 95th Cong., 1st sess., August 3, 1977 (Washington, DC: Government Printing Office, 1977), 1, 3.

39. US Senate, "Project MKULTRA," 28.

40. US Senate, "Project MKULTRA," 32.

41. James E. Mitchell and Bill Harlow, *Enhanced Interrogation: Inside the Minds and Motives of the Islamic Terrorists Trying to Destroy America* (New York: Crown Forum, 2016), 17–21.

42. Scott Shane, "2 U.S. Architects of Harsh Tactics in 9/11's Wake," *New York Times,* August 11, 2009, www.nytimes.com/2009/08/12/us/12psychs.html.

43. Shane; US Senate, Select Committee on Intelligence, *The Senate Intelligence Committee Report on Torture: Committee Study of the Central Intelligence Agency's Detention and Interrogation Program* (Brooklyn, NY: Melville House, 2014), 35 [hereafter US Senate, *Report on Torture*].

44. Adam Goldman and Kathy Gannon, Associated Press; reprinted by NBC News, March 28, 2010. The AP was the first to report on Rahmen's death.

45. US Senate, *Report on Torture*, 61–62; and Mitchell and Harlow, *Enhanced Interrogation*, 89.

46. CIA, Memorandum for Deputy Director of Operations, Subject: Death Investigation—Gul Rahman, January 28, 2003, FOIA Electronic Reading Room, C06555318, released June 10, 2016.

47. US Senate, *Report on Torture*, 58, 240.

48. US Senate, 62–63.

49. Mitchell and Harlow, *Enhanced Interrogation*, 9–10; US Senate, *Report on Torture*, 37–39.

50. US Senate, *Report on Torture*, 38–39.

51. US Senate, 40–42.

52. US Senate, 41.

53. US Senate, 44.

54. US Senate.

55. US Senate.

56. US Senate, 83–85.

57. US Senate, 87–89.

58. US Senate, 90–91.

59. US Senate, 3–4.

60. US Senate, 151–52.

61. US Senate, ix, xii.

62. US Senate, ix, xii.

63. Interview with Jane Harman, Wilson Center, March 9, 2016.

II

GOING GLOBAL

4

OUR MACHINE IN HAVANA

On September 12, 1962, Esteban Márquez Novo, a CIA agent in Cuba, mailed an ordinary-looking letter to the United States. But between the lines of the letter was a note in secret writing describing a restricted military area in western Cuba in the province of Pinar del Río connected by the cities of San Cristóbal, San Diego de los Banos, Consolación del Norte, and Las Pozas. There was even more security surrounding the plantation (*finca*) formerly owned by José Manuel Cortina García where it was rumored that top-secret work on missiles was being conducted. CIA headquarters added the coordinates for the very large grid in the information report when the September 7, observation was disseminated on September 18. As the CIA official Samuel Halpern later recalled, "If you take a pencil and hook up these four towns with a pencil line, you find yourself with a trapezoid. And so it became known as the trapezoid area."[1]

Around the same time, reports came streaming in from other agents and refugees. Claudio Morinas, Castro's personal pilot, reported to a source that Cuba had "40-mile range guided missiles, both surface-to-surface and surface-to-air. . . . There are also many mobile ramps for intermediate range rockets. They don't know what is awaiting them." This was September 20.[2] Another agent report disseminated to the intelligence community the next day recorded that the Cuban army's chief of war plans said, "We will fight to the death and perhaps we can win because we have everything including atomic weapons."[3]

In mid-September, a middle-aged accountant walked into the Opa-Locka refugee center near Miami, Florida. His report, distributed on September 21, was based on an early September sighting of a convoy of twenty Soviet trucks pulling twenty trailers carrying long canvas-covered, missile-like objects with tail fin silhouettes near Havana. When debriefers placed photographs in front of the refugee, he identified the SS-4/R12s. He described the scene as follows:

> The trailers, the longest I have ever seen in Cuba, were two-axle, four-wheeled. They were 65 to 70 feet in length and about eight feet in width.
>
> I believe the transport trailers were carrying long missiles, so long that the tail end extended over the end of the trailer. I would guess that the missiles were a few feet longer than the trailers. . . . It looked as if the tail end of the canvas silhouetted the two top fins of the four fins of the missile.[4]

Long missiles were always offensive missiles.

A second refugee report included an observation on September 17 of a convoy heading toward the San Cristóbal area. This information was received on September 27 and was remarkably similar to the previous refugee reports about Russian missile-carrying convoys.

These were all human intelligence reports describing offensive missiles in Cuba. But the traditional narrative about how we found missiles in Cuba showcases the U-2 spy plane flight over Cuba, almost a month later, as I describe in the next paragraph.

On the morning of October 14, 1962, about an hour after sunrise, Maj. Richard S. Heyser's U-2 spy plane soared over Cuba's airspace flying at an altitude of 72,500 feet—twice as high as a commercial airliner. With very few clouds in the sky, he had perfect visibility for a reconnaissance mission. Swooping in from the south, he headed to the northwest of the island, an area neglected in previous missions. As his plane flew over San Cristóbal, on the western side of the island about sixty miles from Havana, he switched on the camera located under the cockpit. The camera thumped and its motor whined as it swung back and forth scanning the landscape, furiously snapping pictures. After taking three thousand photographs in twelve minutes, Heyser left hostile airspace and flew back to McCoy Air Force Base in Orlando, Florida.[5]

As soon as Heyser landed, he took out two big rolls of film and put them in special shipping containers. The darkly handsome man with a permanent scowl on his face then handed the containers to two generals, who personally couriered them to the Naval Photographic Intelligence Center in Suitland, Maryland. From there the film was taken to Arthur (Art) C. Lundahl's photointerpretation shop located on the top four floors of a car dealership—the Steuart Motor Co. Building on Fifth and K Streets—in a seedy part of Washington, DC, where CIA photo-interpreters had to pick their way through littered trash, abandoned cars, and broken bottles before getting to the office. It was a good cover for the CIA's National Photographic Interpretation Center (NPIC) housed in the seven-story World War II building.[6]

When the take from Heyser's so-called Mission 3101 arrived under armed guard at the Steuart building at 9:55 the next morning, it may have had more "premonitory rattle" (to borrow a phrase from Barbara Tuchman's description of the World War I interception of the Zimmerman telegram) than any other U-2 film from Cuba, but it was handled like all the other films. The duty officer accepted the eight cans from the US Navy truck and plopped them in a wire basket for delivery to the photo-interpreter teams.

These are the iconic images that led to the US discovery of missiles on Cuba, according to the received narrative. The mighty U-2 spy plane's fuzzy reconnaissance photographs provided visual proof of nuclear-tipped missiles ready to attack America.

But there is a big problem with concentrating so heavily on the technological wizardry, no matter how impressive it is, in the story of how we found the menacing missiles on Cuba. It shortchanges the role of humans described at the beginning of the chapter. For it was information that came from human spies that provided the target for the U-2 spy plane's mission. It was the information from human spies that told the U-2 pilot where to look. And it was information from human spies that told the intelligence community what to look for.

One of the reasons that the role of humans is not widely known and has been soft-pedaled is that Americans are so enamored by technology that it has been bestowed with heroic stature. In this case, the machine's renown has been perpetuated because US intelligence agencies place so much weight on using technology in intelligence. The other reason the role of humans is lesser known is that the names of the agents and refugees have never been revealed by the CIA. The reconnaissance photographs were shown publicly as proof, while the agents' role was obscured.

In an effort to ferret out the names of the agents and refugees, I visited CIA headquarters in Langley, Virginia, in February 2016 during my stay

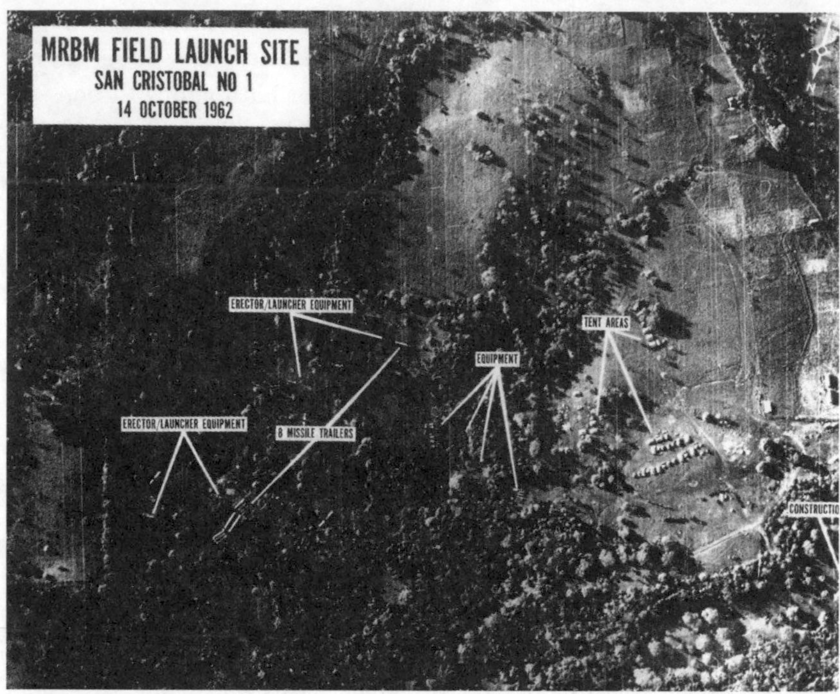

Figure 4.1 One of the first images of missile bases under construction shown to President John F. Kennedy on the morning of October 16, 1962. *John F. Kennedy Presidential Library and Museum, Boston*

in Washington, DC, in order to have them release the names of people who were the unsung heroes of the Cuban Missile Crisis. The meeting took place at the Public Affairs Office secure meeting room, a Sensitive Compartmented Information Facility (SCIF), a little beyond the CIA's museum, which featured an exhibit showing trophies from the CIA's successful mission against Osama bin Laden. Ryan, the public affairs officer, pointed to bin Laden's rifle in a glass case.

During the meeting with Ryan and the CIA historian David Robarge, I hit a brick wall when I brought up the topic of the identities of the agents. Although the event occurred over fifty years ago, the CIA could never reveal the identity of the agents because it would set a bad precedent, said Ryan. It would make it hard for the CIA to recruit agents because they are assured that their identities will remain secret forever. And even if the agent were dead, the agent still had living family members. Unlike well-known and celebrated defectors-in-place like Oleg Penkovsky and Adolf

Tolkachev, who were killed and outed by the KGB and have been lionized in books and articles, the Cuban agents have not been made public by other sources. And researchers cannot obtain information about sources and their names using the Freedom of Information Act.

Despite the CIA's refusal to release the names of the agents and refugees who reported on offensive missiles in Cuba, at least the name of an on-island agent, Esteban Márquez Novo, is now known even though the refugees, names have not yet been uncovered.[7]

To understand the role of human spies, we need to step back in time to the summer before the spy plane mission, when two new sources of human intelligence started to document a stunning Soviet military buildup in Cuba.

Opa-Locka

First the refugees came in their yachts hauling works of art and jewelry, then on boats, on small tramp steamers, on rafts made of old truck tire inner tubes, and finally on planes. The people started coming to America in the hundreds, then thousands, then tens of thousands, then hundreds of thousands. The final tally estimates that about half a million people fled Castro's Cuba. In 1962 alone, the Immigration and Naturalization Service (INS) processed 1,700 to 2,000 refugees a week, and the majority landed in Miami.[8]

Within weeks of Fidel Castro's seizure of power in January 1959, the CIA had established a field office of the Domestic Contacts Division in the Directorate of Intelligence in Miami "to monitor and report on developments in Cuba." In addition to the expected governmental agencies like INS, other intelligence or counterintelligence agencies actively involved with Cubans included the FBI, the army CIC, the navy ONI, and the air force OSI. Naturally, the intelligence community was eager to get any current information they could about Cuba.[9]

But they did not have a lot and were not tapping the rich information coming from the refugees. The need for information about Cuba only increased after the failed Bay of Pigs invasion in April 1961. In fact, by Christmastime, George McManus, special assistant to CIA chief Allen Dulles, paid a visit to Justin F. Gleichauf, head of the Miami field office, to find out why there were so few reports about Cuba. Gleichauf complained that he had only four interrogators and no space. As a result of this visit, he got what he had been recommending for years: "a formal reception and interrogation center" modeled on the successful one in Germany.[10]

The Refugee Interrogation Center opened in March 1962 in Opa-Locka, a Moorish revival town near Miami, where most Cubans arrived. It was officially called the Caribbean Admission Center (CAC), but it was run by the CIA and the Defense Department and used the INS as official cover. Located in an old Marine Corps Air Station, the center consisted of two renovated barracks and about forty officers: twenty-five military personnel from all services and fifteen from the CIA, most of whom knew Spanish. To assist interrogators who debriefed this deluge of refugees, the CIA had prepared the "Interrogation Guide: Cuba." The guide was enormous, with over 116 pages of questions to use when interrogating selected refugees. The government seemed interested in everything ranging from politics, economics, and culture to military installations.[11]

Given the large number of refugees, the CIA felt it had to do a kind of triage. After INS interviewed selected men between the ages of sixteen and sixty at the airport, those deemed to have interesting information were passed on to the Interrogation Center. Although 75 percent of the refugees were women or children, only these men were interviewed. To give these numbers some context: between March and October 1962, 55,000 refugees had arrived from Cuba by airplane alone. By the time the CIA had finished its interrogations in 1962, it had processed 11,500 men, produced 5,500 information reports, and collected 3,000 documents. CIA debriefers had interviewed about 150 people a day.[12] The painstaking work would soon turn up some gold nuggets from several refugees that would alter the course of history.

JMWAVE and Operation Mongoose

In 1961, the CIA created its largest station in the world outside of its Langley headquarters. It was located on the South Campus of the University of Miami. It was code-named JMWAVE and founded to launch operations against Communist Cuba. It was this station that orchestrated Operation Mongoose, a Kennedy administration–sponsored operation to overthrow Fidel Castro by destabilizing Cuba. The CIA's Miami station used the cover of a business, Zenith Technological Enterprises, which employed three to four hundred CIA operatives at first. Ted Shackley, nicknamed the "Blond Ghost," became chief of station in 1962 and oversaw a massive expansion of resources. By the time Operation Mongoose had ended, the station employed about six hundred staff members and five thousand contractors. According to DCI Richard Helms, the CIA had a private navy, which was the third largest in the Caribbean. The CIA modified yachts, fishing boats, and speed boats for operations against Cuba.[13]

On March 11, 1962, Esteban Márquez Novo and his radioman, Yeyo Napoleón, left Miami in a landing craft with a CIA crew, towing a wooden speed boat, which eventually dropped them in a canoe as they approached the shore of southwestern Cuba; then they paddled up the San Diego River into Pinar del Río Province. They were armed with fifteen hundred pounds of munitions and had received six months of spy tradecraft training in the Miami station under a CIA officer, Tom Hewitt. The operation was initially code-named AMCOBRA, but later Novo received the code name AMBANTY-1 and Yeyo Napoleón, AMBANTY-2 ("AM" is the code prefix for Cuba operations). By July 1962, eleven CIA teams had infiltrated Cuba using the CIA's mini naval force to land on the shores of Cuba. This team was the only successful one.[14]

Novo was born in Los Palacios in Pinar del Río Province on August 3, 1909, and came from a well-off family; he was fifty-two years old by the time he landed in his homeland as part of an Operation Mongoose team. He had served in the Cuban army under the Cuban dictator Fulgencio Batista and was fiercely anticommunist. According to the Cuban state newspaper, *Granma*, Novo had attempted a revolt against the new Communist government under Castro together with other former Batista soldiers from the perch of the Sierra del Rosarío in Pinar del Río on February 19, 1961. Cuban soldiers captured many members of Novo's group, and by April 1961 he had fled to the Argentine embassy in Havana where he asked for political asylum. He then flew to the US embassy in Venezuela on May 24, 1962, where he visited a CIA official code-named Otto who co-opted him to work for the CIA. Novo eagerly took up the assignment and training in Miami to become an on-island spy and saboteur under the direction of Tom Hewitt ("Otto").[15] But his days were going to be numbered after returning to his homeland.

The Arms Buildup

Soon after Castro's seizure of power, the Soviet Union began supplying the country with an ever-increasing number of arms. After the Bay of Pigs fiasco in April 1961, during which the US-backed Cuban guerrillas, along with American mercenaries, tried to invade Cuba, the Soviet Union's supplies of arms and munitions increased because the Soviet Union and Cuba feared another invasion. Apparently, the US government did not know about this early military buildup or did not believe it was happening. After the offensive missile verification on October 14, 1962, postmortems claimed that there had been several hundred reports about "Soviet weapons shipments and missiles installations in Cuba . . . before August 1960, i.e. before the USSR had supplied Cuba with any weapons at all." In fact, there were 211 reports of missiles in Cuba before January 1,1962. But the US government claimed that none of the reports could be verified.[16]

By January 1, 1962, the US intelligence community became aware of Soviet Bloc arms delivered to Cuba, including sixty Soviet-built jet fighters, helicopters, and other aircraft. They were clearly displayed at the New Year's Day parade.[17]

The Soviet Bloc arms deliveries were likely Moscow's response to help defend Cuba against the CIA's covert Operation Mongoose, which performed sabotage, subversion, and espionage in Cuba and against Cuban interests around the world in the wake of the failed Bay of Pigs operation.

Meanwhile, the United States had installed Jupiter missiles in Turkey, which had become operational in April. General Secretary Nikita Khrushchev responded by secretly ordering the deployment of offensive medium-range ballistic missiles (MRBMs) and intermediate-range ballistic missiles (IRBMs)—the SS-4 and SS-5 surface-to-surface missiles (SSMs)—to Cuba in May. The United States did not know about this action and subsequent deception operations at the time.[18] By August, however, the CIA did become aware of a rapid influx to Cuba of equipment as well as thousands of military personnel. This alarming information came from reports by refugees arriving in the United States at the Opa-Locka Refugee Center.

By summer 1962, the CIA had received forty reports from Opa-Locka chronicling the arrival of four thousand Soviet Bloc technical and six thousand military personnel in Cuba and an increasing number of ships arriving in Havana Harbor. Many sources reported that "foreign personnel were dressed in dirty, dusty, slept-in, red-checkered shirts and faded blue trousers." Over a dozen sources reported on two major construction sites and many more on the eviction of tenant farmers to make way for restricted military sites.[19]

By the beginning of August, the Committee on Overhead Reconnaissance (COMOR) set up a card file system to start targeting the newly vacant farms for U-2 reconnaissance photography. By the end of August, the CIA had reconnaissance photographs of four farms, including one showing an SA-2 site near Sagua La Grande, 319 kilometers east of Havana. The targeted flights also found eight surface-to-air missile (SAM) sites scattered throughout western Cuba. All the sites were still under construction. Of course, these installations were only for defensive missiles and were designed for air defense against US aerial attacks or U-2 overflights. Some officials, as discussed below, thought this step was a prelude to offensive weapons.[20]

Remarkably, as early as June and July 1962, these reports also included information about offensive missiles and military installations. At that point, refugees reported on rumors that offensive military weapons like long-range missiles were going to be built in Cuba. Later, the CIA said they had checked out every report of missiles using U-2 overflights but never found any offensive missiles. This is not surprising given the fact that the refugees gave only a *forewarning* that missiles were going to be installed, not that they were actually there already.[21]

Although DCI John McCone (1961–65) became increasingly alarmed by this buildup and warned the military that he thought "measures . . . were being taken . . . for the purpose of insuring some secrecy of offensive capability such as MRBM's to be installed by Soviets after the present phase was completed," his voice was ignored in favor of the belief that the Soviet Union would not place offensive missiles on Cuba because it was "incompatible with Soviet policy as we presently estimate it."[22] In other words, they had never done it before and therefore would not do it now.

The CIA's Special National Intelligence Estimate (SNIE 85-3-62), approved by the US intelligence board on September 19, 1962, stated that the USSR recognized "that the development of an offensive military base in Cuba might provoke US military intervention and thus defeat their present purpose."[23] The general consensus was that the missiles observed were defensive against a possible US invasion. This estimate proved to be a huge mistake. And if it were not for a lucky constellation of factors, it would have remained a cornerstone of policy.

In fact, as this estimate was being written, refugee and agent reports were pouring into the hands of the CIA with contradictory information. Between April and October 1962, there were over a thousand human source reports about the arms buildup. But there was one problem. Although refugees and CIA agents observed offensive missiles, by the time the information was communicated to the CIA there was a considerable time lag. In the case of the refugee reports, the lag lay in the travel time between departure from Cuba, processing by the INS, and arrival at the Interrogation Center. It took from one week to one month for the CIA to receive the information. Nevertheless, it was timely enough to take action. A time lag was not unique to the refugee agents. Information from technology was also delayed because there were blackout periods when the U-2 could not fly, and flights depended on cloud-free weather.

In the case of CIA agents based in Cuba, communicating with their handlers in the United States was dangerous and tricky. The director of the CIA admitted that "agents existed and worked in peril of their lives." Some agents were killed by firing squad, and others went missing. Agents based in Cuba could send brief messages in secret writing through the post office to addresses controlled by the CIA (the invisible ink could be developed only by the CIA), or they could send "quick and furtive radio transmissions," or they could meet with couriers to pass on information. Although on-island agents were in danger, communication was often quicker than in the case of the refugee sources.[24]

Royal Palm Tree–Size Missiles

The reports on offensive missiles kept piling up in September and October 1962. In fact, there were 123 reports describing missiles. Of the eight reports included in an Inspector General postmortem, five also described trailer convoys with canvas-covered objects so long that the convoy personnel had to get out and remove streetlight posts and mailboxes in order to turn the corners.[25] Other people reported on missiles as long as royal palm trees—the kind of palms that soar into the sky. As the panelists at the CIA Cuba Missile Crisis conference said in a videotaped session of 1992, the reports about moving mailboxes and lampposts and seeing missiles as tall as royal palms were not included in their packets or the conference booklet.[26] This is another reason to think that the CIA has withheld important material.

Yet the CIA claims that only two reports provided reliable information about offensive missiles near Havana. This assertion, first made and brought to light in the agency's thirtieth anniversary collection of selected documents, published in 1992, is repeated over and over again after 1992. Before 1992, the myth of the machine reigned. There was little to no discussion about the role of human intelligence.[27] Part of the reason for this neglect of the CIA agent Esteban Márquez Novo and his network may have been that the CIA wanted to preserve Novo's security; he was still in Cuba during the Cuban Missile Crisis and even reported on convoys returning mobile missiles to the Soviet Union. But Novo's initial mission was to help overthrow Castro, and he wanted more action.

In fall 1963, Novo had wanted to launch an insurrection against Cuba. He sent a coded radio message to "Otto" (Hewitt) asking for help and weapons. Hewitt refused. It was too early, and such an uprising could not take place throughout the island. By spring 1964, the network in Pinar del Río faced losses and bad luck. One agent was arrested and executed in April. By May, a coal delivery man found a cache of communication equipment and munitions. When security forces came to investigate they found a spy's diary with messages from "Otto" to "Placido" (one of Novo's code names). Agents were rounded up. Novo cut off communication with Hewitt.[28]

According to *Granma*, Novo spent his last days in hiding in a tobacco house. By May 20, 1964, police had surrounded the building, but Novo had burned the documents, and when they entered they allegedly found Novo dead with a gunshot wound to the temple, an apparent suicide, and lots of money in a briefcase.[29]

According to Hewitt, BANTY-1 was "beaten to death by Cuban intelligence."[30] However he died, whether by suicide or murder, the fact that Novo died and was not exfiltrated to the United States may be embarrassing to the CIA and another reason to downplay the role of the agents. Another reason to emphasize technology may be that the CIA still sought funding to finance expensive reconnaissance technology for the U-2 and the SR-71 Blackbird, a fast, jet-powered, high-altitude spy plane.

Surprisingly, one of the first people to be critical of the CIA's handling of the information from human sources was an employee at the CIA itself. In 1964, a J. J. Rumpelmayer (likely a pseudonym), who was a "collector" of information, not an analyst, criticized the analysts who seemed to have overlooked many reports indicating that there were offensive missiles in Cuba in the CIA's in-house journal, *Studies in Intelligence*.[31] But this journal article was not declassified until 1995.

Sherman Kent, a former Yale University professor of history and founding father of estimative intelligence, was head of the CIA Office of National Estimates (ONE) and the principal drafter of the September 1962 SNIE about Cuba. He especially downplayed the number of reports that may have indicated offensive missiles in Cuba. He claimed that "with the benefit of hindsight one can go back over the thousand and more bits of information collected from human observers" in the six months preceding the crisis and find only "a few—a very few" that would indicate offensive missiles. Rumpelmayer refuted this claim by listing more than ten reports whose content indicated missiles, half of which were issued before the faulty estimate. He argues that the quantity of reports wasn't important but rather that the "nugget" pulled from the mass of information was the key to good collection. Finally, most telling is Rumpelmayer's suggestion that the reports were dismissed because of "skepticism regarding the capabilities of human observation . . . and the absence of confirming photographic evidence." In addition, he said, Americans have more "confidence in machines than human observations."[32] There is no doubt that Sherman Kent himself was enamored of technology. He referred to the intelligence gathered from the U-2 spy plane as a "holy miracle."[33]

In contrast to Rumpelmeyer, Kent and other CIA analysts were skeptical of agent reports because they assumed the agents were hostile to the Castro regime and exaggerated or fabricated their reports to damage Cuba and provoke a war against it. However, Rumpelmeyer and others could easily show that this was not the case, given the number and quality of reports and the credibility of the reporters. In the end, of course, photoreconnaissance confirmed the human claims.

In the same issue of the CIA journal, two analysts quickly rebutted Rumpelmayer and claimed to have analyzed fourteen thousand reports, none of which provided enough conclusive evidence. Moreover, they claimed they had received many false reports in previous months. Before January 1962, they had received two hundred reports about Soviet missiles on Cuba, which they claimed were all false and not verified by U-2 photography.[34] The CIA analysts thought human sources were crying wolf again.

Others like Roberta Wohlstetter rationalized the failure and characterized the reporting as a "signal to noise" problem comparable to the attack on Pearl Harbor. The United States had some warnings about a Japanese attack on Pearl Harbor, but there were so many false alarms and reports that they were ignored. The real warning, the "signal," was obscured by "the noise" of false reporting.[35]

Another reason analysts may have dismissed the reports was because of fear of fabricators brought on by the film and book *Our Man in Havana* by Graham Greene. The book, first published in 1958, then released as a film in 1959, tells the story of a vacuum cleaner salesman, James Wormold, who makes up agents and passes off his vacuum cleaner manual blueprints as missile parts (in addition to providing his own sketches depicting weapons based on the vacuum cleaner parts) when reporting to his MI6 British intelligence handlers. Since the CIA had already dealt with false reporting and the film and the book were in the public sphere, they also suffered from the *Our Man in Havana* syndrome.

The Role of the U-2

Even if human intelligence reporting was downplayed, there is no doubt that the agent and refugee reports about the restricted military area and sightings of missiles west of Havana near San Cristóbal led to the targeting of that area for the famed October 14 U-2 flight. As a result of reports describing convoys traveling toward San Cristóbal, a new Committee on Overhead Reconnaissance target card was created between October 1 and 3 and was a "priority requirement for photographic coverage." The card read, "Collateral reports indicate the existence of a restricted area in Pinar del Río Province which is suspected of including an SSM site under construction. . . . Requirement: Search the area delineated for possible surface missile construction, with particular attention to SS-4 Shyster."[36] They were acting on the tips from the CIA on-island agent Esteban Márquez Novo and the middle-aged accountant refugee.

But sending a U-2 spy plane to Cuba became more difficult. On August 30, 1962, a U-2 on a SIGINT mission (in this case, electronic emissions from radar sites and communication channels) flew over Sakhalin Island in Russia, creating another diplomatic furor when the Russians protested. Then on September 8 a U-2 plane flown by a Chinese pilot was shot down over mainland China. In addition, the CIA was reluctant to send planes over the area building SAMs, which could shoot them down. As a result, there was a brief period when the CIA halted U-2 flights over Cuba.[37]

These incidents also triggered a change in who would fly the Cuba missions. The CIA and the Strategic Air Command waged a typical government bureaucratic fight over who should be in control. The CIA thought its cover story that the CIA pilots were Lockheed Martin employees on a "ferry flight to Puerto Rico" was good and that they should simply wear a blue uniform. The air force thought it was safer for their pilots to fly the planes because they could say the pilots simply strayed as a result of a peripheral reconnaissance mission. The CIA then countered that its U-2s had "superior electronic countermeasures and a higher maximum altitude." In the end, the Cuba missions were handed over to SAC pilots who borrowed a couple of the CIA's U-2Cs.[38]

In addition to the reduction of the spy plane flights as a result of the two U-2 incidents, the weather was a continual problem. To fly an effective mission with enough visibility to take good pictures, pilots needed less than 25 percent cloud cover. This meant that the September missile sightings could not be confirmed with overhead photography until Heyser's famous 1962, October 14, flight.

Despite the fact that these flights were illegal, the air force, navy, and CIA flew them with impunity. Not only were the pilots in grave danger of losing their lives if hit by surface-to-air missiles, but the United States risked sparking another diplomatic incident like the famous shoot-down of Gary Powers's U-2 spy plane over Soviet airspace on May Day 1960. At first Eisenhower issued a cover story that the plane strayed into Soviet airspace while on a weather data-collection mission. Once Eisenhower found out that Powers had survived, he admitted that Powers was on a spy mission.

The incident occurred two weeks before the much-anticipated Big Four (Eisenhower, Khrushchev, Charles de Gaulle, and Harold Macmillan) were to attend the East-West Peace Summit in Paris. It created an international crisis contributing to the deterioration of US-Soviet relations because Eisenhower refused to apologize to Khrushchev for the spy plane incident; the summit never took place.

Heyser's October 14 flight was a success—"a milk run," according to him—but other pilots were not so lucky. On October 27, at the height of the Cuban Missile Crisis, Maj. Rudolf Anderson flew over eastern Cuba near the US Guantánamo Bay Naval Base to monitor a possible attack against the American base and was shot down by a SAM over Banes. He died instantly. Despite this death, U-2 and navy overflights continued both during and after the crisis. Although Anderson's remains were returned to

America, the debris from the fateful flight can be found in Cuban outdoor museums, with most of the parts on display at the Museo de Revolucíon in downtown Havana and the Fortaleza de la Cabaña. The museum displays the needle-tipped, slender, fin-adorned surface-to-air missile next to the fuselage of Anderson's plane against the backdrop of soaring majestic palm trees and green trees.[39]

Not only were these missions dangerous; they were also illegal. U-2 overflights violated Cuba's airspace. A statement by William Webster, a former CIA director (1987–91), at a congressional hearing sums up best the CIA's attitude to the illegality of its missions. When a senator asked Webster about a certain secret mission, he said, "Isn't that illegal?" Webster replied, "In the US we obey the law." The senator asked again, "Isn't that illegal?" Webster answered again, "In America we obey the law." The senator repeated the question a third time. Webster replied, "Overseas we pursue our interests."[40]

The Heroic Machine

The CIA worshipped technology and its power to solve operational problems. Agency employees saw the U-2 spy plane as an example of technological ingenuity. The CIA gift shop in Langley used to feature a Christmas ornament of a U-2 spy plane placed within a gold ring hovering above a map of Cuba and the Soviet Union.[41] The CIA also frequently celebrates the success of the U-2 in operations. For example, the United States thought the Soviet Union had more missiles and bombers than the United States, a situation that came to be known as a missile or bomber gap. The U-2 spy plane is credited with determining that there was no missile or bomber gap.

When I have asked students, friends, and colleagues in lectures how the United States discovered missiles on Cuba, the audience invariably answers through photography taken by aerial reconnaissance (some respondents say satellites; others say planes).[42] Part of the reason for this popular perception is the iconic black-and-white aerial photographs of missiles in Cuba displayed on the briefing boards in President Kennedy's Cabinet Room and the more extensive images viewed by millions at the Adlai Stevenson UN briefing, as mentioned in the preface. They continued to be shown in newspaper articles and documentaries. These images are stamped on Americans' collective memory.

There is no doubt that the images captured by U-2 spy planes provided the visual evidence for missiles in Cuba. Interestingly, while the highly classified aerial photographs were revealed publicly for the first time, it was actually an inadvertent release of intelligence capabilities at first. The US embassy in London released the photographs to the British. The Department of Defense took credit for the aerial photography and refused to admit it was a U-2 spy plane. After the mistaken release, government officials (except for the CIA) thought the photographs provided the evidence needed to convince the free world that an attack on Cuba was justified should the Kennedy administration decide to carry it out. That it was a U-2 spy plane was not included in the official release. Nor was the public made aware of the risk taken by human agents. The point is that the images became indelibly imprinted on the consciousness of many Americans and shaped their view of the way in which the US government found missiles on Cuba.[43]

Another reason for neglecting the humans who provided intelligence about the missiles is that most books and films about the Cuban Missile Crisis focus on the crisis itself—those tense thirteen days—and the skillful handling of it by the president that averted a nuclear war. Kennedy is made out to be a hero. In fact, almost all the hundreds of books on the topic deal only with the period *after* missiles were found and how it was handled. Before the 1990s, there were no books that examined what led up to the crisis and how we found the missiles, except to imply that they were "discovered" by the U-2.

For example, Graham T. Allison and Philip Zelikow's influential and widely read book, *Essence of Decision: Explaining the Cuban Missile Crisis*, uses political science models to analyze why the Soviets placed missiles in Cuba and to examine Kennedy's decision-making process. They are not interested in how the United States discovered the missiles in the first place. Much of the literature that followed was written with the same objective.

More generally, sources like encyclopedias perpetuate the myth of the machine. Encyclopedia.com writes, "On October 14, 1962, a U2 spy plane, flying a routine Strategic Air Command mission over Cuba, snapped a series of photographs that became the first direct evidence of Soviet medium-range ballistic nuclear missiles in Cuba." As we have seen, the October 14 flight was anything but routine. The venerable *Encyclopedia*

Britannica is not much better, mentioning the discovery of missiles by the U-2 only in passing, without referring to human intelligence at all.[44]

As late as 2012 Jon Wiener wrote, "The CIA's discovery of the missile sites using aerial photography from a U-2 spy plane was a triumph of technical intelligence." Even the distinguished historian of the Cold War, John Lewis Gaddis, wrote, "The story begins with the discovery, by means of U-2 spy plane photoreconnaissance, of the missiles themselves."[45] As we know, however, the plane verified their existence after humans made the initial discovery.

The literature on the U-2 plane itself usually emphasizes the technical history, the people who championed it, and its role in air force and CIA reconnaissance. I have not found any references to the role of humans in these specialized books. For example, the preeminent historian of the U-2, Chris Pocock, describes the history of the U-2 and its applications in detecting missiles without mentioning the human aspect in two of his books, including one whole chapter, "The Missiles of October," in his book *Dragon Lady*.[46]

The two major exceptions to the public narrative emphasizing the role of the U-2 come from two former intelligence officials. One of them, Roger Hilsman, was director of the Bureau of Intelligence and Research in the State Department and was on the committee that produced the Killian Report postmortem, a critique of the events leading up to the crisis. He allegedly had a political motive for discrediting the CIA because he wanted to rein in the CIA and presumably increase the role of intelligence from the State Department in advising the White House.[47]

Hilsman wrote two books relating to the Cuban Missile Crisis and intelligence. The first book, published in 1967, *To Move a Nation*, which is about foreign policy more generally, is the only public work published before 1992 in which the role of agents and refugees is mentioned. The second book, specifically about the crisis, *The Cuban Missile Crisis: The Struggle over Policy*, was published in 1996 and includes more material on intelligence and the role of human agents. But Hilsman still found that the U-2 was a more reliable source: "Given the accuracy of the U-2 photographs and the uncertainty of agent and refugee reports, everyone realized that the only intelligence convincing enough to justify the kind of action that would be needed to remove the Soviet missiles would have to be supplied by the U-2."[48]

The second exception to the neglect of the role of humans in the specialized literature is a limited print run policy report (and thus with little ability to shape public discourse) for the Strategic Studies Institute published in 2009 by Kenneth Michael Absher, a cigar-smoking former CIA analyst and Latin America specialist: "Mind-Sets and Missiles: A First Hand Account of the Cuban Missile Crisis." One of Absher's points is that US intelligence favored technical intelligence over human intelligence to the detriment of good intelligence, suggesting that even some insider members of the intelligence community, unlike Hilsman, are critical of this approach or mind-set.[49]

Absher is particularly adept at applying this observation to the role of Penkovsky. In June 1961, a National Intelligence Estimate (NIE) "concluded that the Soviets had 50–100 intercontinental ballistic missiles." But a June 2, 1961 memorandum written on the basis of a Clandestine Service report about Penkovsky produced a much lower number. Penkovsky provided information suggesting that the Soviets probably had only twenty-five or fewer ICBMs on launchers and that the program was much smaller than estimated. But no revision was made to the June NIE because there was no confirmatory technical evidence. He quotes Howard Stoertz, the Board of National Estimates officer for the Soviet Missile Program:

> If a photo had been taken by a U-2, I knew what it was. There was an interpreter who could tell me what was being seen. I could never talk to this source [Penkovsky] and could never find out anything about who he was. That was protecting his life, but to that extent it somewhat diminished the utility of it to me. I accepted their word, but I was looking for other confirmation.[50]

In the end, Penkovsky never provided information that the Soviets were shipping MRBMs and IRBMs to Cuba, but he did provide manuals that featured descriptions of the missiles found on Cuba. In addition to the Penkovsky example, Absher's point can be applied to the fact that information about offensive missiles from human agents was also ignored until technical intelligence confirmed it.

It was not until 2005 that there was any public CIA confirmation that an agent had pinpointed a suspect area on Cuba that led to the successful U-2 spy plane mission. This occurred in Ted Shackley's memoirs in which he refers to an on-island agent he code-named Julio.[51] Finally, in 2019, Sean D. Naylor published a Yahoo news report about the CIA maritime specialist Thomas Hewitt ("Otto") training a team sent to southwestern Cuba on a landing craft that towed a wooden speed boat with a canoe, as part of Operation Mongoose. Here we could verify the real name of Ted Shackley's "Julio": Esteban Márquez Novo and his radioman, Yeyo Napoleón.[52]

The top-secret postmortems, declassified only recently—between 2006 and 2010—paint quite a different picture of what led to the discovery of missiles on Cuba and the strengths and weaknesses of the process. While they praise how the intelligence community handled the crisis after offensive missiles were verified in Cuba, they are critical of the period leading up to the crisis.

The four postmortems were highly secret intelligence investigations conducted from fall 1962 to 1963. John McCone, head of the CIA, asked Richard Lehman, a thirteen-year veteran of the CIA, to write the first report, dubbed the Lehman Report. Scarcely before Lehman finished his report, McCone asked the CIA's Inspector General, Jack Earman, to write another report on the topic, dubbed the IG Report. The third report was written by the United States Intelligence Board (USIB) for the President's Foreign Intelligence Board and is sometimes called the Killian Report. The fourth report was written by the PFIAB, headed by James T. Killian, the scientist and president of MIT whom McCone disliked because he objected to an outside body overseeing and interfering with the CIA.[53]

The first major criticism is of the faulty NIE from September 19, 1962, in which analysts wrote that the Soviet Union would not place offensive missiles in Cuba. This claim was made despite the fact that the CIA received reports from agents and refugees two days before the estimate was disseminated that would indicate offensive missiles, despite intelligence agencies having observed many ships coming into the Mariel Harbor overloaded with long objects and hatches covered with canvas, and despite McCone having been convinced the Soviets were placing offensive missiles in Cuba. The CIA also learned about new construction, convoys carrying trailers with tubular structures at night, new restricted military areas, evacuations of people, Soviet supervision of ship unloading, and references to SAMs, cruise missiles, and missile sites. Still analysts didn't change the estimate.[54]

Unlike the public literature, the postmortem reports showed awareness ination of human and technical intelligence that led to the f missiles in Cuba. But many of them were also critical of the ch human intelligence was handled.

terim Report by the PFIAB was particularly scathing. It recommen "hard-hitting efforts to increase" capabilities in acquiring important intelligence through human espionage. Although it praised the "noteworthy intelligence results" achieved by "scientific and technical means," it thought there was still a "great need as ever for carefully selected human-resource espionage operations." It thought the new recent advances in technology like "high altitude satellite photography" had "obscured the roles of human beings as collection and transmission media, trained and equipped with the most sophisticated technical aids." Finally, the board recommended "launching at the earliest possible date" a "vigorous clandestine agent program to provide surreptitious collection of on-the-ground photography of intelligence targets in Cuba, as an essential supplement to aerial surveillance of the island.[55]

Technical versus Human Intelligence

Technology worship is not unique to the CIA. Technophilia is part of American culture and society. Not only is the United States a leading technical innovator but technology promises a quick fix for nagging societal problems. There is no doubt that the US intelligence community displayed "stunning technological virtuosity" during the Cuban Missile Crisis.[56] Yet this wasn't enough.

By the early 1960s, technology had begun to play an increasingly large role in espionage. In fact, agencies began to rely on it at the expense of human intelligence. Unlike the situation in closed societies like the Soviet Union during the Cold War where the United States did not have human sources, they did have some sources of human intelligence: agents in Cuba and refugees fleeing Cuba. While many agents had been imprisoned or killed after the Bay of Pigs invasion, Operation Mongoose replenished the supply of on-island agents. They also had more than enough refugees and the one agent on the ground in Cuba who reported to Miami in invisible ink. Yet these sources were dismissed. If the CIA had listened to them, the missiles would have been found earlier.

Another point to consider is what would have happened if the United States was not able to fly over Cuba to verify the missiles. What if there was a risk that every plane flying over Cuba would be shot down? Or what if the technology did not exist at all? This would have meant that the faulty September estimate would have become operational and that the intelligence community would have had to rely on the human agents. Maybe they would at least have been forced to develop a better stable of human spies and respect the ones they had. Clearly, without proof in the form of pictures, Kennedy could not have launched a blockade or any other military action. If the United States had done nothing, the missiles would have stayed there, and it is doubtful that they would have become operational unless the United States tried to invade Cuba. In fact, the United States had Jupiter missiles in Turkey pointing toward the Soviet Union, and they were never used. This point reminds me of a conversation I had with the retired head of the East German foreign intelligence Sector for Science and Technology. He told me the main reason the Soviet Union placed missiles in Cuba was because they wanted to force the United States to remove the missiles in Turkey. And without much publicity, the United States did remove the missiles in Turkey around the same time the Soviets pulled theirs out from Cuba.

This chapter has highlighted the roles of human and technical intelligence in finding missiles on Cuba in order to showcase how much faith US intelligence placed in technology. But there is another aspect of the story that highlights the US trajectory toward becoming a global espionage power.

With Cuba only ninety miles from Florida, the Soviet Union was flexing its own global muscles by placing missiles there. After all, Cuba was one of the Cold War's most strategic locations for the face off between the Soviet Union and the United States. If the long-range missiles had stayed in Cuba, the Soviet Union would have had the capability to nuke major cities in the United States. Instead, the Soviet Union withdrew them. The United States could now send its spy planes and satellites to other parts of the world as it built its globe-spanning technology.

Notes

1. Information Report, September 18, 1962, in Mary S. McAuliffe, *CIA Documents on the Cuban Missile Crisis, 1962* (Washington, DC: History Staff, Central Intelligence Agency, 1992), 103. In his memoirs, Ted Shackley writes that this agent used the war name "Julio." See Ted Shackley, *Spymaster: My Life in the CIA* (Dulles, VA: Potomac Books, 2005), 59. The Communist newspaper identifies

Esteban Márquez as a CIA spy. Samuel Halpern interview for CNN series on the Cold War; transcript of the interview at https://nsarchive2.gwu.edu/coldwar/interviews/episode-10/halpern1.html. Sean D. Naylor, "Operation Cobra: The Untold Story of How a CIA Officer Trained a Network of Agents Who Found the Soviet Missiles in Cuba," Yahoo News, January 23, 2019, shows how CIA officer Thomas Hewitt trained Novo and his network and how they arrived on the island; see www.yahoo.com/entertainment/operation-cobra-untold-story-cia-officer-trained-network-agents-found-soviet-missiles-cuba-100005794.html.

2. Information Report, 105.

3. "Report to the President's Foreign Intelligence Advisory Board on Intelligence Community Activities Relating to the Cuban Arms Build-Up by the Director of Central Intelligence," 25. This report is available in the John F. Kennedy Presidential Library as well as in CREST. The JFK Library version is less sanitized.

4. McAuliffe, *CIA Documents*, 107.

5. Dino Brugioni, *Eyeball to Eyeball: The Inside Story of the Cuban Missile Crisis* (New York: Random House, 1991), 182–84; and Michael Dobbs, "Into Thin Air," *Washington Post*, October 26, 2003, W14.

6. Brugioni, *Eyeball to Eyeball*, 190.

7. Sean Naylor included the name of the agent, previously dubbed "Julio" by Ted Shackley, in his article about Thomas Hewitt, Novo's case officer, in 2019. See Naylor, "Operation Cobra."

8. C. J. Bon Tempo, *Americans at the Gate: The United States and Refugees during the Cold War* (Princeton, NJ: Princeton University Press, 2008), 109, 132.

9. Justin F. Gleichauf, "A Listening Post in Miami," *Studies in Intelligence*, no. 10 (2001): 49–53.

10. Gleichauf, 51; and Helms and Hood, *Look over My Shoulder*, 210.

11. The figures come from the "Report to the President's Foreign Intelligence Advisory Board on Intelligence Community Activities Relating to the Cuban Arms Build-Up by the Director of Central Intelligence," 13. For the guide, see National Archives, *Interrogation Guide: Cuba*, declassified December 19, 2013, www.archives.gov/declassification/iscap/pdf/2011-063-doc3.pdf.

12. "Report to the President's Foreign Intelligence Advisory Board on Intelligence Community Activities Relating to the Cuban Arms Build-Up by the Director of Central Intelligence"; and Judith Edgette, "Domestic Collection on Cuba," *Studies in Intelligence* 7 (Fall 1963): 41–42.

13. Helms and Hood, *Look over My Shoulder*, 202; and David Corn, *Blond Ghost: Ted Shackley and the CIA's Crusade* (New York: Simon & Schuster, 1994), 74–75.

14. Memorandum for the Record, Subject: AMCOBRA, www.maryferrell.org/showDoc.html?docId=18070&relPageId=2.

15. Pedro Etcheverry Vázquez, "El fracaso de una causa que nunca triunfaría," *Granma*, October 8, 2014, www.granma.cu/cuba/2014-10-08/el-fracaso-de-una-causa-que-nunca-triunfaria; and www.maryferrell.org/php/cryptdb.php?id=AMCOBRA.

16. Quote from Lehman Report, "CIA Handling of the Soviet Build-Up in Cuba, 1 July–16 October 1962," 23; and Graham T. Allison and Philip Zelikow, *Essence of Decision: Explaining the Cuban Missile Crisis* (New York: Longman, [1971] 1999), 83.

17. Milo Jones and Philippe Silberzahn, *Constructing Cassandra: Reframing Intelligence Failure at the CIA, 1947–2001* (Stanford, CA: Stanford University Press, 2014), 137.

18. Jones and Silberzahn, 137.

19. CIA Memorandum, "Recent Soviet Military Aid to Cuba," August 22, 1962; and Laurence Chang and Peter Kornbluh, *The Cuban Missile Crisis, 1962: A National Security Archive Documents Reader* (New York: New Press, 1998), 68.

20. "U-2 Overflights of Cuba, 29 August through 14 October 1962," February 27, 1963, in McAuliffe, *CIA Documents*, 129.

21. "U-2 Overflights of Cuba," 45.

22. Special National Intelligence Estimate (SNIE 85-3-62), "The Military Build-Up in Cuba," submitted by the Director of Central Intelligence, September 19, 1962, 2, www.cia.gov/library/readingroom/docs/DOC_0000242425.pdf.

23. SNIE 85-3-62, "The Military Build-Up in Cuba," John McCone memorandum.

24. "Report to the President's Foreign Intelligence Advisory Board on Intelligence Community Activities Relating to the Cuban Arms Build-Up by the Director of Central Intelligence," 12, Papers of John F. Kennedy, Presidential Papers, National Security Files, Foreign Intelligence Advisory Board (FIAB): Volume III, Annexes to the Report to the President's Foreign Intelligence Advisory Board on Intelligence Community Activities Relating to the Cuban Arms Build-Up, 1962: 14 April–14 October (Copy 1) (2 of 2 Folders), JFKNSF-472-006, John F. Kennedy Presidential Library and Museum.

25. "Report to the President's Foreign Intelligence Advisory Board."

26. The videotape of this 1992 Symposium on the Cuban Missile Crisis is available on YouTube: www.youtube.com/watch?v=_iAJM_Q4nvU.

27. McAuliffe, *CIA Documents*, 103, 105. Reference to these two reports is repeated by Raymond L. Gartoff, "US Intelligence in the Cuban Missile Crisis," in *Intelligence and the Cuban Missile Crisis*, ed. James G. Blight and David A. Welch (London: Frank Cass, 1998), 23–24.

28. Cable, Otto to Placido, November 17, 1963, www.maryferrell.org/showDoc.html?docId=18191&relPageId=3; Pedro Etcheverry Vázquez, "El fracaso de una causa que nunca triunfaría," *Granma*, October 8, 2014, www.granma.cu/cuba/2014-10-08/el-fracaso-de-una-causa-que-nunca-triunfaria; and Pedro Etcheverry Vázquez, "Los crímenes del bandidismo," *Granma*, March 28, 2017, www.granma.cu/cuba/2017-03-28/los-crimenes-del-bandidismo-28-03-2017-17-03-04. On Hewitt, see Naylor, "Operation Cobra."

29. Cable, Otto to Placido; Vázquez, "El fracaso"; and Vázquez, "Los crímenes."

30. Naylor, "Operation Cobra."

31. J. J. Rumpelmayer, "The Missiles in Cuba," *Studies in Intelligence* 8 (Fall 1964): 87–92.

32. Rumpelmayer, 90–91.

33. Dino Brugioni, *Eyes in the Sky: Eisenhower, the CIA, and Cold War Aerial Espionage* (New York: Naval Institute Press, 2011), 357.

34. Harlow T. Munson and W. P. Southard, “Two Witnesses for the Defense,” *Studies in Intelligence* 8 (Fall 1964): 94–98.

35. Roberta Wohlstetter, “Cuba and Pearl Harbor: Hindsight and Foresight,” *Foreign Affairs* 43, no. 4 (July 1965): 691–707.

36. CREST, “Lehman Report,” Memorandum for: Director of Central Intelligence, CIA Handling of the Soviet Build-Up in Cuba, July 1–October 16 1962, November 14, 1962, 25.

37. Pedlow and Welzenbach, *Central Intelligence Agency and Overhead Reconnaissance*. The report is available at www.foia.cia.gov/sites/default/files/document_conversions/18/1992-04-01.pdf; and http://nsarchive.gwu.edu/NSAEBB/NSAEBB434/docs/U2%20-%20Chapter%205.pdf.

38. Pedlow and Welzenbach, 207–8.

39. Author’s visit to the Museo de Revolucíon, Havana, Cuba, May 2018.

40. Anecdote told at an NSA history conference, October 22, 2015.

41. John Diamond, *The CIA and the Culture of Failure: U.S. Intelligence from the End of the Cold War to the Invasion of Iraq* (Stanford, CA: Stanford University Press, 2008), 3.

42. Although satellite reconnaissance existed, the CORONA was unable to provide clear images of Cuba. See Joseph W. Caddell Jr., “Corona over Cuba: The Missile Crisis and the Early Limitations of Satellite Imagery Intelligence,” *Intelligence and National Security* 31, no. 3 (2015): 1–23.

43. John W. Finney, “Aerial Cameras Traced Cuban Missile Build-Up,” *New York Times*, October 24, 1962, 21; and Howard Simons, “USIA Distributing Aerial Photos of Cuba Buildup to the Free World,” *Washington Post, Times Herald*, October 25, 1962, A10.

44. “Cuban Missile Crisis,” *International Encyclopedia of the Social Sciences*, 2008, www.encyclopedia.com/topic/Cuban_Missile_Crisis.aspx; and “Cuban Missile Crisis,” *Encyclopaedia Britannica*, www.britannica.com/event/Cuban-missile-crisis.

45. Jon Wiener, *How We Forgot the Cold War: A Historical Journey across America* (Berkeley: University of California Press, 2012), 83; and John L. Gaddis, *The Landscape of History: How Historians Map the Past* (Oxford: Oxford University Press, 2004), 44.

46. Chris Pocock, *Dragon Lady: The History of the U-2 Spyplane* (Osceola, WI: Motorbooks International, 1989), 75–89; and Chris Pocock, *The U-2 Spyplane, toward the Unknown: A New History of the Early Years* (Atglen, PA: Schiffer Military History, 2000).

47. David M. Barrett and Max Holland, *Blind over Cuba: The Photo Gap and the Missile Crisis* (College Station: Texas A&M University Press, 2012), 45.

48. Roger Hilsman, *The Cuban Missile Crisis: The Struggle over Policy*

(Westport, CT: Praeger, 1996), 26. See also Roger Hilsman, *To Move a Nation: The Politics of Foreign Policy in the Administration of John F. Kennedy* (Garden City, NY: Doubleday, 1967).

49. Kenneth Michael Absher, "Mind-Sets and Missiles: A First Hand Account of the Cuban Missile Crisis" (Strategic Studies Institute, Carlisle, PA, September 2009). [Pamphlet.] One of his mentors described him as a cigar smoker.

50. Absher, 15.

51. Shackley, *Spymaster*, 59.

52. Naylor, "Operation Cobra."

53. Naylor. All these reports are available on CREST. I found a less redacted version of the so-called Killian Report also at the Kennedy Presidential Library.

54. Inspector General's Survey of Handling of Intelligence Information during the Cuban Arms Build-Up, August to mid-October 1962, CREST Version, National Archives, CIA-RDP80BO1676R001800060005-4.

55. Interim Report to the President by the President's Foreign Intelligence Advisory Board, dated December 28, 1962. Accessed at the Digital National Security Archive, Proquest, http://gateway.proquestcom/openurl?url_ver-Z39.88-2004&res, 3, 4.

56. Comment made by Graham Allison at the 1992 Symposium on the Cuban Missile Crisis is available on YouTube: www.youtube.com/watch?v=_iAJM_Q4nvU.

5

BETRAYAL UNDER THE OCEAN

In October 1967, Chief Warrant Officer John Walker drove his red MG convertible from Norfolk, Virginia, to Washington, DC. He parked his car around G and Sixth Streets near a phone booth, about half a mile from the Capitol, changed into a sport coat, and called a taxi to take him to the 1000 block of Sixteenth Street. When he arrived at the city block, he walked to 1125 Sixteenth Street NW, a stately old gray mansion. It was the Russian embassy.[1]

After he slipped in behind another gentleman, he quickly asked to see Security. A few minutes later, Boris Solomatin entered the foyer, shook Walker's hand, and escorted him to a private room. As soon as Solomatin saw the Navy KL-47 cryptographic machine key list Walker had stolen from his office the night before, he knew the material was authentic. The daily key lists were used to unscramble all messages sent through the navy's code machines. Walker told Solomatin he was a watch officer in Norfolk, handling communications with US submarines in the Atlantic Ocean. Walker did not hide his motive: "I'm a naval officer. I'd like to make some money and I'll give you some genuine stuff in return."[2]

In March 1968, US intelligence learned that there was a sunken Soviet submarine about three miles deep at the bottom of the central North Pacific Ocean. No one knew what caused the sub to sink, but one of the first thoughts was, "How can we access it and retrieve valuable information, like cryptographic materials, that would be on board?" By the end of the year, there were discussions in Washington about the technical feasibility of accessing the material. By April 1969, the deputy director of defense had written to the director of the CIA, Richard Helms, instructing him to form a working group at the CIA to examine the issue. By summer 1969, the CIA launched Project Azorian to lift the sub from the bottom of the ocean.

In summer 1968, US intelligence developed another technical project to target the Soviet Union under the ocean. The USS *Halibut*, originally a nuclear-powered sub outfitted to launch Regulus missiles from its flat top, was refurbished as a spy sub, complete with a decompression chamber disguised as a deep sea submersible, sonar, and hanging "fish" with cameras and video feeds. This spy sub would eventually take part in a joint navy-NSA operation code-named Ivy Bells to tap underwater cables in the Soviet Sea of Okhotsk.

These three episodes illustrate two different ways of going about intelligence collection. One method is the Soviet's use of a human source in espionage; the other two feature America's use of technical means to access similar material. Walker did not know about Project Azorian or Operation Ivy Bells, and American officials did not know about Walker's treachery when the two undersea operations took place, but all three stories unfolded at about the same time and reflected the different emphasis each country placed on methods of intelligence collection. While the Walker case was the most successful KGB espionage coup since the World War II atomic spy ring and cost a mere million dollars to run, the Azorian project was often seen as a CIA failure and cost $500 million.[3] Ivy Bells, which cost a million dollars a day when the submarine was operational, was a great success until Ronald Pelton betrayed the secret to the KGB around 1980.

All three episodes also took place during a period of détente, an easing of tensions between the superpowers and a period when the Soviets and the United States negotiated a reduction of strategic arms. This did not mean a reduction in spying. In fact, both sides claimed their spying helped verify the negotiated terms of the arms limitations.

Both Project Azorian and Operation Ivy Bells helped extend US intelligence's reach around the globe using sophisticated technology—one more step to becoming a global espionage power. And both projects used contractors to buy the best technology to solve underwater technology problems.

John A. Walker, Soviet Spy

The KGB doesn't trust every American who walks into its embassy offering to spy. Nor does American intelligence trust every Russian who walks into a US embassy volunteering to spy. "Walk-ins," as they are known in the trade, are suspect from the start. Both sides had to consider that the walk-in might be a "dangle," a double agent controlled by the initiating spy agency. Walker could have been an FBI trap. But as soon as Solomatin saw the key list and assessed the navy man, he knew he had hit gold. Walker did not pretend to have noble ideological reasons for spying. He just wanted the money. Solomatin appreciated the candor.[4]

Acquiring a walk-in was not necessarily an example of skillful recruitment of a human source by the KGB. The KGB did not recruit him, but they handled him skillfully and avoided his capture for eighteen years once he volunteered his services. He fell into its lap, and he was genuine, not a plant. During the Cold War, the Soviet Union and the Eastern Bloc benefited from many military walk-ins; the enlisted men (they were mostly men) were poorly paid and often disgruntled. This marked a shift to monetary greed from the earlier ideological spies such as the atomic spy ring and the Cambridge Five. The KGB became a second job. But there is no doubt that the spies were usually well run because the KGB knew how to use human weaknesses for its own ends. And it made the agent feel like it cared about their well-being. Its tradecraft decreased the chances that its spies would be caught. The walk-ins were valuable additions to the KGB's stable of recruited spies.

Walker's Haul

When Walker volunteered to spy for the KGB he worked at the Operations Headquarters of the US Atlantic Fleet. The navy divided the world into four geographic regions at that time: the Atlantic, the Mediterranean, the Western Pacific, and the Eastern Pacific. Each region had its own huge communications center called Naval Communication Area Master Stations. Thousands of scrambled messages came into those stations every day from warships, naval stations, submarines, and spy satellites. All ships in the Atlantic were run from the windowless building in Norfolk, Virginia, where Walker worked. The officer on duty read every communication between the submarines and shore after decrypting the messages. During the 1960s, the navy still used high-frequency radio transmissions.[5]

The KL-47 cryptographic machine settings were valuable secrets, but in order to read the messages, one needed the actual machine. Since the machine was outdated, the settings needed to be changed every day by hand. Walker chose that model because the key list was stamped "TOP

SECRET" and it would be harder to trace back to his office. The sample was meant to whet the KGB's appetite.[6]

Before Walker left his first meeting with KGB officials at the embassy, they said they would schedule one more personal meeting in two weeks. To ensure that he left the embassy safely without being caught by FBI surveillance, Walker was dressed up in an oversized coat and hat and shoved to the bottom of the backseat of a Soviet embassy car sandwiched between two KGB officers and spirited out of the embassy. When the car was far enough away and the driver was sure he had not been followed, they let Walker out.[7]

For the next meeting, Solomatin told him one of their officers would meet him in front of a Zayre's shopping center in a northern Virginia suburb to set a salary, describe dead drops, and retrieve a shopping list of the kinds of documents he could supply. When Walker met his new case officer, Yuri Linkov, he brought with him the KW-7 key list, along with technical manuals; the adversary could now read tactical intelligence—real-time intelligence of thousands of messages a day. Linkov warned Walker not to spend his new $4,000-a-month salary lavishly and not to tell his wife about his new spy job. He also told Walker that this was going to be the last personal meeting for a long time. Instead, the KGB would communicate with him and pass on secret material using dead drops in the Washington, DC, area.[8]

A dead drop is an impersonal form of communication, not requiring dangerous personal meetings with a spy's handler. Instead, the secret material, instructions, or money is deposited at a predetermined secret location. It is also a classic KGB method. Maj. Gen. Oleg Kalugin, who was stationed at the Soviet embassy when Walker walked in, spent "countless hours" planning the dead drops, and in the two years he helped handle Walker, none of the "drops went awry."[9] This was also part of the reason Walker was able to spy for the Soviets for so long without being caught.

Walker was given a time and exact place for the next drop during his meeting at the Zayre department store. There he would deposit his material while collecting the money and instructions at the next drop. Kalugin and Linkov spent hours scouring remote places in Maryland and Virginia looking for appropriate drop sites; they had to be remote and accessible. At first they provided Walker with detailed written instructions and a map; later they provided a photograph. At first, Walker delivered garbage bags full of documents at drop sites in the woods. After Walker dropped off the goods and picked up his money, he would leave a sign that he made his drop. Usually he would place an *X* on a utility pole. About fifteen to thirty minutes after Walker's drop, Linkov would locate the *X* and proceed to the drop site to pick up the material. Then Linkov would leave an *X* on another telephone pole, and Walker would see it and know his material had been picked up. Then he would drive home.[10]

In January 1968, a few months after Walker's delivery of material to the Soviets, the North Koreans captured the US Navy communication ship, the USS *Pueblo*, off the coast of North Korea. As they boarded the ship, North Korean soldiers sprayed bullets and killed one crewman and injured many more. Some intelligence officials suspected the ship was captured in order to steal the cryptographic machines for which Walker supplied the key lists. It seems that a KW-7 machine was indeed taken from the ship before it could be destroyed like other cryptographic equipment. This may have been done at the behest of the Soviets. Apparently, within two days of capturing the spy ship, the North Koreans sent an airplane to Moscow containing 792 pounds of cargo. The KGB also sent a team of intelligence experts to the Wonson Port in North Korea. Now the National Security Agency was aware that the Soviets had the machine. Instead of discontinuing the use of this widely used machine, however, the NSA simply modified it and changed the key lists every month with new settings. The only problem was that Walker kept the Soviets up to date on the new settings.[11]

Walker's haul allowed the Soviets to read all messages about naval affairs. One of the most telling pieces of information the Soviets acquired was the US techniques for silencing subs. This included engine-cushioning equipment to reduce vibrations through the hull. They were able to glean from the material how quiet the US submarines were and that the noisy Soviet subs made it easy for the United States to follow and track them. The first step the Soviets took was to hide the subs closer to home so that they would be harder to trail. Soon sonar operators began to complain that they did not notice the Soviet attack subs until they were right behind them. In fact, Toshiba had sold the Soviets embargoed computer-guided milling machines to make propeller blades smoother and quieter.[12]

The sheer volume of material Walker stole was staggering. Oleg Kalugin recalls sifting through "mountains of material," translating what was urgent and cabling that information to KGB headquarters in Moscow immediately. After he learned how to use a Minox camera, Walker delivered many rolls of films with pictures of secret documents and would hide them at the drop sites in Coke cans. Walker handed over the battle plans of the US Atlantic Fleet. As a result, the Soviets knew about US naval exercises in advance, and admirals were totally surprised when Soviet ships would turn up at the secret maneuvers. Kalugin and his colleagues were "amazed" at how easy it was for Walker to steal top-secret documents and stuff them in his clothes or briefcase or photograph them and simply walk out of the naval base.[13] Walker would later quip, "A K mart store has better security than the US Navy."[14]

In the meantime, Walker was making a lot of money. He moved into a nicer apartment with his wife and four children. His wife spent lavishly, decorating the place and buying new furniture. If a colleague asked where he got the money, Walker said his bar business was going well. In fact, one of the reasons he needed money was to get out of the debt from his bar business. He bought a sailboat and spent weekends with his buddies sailing. Pretty soon his marriage was on the rocks; his wife started drinking, and they got divorced.[15]

A few years after he started spying for the KGB, Walker moved to San Diego, where he had less access to important top-secret material, but that did not stop him. Instead of doing the spying himself, he began to recruit friends and members of his family, one by one. In 1973, Walker befriended Jerry Whitworth, a navy petty officer at a radio school in San Diego, and recruited him as a spy by telling him the classified material was going to Israel.[16] After he retired in 1976, Walker recruited his older brother Arthur and his son, Michael, who was only twenty years old when he started spying in 1983.

Meanwhile, in fall 1984, Walker's wife had reported her husband's spying to the FBI's Boston office. At first, the FBI officials did not believe her because she was drunk when she called. But the FBI transferred the information to the Virginia office, and they plotted a course of action.

Although Walker had met only twice personally with the KGB on American soil, he met several times with his KGB contacts in Vienna, Austria, a favorite place for KGB spies. During a January 19, 1985, rendezvous Walker handed over a bag full of undeveloped film with naval secrets and his Russian handler gave him detailed instructions in an envelope for a dead drop in Rockville, Maryland, planned for May 19, 1985.[17]

On Sunday, May 19, shortly after noon, Walker left his home in Norfolk and drove four hours to Washington and the Maryland suburbs. He didn't notice any surveillance on his way to Rockville and was anxious to check into the Ramada Inn and relax. Instead, he took a test run to locate the dead drop site because they were sometimes hard to find in the remote rural areas.

After he freshened up and ate a steak dinner at the hotel, Walker drove his van toward Poolesville, a few miles from the banks of the Potomac River, where he found an empty 7-Up can on the edge of the road. This was the signal that the KGB contact was in the area ready to make an exchange. As he drove five miles down the road, he deposited his own 7-Up can to signal he was ready. He then continued to the drop point and left his package of 129 pages of classified material, wrapped in a white plastic trash bag to protect it from rain, near a utility pole. He had hidden the package in the bottom of a brown paper grocery bag topped with a soap wrapper, an empty Diet Coke bottle, an old rubbing alcohol container, and an old box of Q-tips. Simultaneously, the KGB had left a plastic-wrapped package with cash a few miles away for pickup.[18]

Everything had gone smoothly up until he dropped his package off. But when he reached the Soviet drop point, he couldn't find the wrapped cash. And when he returned to his drop spot, his material was missing. He drove back to his hotel room confused and worried because the FBI hadn't arrested him.

Instead of catching him in action, the FBI collected the evidence and devised a plan to lure him out of his room. At 3:30 a.m. on Monday, May 20, the front desk called his room to tell him that there had been an accident. Someone had hit his van. The front desk attendant told him to get down to the van as quickly as possible. As a private investigator, Walker was suspicious and snuck around before opening his door. As he walked toward the elevator, however, two FBI agents appeared and pointed a gun at his face. The game was up.[19]

John Walker was convicted of spying for the Soviet Union and received a life sentence, as did his older brother Arthur. His son received a sentence of twenty-five years in exchange for a plea bargain in which he would provide details of his espionage and testify against Jerry Whitworth, who received 365 years in prison and a hefty fine.[20]

The Walker spy ring was one of the most damaging cases of Soviet espionage against the United States during the Cold War. Vitaly Yurchenko, a defector who re-defected to the Soviet Union, commented after Walker's conviction that the "KGB considered the Walker-Whitworth operation as the greatest in its history even surpassing the atomic spy operations of the 1940s." Not only could the Soviets develop quieter ballistic missile submarines, but the information allowed them to decipher "more than a million" decrypted secret messages. Of course, the greatest damage of the intelligence gleaned from the Walker spy ring was that if the Cold War had turned hot, the Soviet Union would have had the upper hand and the results would have been "devastating" to the United States. In addition, the information the Soviets gathered threatened US hegemony around the globe.[21]

The Halibut *Spy Sub Finds a Sunken Soviet Sub*

While John Walker was launching his long spy career for the Soviet Union in 1968, James F. Bradley Jr., the navy's chief underwater spy, started hatching audacious plans for the underwater war against the Soviet Union. Bradley had assumed his official position as assistant for undersea warfare at the Office of Naval Intelligence in 1966. He came on board at a time when the navy was leveraging US strength in advanced technology and applying it to underwater intelligence. Just as technology was developed and used underground (the tunnel) and in the sky (U-2, Oxcart, and spy satellites) to make up for the lack of human spies, the technological effort started to move underwater.[22]

The first catalyst for Bradley's audacious plans came in March 1968, when the Soviet Union lost a Soviet Golf-II Class diesel submarine, the K-129, 16,500 feet underwater on the ocean floor, about 1,500 miles northwest of Hawaii. The sub had sailed from the Russian naval base at Petropavlovsk toward the middle of the Pacific Ocean on a routine reconnaissance mission. The 1,750-ton submarine carried three SS-N-5 nuclear ballistic missiles on it, each tipped with a one-megaton warhead, in addition to cipher material and ninety-eight crew members. But the submarine disappeared. After twenty-four hours of listening in vain for signs of the sub, the Soviet navy sent a dozen ships that struggled with gale force winds, snow, and forty-five-foot waves to search for it. The Soviets could not locate their missing sub.[23]

The United States, however, had noticed the flotilla of ships and submarines scouting the area and determined some rough coordinates; they rightly assumed that their rivals were looking for a lost submarine. And the US Navy had something the Soviet navy did not possess: the Sound Surveillance System (SOSUS), a global network of underwater hydrophones used to analyze sounds.

By 1958, the US Navy had installed a system of underwater hydrophones, nailed to the seafloor, stretching from the Caribbean to Nova Scotia in the Atlantic Ocean and along California and Hawaii on the Pacific Ocean. These underwater ears could hear the distinctive sounds of submarines such as the propeller, cooling system, or diesel-electric engine.[24]

After conducting a mock trial by sinking an old World War II submarine with the hatches open, the US Navy possessed a sample sound. With the West Coast hydrophones, they found a similar sound and located the Soviet sub by May 1968.

The second major development for submarine spy warfare in 1968, under Bradley's orders, was the completion of the transformation of the Regulus missile toting and launching nuclear submarine the USS *Halibut* into a spy submarine. Bradley had given John P. Craven, the US Navy's chief scientist, $70 million to convert it; it was now ready for deployment.

Craven had joined the navy's deep submergence group to analyze ways submarines could dive deeper than 1,000 to 1,500 feet, the average depth a sub could withstand without imploding from the extreme water pressure in deep oceans. The navy selected Craven for this project because he had successfully worked on the *Polaris*, a nuclear-powered submarine, as chief scientist, and he was an iconoclastic blend of ideas and intelligence. He completed high school when he was eleven years old; though he was not admitted into the Naval Academy, he received a BA from Cornell University, a master's degree from the California Institute of Technology, and a PhD in ocean engineering from the University of Iowa. He was proud of his navy lineage and boasted of his heritage from a Moorish pirate on his mother's side and the Union ship *Tecumseh* on his father's side. He eventually became head of the Deep Submergence Systems Project (DSSP), created in order to dive to the seafloor, rescue submariners, and retrieve materials like a stray Soviet ICBM nose cone.[25]

When Craven was given $70 million to convert the USS *Halibut* into a spy ship, he was one of the few people who liked the *Halibut*'s odd design and features. Flat on the top like a halibut, in order to launch Regulus missiles, the resemblance stopped there. Instead, it sported a huge hump on the top that opened up into a "large sharks-mouth hatch, part of the original missile hangar." It was loud at a time when engineers sought utmost quiet, and its shape made it the least hydrodynamic sub in the nuclear-powered fleet. For Craven, though, the three-level cavernous space stretching fifty feet long and climbing thirty feet high would allow him to create his dream spy lab, complete with a data analysis room, a darkroom, and a computer room taken up by an enormous Univac 1124 with blinking lights and reel-to-reel tape machines. He christened the hump with its gaping hatch the "Bat Cave," a real technological James Bond film reminiscent of a Dr. No–style hideout.[26]

This new submersible would be outfitted with an array of intelligence-gathering technology like cameras, sonar gear, electronics, and sound recorders.[27] Craven also developed aluminum "fish" that could swim through deep water outfitted with battery-powered strobe light eyes, sonar whiskers, and rudders as fins. A cable from the Bat Cave reaching to the bottom of the ocean towed the aluminum fish, which cost $5 million each.[28]

In summer 1968, Craven lowered the thick steel cable with the dangling cameras and lights from the *Halibut* to the ocean floor searching for the Soviet sub. Earlier missions to find Soviet missile debris failed, but this time the *Halibut*'s cameras photographed the lost sub. The pictures showed three missile tubes with one intact in the front and middle of the sub, the sail, and the skeleton of a sailor. The submarine's rear end was split off from the center and the middle. The photography project, code-named Velvet Fist, eventually sent back 22,000 photographs to the navy and the Pentagon.[29]

But the navy and the CIA wanted more than pictures. Soon after acquiring the photographs, the two departments hatched plans to retrieve material on the sunken submarine, technology like warheads and cryptographic materials stored in watertight safes. The contents promised to reveal valuable information on Soviet strategic capabilities.

Bradley met frequently with Craven at his office hidden deep in the inner ring of the Pentagon. Barricaded behind a succession of three doors, they discussed how they could acquire the material on the sub. They proposed using a submersible to approach the sunken submarine and create a hole in the hull with an explosion in order to grab material like the safe containing the codebooks, burst transmitters and receivers, and a nuclear warhead.[30]

Enter the CIA

Meanwhile, the secretary of defense, Packard, had written to DCI Helms at the CIA in April 1969 asking him to assemble a working group to look at the technical feasibility of accessing the material on the sunken submarine.

Although the CIA had no experience conducting submarine espionage, it had successfully completed major feats of technical intelligence, including overhead reconnaissance with the U-2 spy plane, the Oxcart supersonic spy plane, and spy satellites.

Initially, Helms was reluctant to embark on a new course of ocean engineering precisely because the CIA had experience with spy planes and satellites but not spy boats. In addition, while he appreciated technical collection methods, he thought that satellites and sensors would never replace human spies as a way to learn about the enemy's intentions.[31] Nevertheless, he passed on Packard's request to the CIA's new deputy head of the Directorate for Science and Technology (DST), Carl Duckett, to look into what the CIA would do with sunken sub.[32]

Duckett was enthusiastic about the project and asked for a couple of months to assemble a team of scientists to study the problem. Duckett had been a controversial choice to lead the directorate. Unlike his predecessor, Bud Wheelon, he did not have advanced degrees from prestigious institutions and a long list of scientific publications. In fact, he didn't even have a college degree, though he did have a background in missile technology. Whatever Duckett lacked in formal scientific training and accomplishments, he made up for as a "smooth talker"; he "could sell Congress anything." He also had a talent for turning "technical data into laymanese."[33]

Duckett quickly appointed John Parangosky to assemble and head up the CIA working group of seven scientists and engineers from the DST in summer 1969 to assess the technical feasibility of gaining access to the materials on the sunken submarine. A rather rotund, handsome man who liked to eat alone at French restaurants, Parangosky was a workaholic and already had served as project manager for the CIA's vaunted U-2, Oxcart, and Corona technical programs in Richard Bissell's office. He was seen as a "miracle worker" by colleagues. In his capacity as program manager for the previous programs he also forged valuable relationships with industry partners. Like Duckett, he didn't have a degree in a technical subject, since he studied law, but he read in the field and trusted the experts to guide him.[34]

One of the first ideas the Azorian team proposed was to attach rocket boosters to the K-129 using mini-subs, launching it to the surface. It wasn't clear to the DST scientists and engineers, whose previous experience lay in airplanes, missiles, and satellites, what they would do next. Duckett, sometimes referred to as "Mr. Rocket" in Congress, who had led a ballistic missile group in Alabama, thought it was "reasonable." As David Sharp, one of the participants, remarked in his memoirs, "To a hammer, every problem looks like a nail." He admits they all had "zero experience in ocean engineering."[35]

The CIA group came back with another idea to lift the submarine from the ocean floor using a so-called capture vehicle. Obviously, the CIA was not going to build the contraption itself. Instead, Parangosky decided to contract it out, as he had with the U-2 spy plane and the Corona satellite. He started knocking on the doors of old aerospace associates from the National Reconnaissance Office like McDonnell Douglas and Lockheed. It turned out that Lockheed's oceans division knew how to apply space technology to deep-sea problems. Finally, he found Curtis Crooke at Global Marine who was interested in working on the problem.[36]

When Craven and Bradley heard this news, they thought the CIA was crazy and were very much opposed to it. Bradley reportedly said, "Oh, no, Jesus Christ almighty! You people are in a tank! That's a pipe dream!" Despite the navy's strong opposition, the CIA project survived.[37] The conflict was reminiscent of the one surrounding the U-2 spy plane and the air force's lack of interest in a flimsy plane that couldn't drop bombs. In the end, the CIA took over a plane project that traditionally belonged to the air force. In both cases, the military agencies felt they lost moneys that belonged to them to a civilian organization tasked with human intelligence gathering.

Although the director of central intelligence and a member of the US Intelligence Board, Richard Helms, was not supportive of the project at first, he slowly became a convert and was as enthusiastic about lifting the submarine with innovative technology as he had been about the agency's use of spy planes and satellites. According to David Sharp, he "consistently urged the Directorate of Science and Technology to push the envelope of what was possible." He was particularly keen on acquiring the cryptographic material on the sub.[38]

One of the first steps Parangosky took to salvage the relationship with the navy and to provide a way to protect CIA sources and methods was to create the National Underwater Reconnaissance Office (NURO), similar to the NRO, which was created to facilitate relations with the air force and to share photoreconnaissance images from planes and satellites.

Parangosky called Gene Poteat, who had worked on missile guidance and electronic warfare at the DST; they had become friends when Parangosky recruited him to work on the OXCART supersonic plane in Nevada. Poteat had helped design the NRO, and Parangosky wanted advice on how to organize it. Poteat replied, "You mean fighting and struggles?"[39]

In August 1969, Duckett brought the idea of the NURO to the National Security Council's 40 Executive Committee, an advisory group that included Henry Kissinger and Richard Helms. Just as the NRO had overseen and distributed aerial reconnaissance, the NURO would do the same for underwater reconnaissance, he explained. Kissinger told President Richard Nixon about the NURO and about the submarine recovery operation; both the new office and the elaborate plan appealed to him.[40]

Operation Ivy Bells

Meanwhile, in his backroom at the Pentagon, Bradley started hatching a new naval spy mission for *Halibut*, one that would entail more than simply taking pictures of a sunken submarine. He imagined finding a communication cable in the bottom of Soviet waters to tap into the innermost thoughts of the Soviet navy. As Sherry Sontag and Christopher Drew write in *Blind Man's Bluff*, "If Halibut's camera toting fish could find that cable, and her crew could tap it, then the United States would violate the very soul of Soviet secrecy."[41] For US intelligence, eavesdropping was the closest equivalent to having a human spy in place.

But a communication cable beneath the ocean would be no wider than five inches, and this would be the proverbial needle in a haystack mission. The story goes that Bradley started daydreaming, and his mind focused on his childhood on river shores in Missouri. He recalled seeing signs that said to watch for underwater cables as boats floated down the river. He thought the Soviets might similarly have signs along the shore warning of cables.[42]

Aside from solving the problem of locating the cables, another scientific hurdle was the depth of the ocean. Divers could dive only about 130 feet before suffering from nitrogen narcosis. The *Halibut* would need a decompression and lockout chamber for saturation divers, and its hump was the perfect place to hide it. Publicly, the hump contained a deep submergence rescue vehicle (DSVR).

Bradley decided to search for the cables in the Sea of Okhotsk in the western Pacific Ocean because they would connect the Soviet Naval Pacific Headquarters in Vladivostok to the Soviet ballistic missile submarine base at Petropavlovsk. In October 1971, he sent Cmdr. "Smiling Jack"

McNish with a crew on the *Halibut*'s first reconnaissance mission for the cable tapping project. As the sub approached the Siberian coast with its periscope up, McNish did indeed see small signs on the beach warning of cables beneath the sea. Using the fish with dangling cameras, the crew took rolls of film and finally captured color images of a three-inch-diameter communication cable. They brought the evidence back to Washington, DC, for Bradley. They also attempted to tap the cable.[43]

The tapes from the cable tap were then sent to the NSA, often nicknamed "No Such Agency." Perched in Fort Meade, Maryland, the NSA worked with all intelligence agencies on eavesdropping projects, decrypting messages and collecting signals from the ether and from cables beneath the water. This sort of signals collection was called SIGINT in intelligence circles.

The SIGINT spies on board tried to siphon off some signals, but they were of poor quality. When the *Halibut* went on a second mission in August 1972, the quality was no better. Instead of halting the mission, the NSA and the navy became more determined; they were "convinced that intelligence pearls" lay in those communication cables. The NSA considered Ivy Bells a priority project, which helped justify the one-million-dollar-a-day navy expense. In addition to sending the sub to the Pacific, the dangerous mission on Soviet territory required a SR-71 spy plane to fly overhead monitoring Soviet traffic along with "decoy" subs to distract Soviet subs suspicious of enemy incursions.[44]

Project Azorian

As the joint navy-NSA project solved technical problems, the Azorian project stumbled over technological hurdles and security protocols. In concert with the NURO, the CIA set up the highest security protocols for Project Azorian. Every effort was made to separate the data from their origin. When information was to be forwarded to the navy or State Department or NSA, it would have a stamp on it with a code. The security system was code-named Jennifer. Almost every folder was labeled "Jennifer." Later, when the program was leaked to the press, it was known as Project Jennifer, not Azorian. The Jennifer security system was named after the young daughter of Paul Eastman (head of the security system) who had just died tragically.[45]

The Jennifer security system was just one way in which the project was hidden and disguised. However, disguising an enormous ship with an oil-like derrick on the top and with a barge to lift a submarine out of the ocean required some ingenuity.

What better way to hide the project in plain sight than to recruit the reclusive, secretive, Howard Hughes to play along? Through his lawyers, Hughes agreed to allow Global Marine and the CIA to use his name as a cover for the ship. It would be named the *Hughes Glomar Explorer* and would be disguised as a deep-ocean mining ship. It took five years before Global Marine got the ship and the barge ready for action in the middle of the Pacific Ocean.

Imagine trying to lift a 1,750-ton Soviet submarine stuck three miles down (almost twice the length of the Golden Gate Bridge) on the ocean floor of the Pacific with five steel claws attached to an enormous crane-like contraption. To reach the sub and grab it around its middle, the contraption must descend from a barge and struggle against powerful currents, crushing pressure, and the darkness of deep water. This was the CIA's Project Azorian undertaken by the CIA's Directorate of Science and Technology with the support of Global Marine and other industry contractor partners.

The NSA's Underwater Eavesdropper

While Project Azorian dragged on and foundered with cost overruns and the threat of cancellation, Operation Ivy Bells overcame many of its technical problems. Since the early tapes had been a "recorded cacophony" of sound but not distinct words, the NSA contacted a navy-NSA technical specialist, John Arnold, who was asked to assemble a team of eavesdropping spies to help decipher the signals.

Together they created advanced systems to capture the signals. While the early tapes had recorded multiple overlapping voices, they succeeded in filtering the signal processes to tape single voices. One of their first recordings included an admiral talking to his wife on one line and his mistress on the other. The team set up shop in the sub's chart room. They used 70 percent off-the-shelf manufactured equipment, not military grade, using analog rather than digital systems. They wired, soldered, tweaked, troubleshot, calibrated, and worried until it worked. A Hewlett-Packard 1730 computer was also on board, interfacing with the radio equipment, when they set sail for the third mission to the Sea of Okhotsk.[46]

Discovery

Meanwhile, an investigative reporter, Seymour Hersh, got whiff of a top-secret, highly classified project with many cost overruns. He had been getting tips for years about waste in the intelligence community. This time a source he met at a northern Virginia restaurant told him about a CIA barge that could reach down deep into the ocean and snatch up a missing submarine. By the time the CIA heard Hersh was on to them in early 1974, the *Hughes Glomar Explorer* hadn't even gone out to sea yet. William E. Colby, the new DCI, did everything in his power to muzzle Hersh, who "scared the living daylights" out of him. He succeeded for a while, until Jack Anderson at the *Los Angeles Times* heard about the story because of a break-in at the Hughes Summa Office and found material revealing the secret project. On February 7, 1975, Anderson scooped Hersh on the story. Anderson felt the CIA had no right to cover up a "boondoggle," especially one that cost $350 million (later estimates put the cost at $500 million).[47]

The project certainly seemed like a boondoggle because once the *Hughes Glomar Explorer* sailed out to the middle of the Pacific in summer 1974, two of the capture vehicle's claws broke as it tried to lift the submarine from the ocean floor. It brought only part of the sub up, and then the sub "dissolved" like "Alka-Seltzer" in the ocean.[48]

Hersh and Anderson were not the only outsiders to dig up the heavily guarded secrets hidden in an open cover story. Otis G. Pike, a Democratic member of the House of Representatives from New York, was leading a broader investigation into the CIA and all the other three-letter entities for abuse and waste. Unlike his more famous counterpart Frank Church, who was also leading an enormous investigation into intelligence abuses, Pike was interested in a cost-benefit analysis. "How much use do they get out of the massive amount of information they collect?" he asked.[49] Pike's report was one of the few that looked into submarine espionage. It shed light on the mystery surrounding high-tech underwater espionage and its perils. He chronicled submarine tailings and collisions.[50]

It shouldn't be surprising that the secret was out. CIA officials assumed it would leak at some point. After all, eighteen hundred people knew about the project. Not only were spy agencies' officials privy to the secret hiding in plain sight, but so were the two major contractors, Global Marine, designer of the *Glomar Explorer*, and Lockheed Missile and Space, designer of the capture vehicle.[51]

To add to the spilled secret, documents released in 2014 show that since the project wasn't tested because of time constraints, it stood only a 20 to 40 percent chance of success. While the National Security Council thought it had a 30 to 40 percent chance of success in its 1972 review, by the time it was ready for launch in 1974, this estimate increased to 40 percent.[52]

Most of Project Azorian, like Ivy Bells, took place during the period of détente between the United States and the Soviet Union, an attempt to relax tensions between the superpowers. When Richard Nixon arrived in office in 1969, he was determined to make détente the centerpiece of his foreign policy. Henry Kissinger, his national security adviser, also sought to negotiate, not confront. During the 1972 Moscow Summit, Nixon and General Secretary Leonid Brezhnev signed an agreement limiting strategic arms and reducing incidents in the ocean. The thrust of the agreement was to "avoid military confrontations and to prevent the outbreak of nuclear war."[53]

Détente didn't mean that spying stopped or slowed down. The John Walker case, Operation Ivy Bells, and Project Azorian illustrate that spying continued with impunity, and each side used its respective strengths to do so. The National Security Council considered the question of détente during the 1972 review of Azorian. Helmut Sonnenfeldt, the NSC's resident Sovietologist, commented, "Détente is not going to terminate mutual intelligence operations which the targeted country will consider obnoxious and the collecting country vital. Either country which wished to exploit a reconnaissance operation could cite airborne, underwater and overhead programs now being conducted."[54]

Even so, there were discussions about the impact of Azorian (if there were discussions about Ivy Bells, they haven't been released) on US-USSR relations led by Kissinger at the National Security Council meetings of the 40 Executive Committee. Project Azorian program managers thought Nixon's détente policy might undermine the project.

Although there were several voices from the State Department and the navy on the committee against continuing the Azorian project, Kissinger was very supportive of the CIA's desire to continue it. Surprisingly, after the first attempt to bring up the submarine failed, Kissinger supported the second attempt, code-named Matador, even more.

When the 40 Committee met on June 5, 1974 in the White House

Situation Room to decide whether the Azorian mission would continue, it was in the context of endangering Nixon's prized détente foreign policy as well as the taint of the recent Watergate scandal. Kissinger asked whether the president would want to risk relations with the Soviet Union in order to achieve an "intelligence coup." He considered arguments against the project and concluded that the issue of "morality" was the strongest one against it. He even tried to second-guess the Soviets' reaction if they found out about the salvage effort. Kissinger quipped, "If the Soviets found out about the project wouldn't they say 'boys will be boys' or would they say 'You dirty SOB's.'"[55]

According to William Colby, they knew they had a "hot potato on [their] hands" that could threaten détente. But Kissinger was always "fully supportive" of the project and considered it Colby's "business[;] . . . it was his problem, it was his money."[56] Whatever qualms the committee had about any political fallout if Project Azorian were to be found out, they overcame them and decided to continue the project.

On March 19, 1975, the day after Jack Anderson's *Los Angeles Times* radio story and the day of Seymour Hersh's *New York Times* article on Project Azorian, James R. Schlesinger, then secretary of defense, met with President Gerald Ford in the Cabinet Room at 11:20 a.m., along with William Colby, to discuss how to handle the stories. Since Colby had already confirmed the project but offered no details of the mission, they decided to leave it at that. But Colby did not want another U-2 episode. He did not want to pressure the Soviet Union to respond.[57]

Schlesinger considered the "episode . . . a major American accomplishment." "The operation is a marvel—technically, and with maintaining secrecy," he said. Even though the claw could not bring up the sunken submarine, the operation certainly was a technical marvel; it succeeded in pulling together America's finest engineers to develop an unprecedented "claw" to lift a very heavy submarine. At the time, the government was also ready to throw a lot of money at the project and the expensive technology. David Sharp, an engineer on the project, thought Azorian was "the most fascinating example of what has sometimes been described as the technical arrogance of the CIA's Directorate of Science and Technology during the Cold War years."[58] Whether technical marvel or technical arrogance, the project showcased US intelligence's faith in the power of technology to solve intelligence problems.

While Project Azorian had been leaked by journalists during the time it was taking place, Operation Ivy Bells stayed secret for about ten years. Ronald Pelton, an NSA analyst in need of money, told the KGB about Ivy Bells for only $36,000 in 1980. Although the Sea of Okhotsk cable tap was exposed, the navy and the NSA continued to tap other undersea cables until the end of the Cold War.

Like Walker before him, Pelton, a human source, betrayed vaunted American technology to the Soviet Union. And like the U-2 spy plane episode in 1962, Project Azorian was exposed and threatened US-Soviet relations. And like the technology created before and after in the service of espionage, Azorian was indeed a technological marvel. But like all the technological marvels before and after it, it was expensive and extravagant. Even if Azorian was a "boondoggle," as Anderson described it, SOSUS, Ivy Bells, and other underwater technology contributed to the United States as a global espionage power.

Notes

1. John A. Walker Jr., *My Life as a Spy* (New York: Prometheus Books, 2008), chap. 1 (Kindle ed.).

2. Walker; and Oleg Kalugin, *Spymaster: My 32 Years in Intelligence and Espionage against the West* (New York: St. Martin's Press, 1994), 84–89.

3. Sherry Sontag and Christopher Drew, *Blind Man's Bluff: The Untold Story of American Submarine Espionage* (New York: Harper Paperbacks, 1998), 272, 469.

4. Interview, Pete Earley with Solomatin, Moscow, 1995. See https://www.cryptomuseum.com/crypto/usa/kw7/files/boris_solomatin_interview.pdf.

5. Pete Earley, *Family of Spies: Inside the John Walker Spy Ring* (New York: Bantam Books, 1989), 68.

6. Earley, 68–69.

7. Walker, *My Life as a Spy*, location 198.

8. Walker.

9. Kalugin, *Spymaster*, 86.

10. Kalugin, 86–87.

11. Mitchell B. Lerner, *The* Pueblo *Incident: A Spy Ship and the Failure of American Foreign Policy* (Lawrence: University Press of Kansas, 2002), 83.

12. Sontag and Drew, *Blind Man's Bluff*, 351–52.

13. Kalugin, *Spymaster*, 84.

14. Earley, *Family of Spies*, 92.

15. Earley, passim.

16. Earley, 154–60.

17. Earley, 3.

18. Earley, 6.

19. Earley, 8–9.

20. John Barron, *Breaking the Ring: The Bizarre Case of the Walker Family Spy Ring* (Boston: Houghton Mifflin, 1987), 201.

21. Jeffrey Richelson, *A Century of Spies: Intelligence in the Twentieth Century* (New York: Oxford University Press, 1995), 397.

22. Richelson, 18.

23. CIA, CREST, "Project AZORIAN: The Story of the Hughes Glomar Explorer," *Studies in Intelligence*, declassified 2010, 1–50, available at https://nsarchive2.gwu.edu/nukevault/ebb305/doc01.pdf; Josh Dean, *The Taking of the K-129: How the CIA Used Howard Hughes to Steal a Russian Sub in the Most Daring Operation in History* (New York: Dutton, 2017), 10; Norman Polmar and Michael White, *Project Azorian: The CIA and the Raising of the K-129* (Annapolis, MD: Naval Institute Press, 2010), 179; and Jeffrey T. Richelson, *The Wizards of Langley: Inside the CIA's Directorate of Science and Technology* (Boulder, CO: Westview Press, 2001), 133. A new book is coming out on Project Azorian in December 2022 that the author was not able to consult as the copyediting review was completed in May 2022: see M. Todd Bennett, *Neither Confirm nor Deny: How the Glomar Mission Shielded the CIA from Transparency* (New York: Columbia University Press, 2022).

24. Dean, *Taking of the K-129*, 19–20.

25. Sontag and Drew, *Blind Man's Bluff*, 65–67; Dean, *Taking of the K-129*, 27–32; and "John Craven, 90, Pioneer of Spying at Sea, Dies," *New York Times*, February 18, 2015.

26. Sontag and Drew, *Blind Man's Bluff*, 75–76, 86.

27. Sontag and Drew, 76; and Dean, *Taking of the K-129*, 31.

28. Sontag and Drew, *Blind Man's Bluff*, 86.

29. Sontag and Drew, 115–16; and Richelson, *Wizards of Langley*, 134.

30. Sontag and Drew, *Blind Man's Bluff*, 92, 117–19.

31. David S. Robarge, "Richard Helms: The Intelligence Professional Personified," *Studies in Intelligence* 46, no. 4 (2002), www.cia.gov/library/center-for-the-study-of-intelligence/csi-publications/csi-studies/studies/vol46no4/article06.html.

32. David H. Sharp, *The CIA's Greatest Covert Operation: Inside the Daring Mission to Recover a Nuclear-Armed Soviet Sub* (Lawrence: University Press of Kansas, 2012), 7.

33. Richelson, *Wizards of Langley*, 132.

34. Sharp, *CIA's Greatest Covert Operation*, 8.

35. Sharp, 11.

36. Sharp, 23–24.

37. Sontag and Drew, *Blind Man's Bluff*, 119.

38. CIA, CREST, "Project AZORIAN"; and Sharp, *CIA's Greatest Covert Operation*, 25.

39. Dean, *Taking of the K-129*, 82–83.

40. Dean.

41. Sontag and Drew, *Blind Man's Bluff*, 222.

42. Sontag and Drew.

43. W. Craig Reed, *Red November: Inside the Secret U.S.-Soviet Submarine War* (New York: Harpers, 2011), 230.

44. Reed, 230–31.

45. Sharp, *CIA's Greatest Covert Operation*, 42–43.

46. Reed, *Red November*, 232–33.

47. Sontag and Drew, *Blind Man's Bluff*, 272, 469.

48. Sontag and Drew, 277.

49. Sontag and Drew, 280.

50. Sontag and Drew, 279–81.

51. Memo for the record, July 1, 1974, doc. 188, in *Foreign Relations of the United States, 1969–1974*, vol. 35, National Security Policy, 1973–1976 (Washington, DC: Government Printing Office, 2014), https://history.state.gov/historicaldocuments/frus1969-76v35/ch4 ; and M. Todd Bennett, "Détente in Deep Water: The CIA Mission to Salvage a Sunken Soviet Submarine and US-USSR Relations, 1968–1975," *Intelligence and National Security* 33, no. 2 (2018): 196–210. Bennett uses the figure 1,700.

52. Memo for the record; and National Security Staff Paper, no date, attachment to doc. 187, FRUS.

53. Bennett, "Détente in Deep Water," 3.

54. "Paper Prepared by the National Security Staff," Washington, DC, no date, 3, https://history.state.gov/historicaldocuments/frus1969-76v35/d187. Newly released 2014 *Foreign Relations of the United States* materials shed new light on Azorian and détente. See also Bennett, "Détente in Deep Water."

55. Bennett, "Détente in Deep Water," 5.

56. Sontag and Drew, *Blind Man's Bluff*, 469.

57. Memorandum of Conversation, March 19, 1975, President Ford, James E. Schlesinger, Philip Buchen, John O. Marsh Jr., Donald Rumsfeld, Brent Snowcroft, and William E. Colby; available at Gerald Ford Library, CREST, and in the FRUS Azorian documents.

58. Sharp, *CIA's Greatest Covert Operation*, ix.

6

TURNER'S TECHNOLOGICAL TURN

The telephone call that would eventually allow a navy admiral to change the way the CIA conducted espionage came at 4:30 in the afternoon on Wednesday, February 2, 1977, when Stansfield Turner was sitting in his enormous Mussolini-style office in Naples, Italy, as the commander of NATO's Southern Flank.

Admiral Turner's aide told him a secure call had just come in from Washington, DC. When Turner pressed the receiver to his ear, he heard the secretary of defense say, "The president would like to see you in Washington tomorrow. Can you get here?" Turner said he could. Within a few hours, he picked up the bag his wife had packed, flew to Paris in a navy plane, and boarded a Concorde jet that flew twice the speed of sound to arrive in Washington, DC, in three hours and fifty-five minutes—in time for a mysterious meeting with the president.[1]

Jimmy Carter was no stranger to Turner. Although Turner didn't remember him from their Naval Academy days, he had met him at their twenty-fifth class reunion in 1971 when Carter was governor of Georgia; he found him warm and sincere. A few years later, Turner, who had been a Rhodes Scholar after his Annapolis days, invited Carter to speak at the Naval War College, where he served as president.

When Turner arrived at the Oval Office, Carter greeted him in the same warm manner he had recalled from their earlier encounters. After complimenting his accomplishments, Carter came to the point: "Stan, I'm considering you for Director of Central Intelligence." As a navy man, Turner was surprised, as he had expected an offer in military affairs. He was not Carter's first choice. Theodore Sorenson, John F. Kennedy's speechwriter, was, but he withdrew after resistance from Congress. Now Turner was competing with another military man, Gen. Bernard W. Rogers, chief of staff of the army.[2]

Turner was a "coldly affable" man of medium height,[3] with a widow's peak at his graying hairline, a robust build, and prominent blue eyes. He had been associated with the navy ever since the Naval Academy and was considered one of their best and brightest. He was fifty-three when the phone call came, ready to trade in his navy blues for civilian attire, and did not expect to don a cloak and dagger. Even so, he accepted the position.

Like Carter, Turner was enamored with technology. He had experienced successful technical collection in the navy and wanted to beef up these techniques at the CIA. Although the CIA already had much success with spy planes and satellites, their official mission, unlike other military intelligence agencies and the NSA, was really to gather intelligence using humans. However, the CIA conducted the technical programs alongside the human ones. Previous leaders had never planned to extinguish human intelligence programs while beefing up technical collection. But Turner would change that course.

Turner's appointment in spring 1977 came at a time when the CIA was still reeling from the Church Committee hearing revelations. Many of the abuses involved science and technology, like the LSD experiments and electronic surveillance, but covert action was also under fire. In fact, Gerald Ford had made assassinations illegal. Other problems also plagued the beleaguered agency, which had become a top-heavy, aging bureaucracy.

Halloween Massacre

As a response to Carter's call for reforms and to the internal reports on the agency, Turner started firing staff members or easing them into early retirement. Some estimates for this unprecedented shakeup are as high as thousands of people eliminated, but Turner claims only 820 *positions* (not people) were eliminated, that it was mostly by attrition, and that 147 people retired early and only 17 were actually fired; but this was still some 20 percent of the workforce, and it was done in two short years. The majority of the pink slips and early retirements went to covert action operators, whose ranks had swelled during the Vietnam War and who were under fire during the Church Committee hearings.[4]

Aside from his decimation of the clandestine services portion of the

Figure 6.1 Adm. Stansfield Turner (*left*) shaking hands with President Jimmy Carter at Turner's swearing-in ceremony after becoming director of the CIA, March 9, 1977. *Jimmy Carter Library*

agency, Turner's way of letting people go was irksome to CIA staff. He asked the personnel office to computerize the way it was done and to use the computerized profiles and formulas to eliminate senior people to make room for younger women and men. Not a diplomat by nature, Turner simply sent staff members a photocopied memorandum informing them of their dismissal on October 31, 1977, Halloween. As a result, few people liked him and everyone was afraid of him. A former aide said of him after the Halloween Massacre, "Stan is deeply suspicious of the clandestine services. He is very uncomfortable with their basic uncontrollability. He doesn't like their fine clothes and accents, their Cosmos and Yale and Georgetown Clubs. They're simply not good sailors. He finds them sneeringly elliptical. It drives him crazy. He just can't get hold of this quicksilver."[5]

In his memoirs, Turner admitted that the way in which the dismissal letter was written was "unconscionable." But he blamed it on the previous director of central intelligence who had let people go. It was an "abrupt two paragraph bureaucratic letter" that concluded, "It has been decided that your services are no longer needed." He says he had drafted a longer, two-page letter outlining in detail gratitude for the staff members' service and his regret, but his colleagues talked him out of sending it for legal reasons.[6]

A victim of Turner's purge complained, "To receive the grateful thanks of a grateful government for services rendered—sometimes overseas at great hazard—in the form of a two-sentence message, without any recognition of past performance, was insulting and humiliating."[7] Turner's victims were so upset with his heartless firings that they circulated an adaptation of the admiral's song in Gilbert and Sullivan's *H.M.S. Pinafore*:

Of Intelligence I had so little grip
That they offered me the directorship
With my brassbound head of oak so Stout
I don't know what it's all about[8]

Techno-Spies

Although Turner denied media reports that by reducing humans he was increasing technical espionage, there is no doubt that he was enamored with technology and supported it throughout his tenure as DCI. In his memoirs he admits, "I did . . . give more of my time to technical systems. Technical systems cost infinitely more money than human ones, and once the Congress appropriates the money for something like a new satellite, the commitment is set; you cannot modify a satellite once it is set."[9]

Like Dulles before him, Turner was well aware of the relationship between the superpower status of the United States and espionage. But in contrast to Dulles, who preferred old-fashioned human intelligence (HUMINT), Turner swooned over the technology that would soon cover the globe, making the United States the preeminent intelligence superpower. He bragged that the United States was the only country in the world with superior technical intelligence capabilities and needed to guard it against counterattack by the Soviet Union.[10]

> Now that we have technical systems ranging from satellites travelling in space over the entire globe, to aircraft flying in free airspace, to miniature sensors surreptitiously positioned close to difficult targets, we are approaching a time when we will be able to survey almost any point on the

> earth's surface. . . . One way or another, we should soon be able to keep track of most activities on the surface of the earth.[11]

The navy tended to use a lot of new technology, and Turner's experience mirrored that of other military men who became leaders in the intelligence community.

In fall 1974, the large naval fleet Turner commanded crossed the Atlantic from Norfolk, Virginia. As the ships approached the Norwegian Sea, he received an official message warning of an escort by two Soviet ships. At the time Turner didn't know how Norfolk headquarters knew of the Soviet surveillance. He later learned it was through satellite reconnaissance. At the time, even a fleet commander was left in the dark.

In fact, spy satellites were officially made public already during the Strategic Arms Limitation Talks (SALT I) in 1972. They were called "technical means of verification," and both the Soviet Union and ordinary Americans knew about them. Carter was very open about using spy satellites because he wanted Americans to know that he needed the satellites to verify his nuclear arms control treaty, SALT II.[12] It wasn't clear if the Soviets could camouflage any violations if they knew they were being watched. However, just the fact that they were being watched was expected to make them more compliant.

According to information from spy satellite photography and electronic listening devices, however, there were times when the Soviets did violate the treaty. In 1979, the United States detected both a ballistic missile site and an antiballistic missile site.[13] Satellites were good at finding certain types of activities, usually related to military capabilities like nuclear weapons, but incapable of determining intentions or getting into the heads of human beings or even preventing terrorist attacks in later years.

In Turner's view, however, human intelligence was flawed because humans had different perceptions of the same event. When Caleb was sent on a mission to "spy out the land of Canaan," he returned with reports of a land that "flowed with milk and honey," but others returning found a land that "eateth up the inhabitants thereof" and that was populated with scary giants. In contrast, he thought technology simply recorded the facts and information without distorting human perceptions.[14]

People reacted strongly to Turner's new emphasis on technology. A Western European fieldsman "snorted" that "there's no technology invented yet that can read minds." He thought it was essential to "cultivate sources and collect human intelligence . . . so political leaders [could] answer questions like 'Who is going to push the button—and when?'"[15]

Turner thought electronic intercepts were a good way of finding out people's intentions. If, for example, the United States intercepted spoken plans by a foreign spy, the transcripts of the conversation were more reliable than filtered, secondhand reports.[16]

Despite Turner's love affair with technology, he was aware that it was difficult to analyze the vast amount of information acquired. He saw this as a challenge to meet, not a weakness. In 1979, before members of the Association of Former Intelligence Officers, he admitted, "Our real problem now is becoming how to process, evaluate, and act on this information which we are able to collect."[17]

In the 1970s, technical intelligence was eclipsing human intelligence in general. While America had developed technical programs in the 1950s, technical advancements accelerated the volume of technical collection year after year. Figures vary over the decades, but most analysts estimated that only about 13 percent of US intelligence came from human sources by the mid-1970s, and 83 percent came from technical intelligence. Another source estimates only 5 percent of US intelligence was gathered by human sources.[18]

Unlike Turner's rose-colored glasses view of the power of satellite photography, a previously top-secret report reveals that the CIA itself concluded that satellite photography had been useless in gleaning intelligence for international crises like the Arab-Israel war of October 1973. The opening lines of the undated report read, "Because of limitations in collection systems, photographic intelligence (PHOTINT) has generally produced little information of immediate value during international crises."[19]

The Iranian Revolution and the Middle East

Curiously, although Turner promoted technical intelligence, President Carter's national security adviser, Zbigniew Brzezinski, had complained to officials at a dinner hosted by Turner himself at CIA headquarters in Langley on October 27, 1977, that the "intelligence community had allowed its human-intelligence . . . skills in gathering political data to decay because of the increased emphasis on technical intelligence."[20]

But when the bottom fell out of political intelligence a few weeks later, Jimmy Carter took Brzezinski to task, along with Secretary of State Cyrus Vance and Turner because he was not informed that a revolution was under way in Iran. There were riots in the streets, and Shah Pahlavi had to impose a military government in his country.

Within weeks after Brzezinski's complaint about the lack of political intelligence, Carter wrote a handwritten note addressed, "To Cy, Zbig, Stan," on a cold November day in 1978: "I am not satisfied with the quality of political intelligence." He wanted them to provide him with an assessment of US "assets" around the world in a report, and he wanted it as soon as possible.[21] But the CIA and the State Department had no sources in Iran. There had been a tacit agreement that the shah took care of domestic issues and the CIA was allowed to install its technological listening devices in northern Iran aimed at the Soviet Union. The CIA had installed telemetry and electronic and communication monitoring equipment to monitor Soviet missiles.

Three months later, in February 1979, the Ayatollah Ruhollah Khomeini returned to Iran from his Paris exile and led the movement to overthrow the shah, which established an Islamic, anti-American revolutionary state. And just eight months after he came to power, Iranian students and militants seized over sixty diplomats, marines, and staff members (including three CIA men) at the US embassy and held them hostage.

Without agents in Iran, US intelligence had to rely on technical intelligence, which could not predict a revolution and hostage crisis. Even so, the hostage rescue mission attempted to use the latest military aircraft technology to seize the hostages instead of using diplomacy. Two of the helicopters crashed, killing eight servicemen, but the hostages were eventually rescued.[22] It turns out that Washington was at an advantage during the negotiations to release the hostages because it could read the weakly encrypted communications of Iran and Algeria, which was serving as a neutral mediator. Both countries had bought and used Crypto AG's doctored encryption machines that the United States could decipher. As detailed in chapter 8, the company was owned by the CIA and the BND, West German intelligence. It turns out that the CIA had more eavesdropping capabilities in Iran than had been acknowledged before the media revealed Crypto AG's capabilities in 2020.[23]

Six of the hostages who had taken refuge at the Canadian ambassador's house were rescued in an exfiltration operation now made famous by the film *Argo*, which was based on Tony Mendez's book on the same subject.[24] The film served to glorify the CIA's seeming success in using humans. However, the rescue mission was an instance of combining technical and human intelligence. Even if it was not a case of collecting information via a human source, it involved using humans to extract people from captivity. However, the operation used disguises developed by Mendez, a master of disguise, in the CIA's Office of Technical Services (OTS).

The Iran crisis was not the only Middle East problem that technical intelligence did not predict or help with alone. The US technological approach to espionage was not appropriate to rooting out terrorism, as the world would discover decades later, after the 9/11 terrorist attacks on American soil.

Robert Baer, a longtime case officer in the Middle East and India (1976–97), was entirely frustrated with Washington's spy-in-the-sky mentality: "The theory was that satellites, the Internet, electronic intercepts . . . would tell us all we needed to know about what went on beyond our borders." They thought allies in Europe and the Middle East would deal with Islamic fundamentalism. During his service, Baer witnessed a systematic shedding of its agents and even many of its case officers. The CIA felt that running agents "had become too messy." Agents didn't always act properly, and they "didn't fit America's moral view of the way the world should run."[25]

During his interview process at the CIA, the recruiters from the operations side of the CIA were still ardent believers in old-fashioned human espionage, reflecting a division in the agency between proponents of technical intelligence and those that favored human intelligence. Baer's mentor, Scott, told him, "Satellites and intercepts can't see inside someone's head. You need a person to do that. Agents and the secrets they steal are the crown jewel of American intelligence. It is what the intelligence business is really about."[26] While on tours in India and the Middle East, Baer recruited and ran agents and also became a firm believer in human intelligence. But he didn't just use money, ideology, compromise, or ego to recruit agents; he also played on common interests. He learned how to hunt in order to hang out with a hunter he wanted to recruit; he also skied with Russians. When he operated in India he ran between nine and fifteen agents.[27]

Baer ran one of his most successful agents in a Middle East country he wasn't allowed to name. The senior military official wanted to work for the United States because he loved the country. He visited a brother in Chicago and told him he wanted to spy for the United States. The asset simply walked into the FBI offices and volunteered; the FBI then passed him on to the CIA. He provided manuals with the latest Soviet technology, saving the United States $5 billion in missile systems. (At the time, the CIA worked in the Middle East primarily against the Soviet Union.) Baer was also a middleman and recruited other agents because he knew everyone in town. Money wasn't his prime motivation for spying, but he never had enough of it. Since he never seemed to be able to get his car out of second gear, he often needed a new transmission; the CIA was happy to buy him replacements.[28]

During his tours abroad in the late 1970s and 1980s, Baer witnessed the decline of the Directorate of Operations (DO) and the increased use of technology: "As the DO went into decline, satellites, not agents, became the touchstone of truth in Washington. Few things are more satisfying for a policymaker than to hold in his hand a clean, glossy black-and-white satellite photo, examine it with his very own 3D viewer, and decide for himself what it means. Not only could he do without analysts, he could do without agents, too."[29]

Clean, black-and-white satellite photos had been "touchstones of truth" for decades already, as the story of the Cuban Missile Crisis showed. They were the evidence John F. Kennedy needed to make a decision about the missiles in Cuba. But technological intelligence fell short when dealing with messy human situations like terrorists. Even so, the technology Carter and Turner worshipped helped catapult the United States to its position as a global espionage power.

Notes

1. Stansfield Turner, *Secrecy and Democracy: The CIA in Transition* (Boston: Houghton Mifflin, 1985), 9, 12.

2. Turner, 16.

3. John Ranelagh, *The Agency: The Rise and Decline of the CIA* (New York: Simon & Schuster, 1987), 634.

4. Michael Ledeen, "Tinker, Turner, Sailor, Spy," *New York Magazine*, March 3, 1980.

5. "Shaping Tomorrow's CIA," *Time*, February 6, 1978, 16.

6. Turner, *Secrecy and Democracy*, 198–99.

7. "The CIA: How Badly Hurt?," *Newsweek*, February 6, 1978, 4.

8. Quote in "Shaping Tomorrow's CIA."

9. Turner, *Secrecy and Democracy*, 206.

10. Turner, 98.

11. Turner, 92.

12. Turner, 90–91.

13. Turner, 93.

14. Turner, 94.

15. "The CIA: How Badly Hurt?"

16. Stansfield Turner, "Intelligence for a New World Order," *Foreign Affairs* 70, no. 4 (1991): 154.

17. National Archives, College Park, MD, CREST, CIA-RDP80BO15540 3000350001-4; and Association of Former Intelligence Officers, Sheraton Hotel, Reston, VA, October 5, 1979.

18. *Foreign and Military Intelligence, Book 1: Final Report of the Select Committee to Study Governmental Operations with Respect to Intelligence Activities, United States Senate, Together with Additional, Supplemental, and Separate Views*, April 26 (Legislative Day, April 14), 1976 (Washington, DC: n.p., 1976), 344; Walter Laqueur, *A World of Secrets: The Uses and Limits of Intelligence* (New York: Basic Books, 1985), 24; and Aid, "National Security Agency and the Cold War," 46.

19. CREST, CIA-RDP82T 00285R000240028-8, "Photographic Intelligence Production during an International Crisis," i.

20. Ted Szulc, "Shaking Up the C.I.A.," *New York Times Magazine*, July 29, 1979, 33.

21. Szulc; and Ranelagh, *The Agency*, 651.

22. Ranelagh, *The Agency*, 651–52.

23. Dover and Aldrich, "Cryptography and the Global South," 1909.

24. Antonio J. Mendez and Matt Baglio, *Argo: How the CIA and Hollywood Pulled Off the Most Audacious Rescue in History* (New York: Viking, 2012); and Ben Affleck, dir., *Argo* (Warner Bros., 2012).

25. Robert Baer, *See No Evil: The True Story of a Ground Soldier in the CIA's War on Terrorism* (New York: Three Rivers Press, 2002), 17.

26. Baer, 18.

27. Baer; and interview with Robert Baer, March 28, 2016.

28. Interview with Robert Baer.

29. Baer, *See No Evil*, 140.

III

FULLY GLOBAL

7

PASSING THE GLOBAL ESPIONAGE TORCH

In March 1945, Sir Edward Travis, then head of Bletchley Park, Great Britain's World War II code-breaking center, left Great Britain with an entourage of code breakers and naval intelligence officials for an around-the-world communications intelligence tour. The group traveled from Great Britain through the hot spots of the British Empire, including Egypt, India, Ceylon, Singapore, Hong Kong, Australia, and New Zealand, before ending up in Washington, DC. The trip helped lay the foundation for postwar worldwide Anglo-American communications intelligence cooperation. But its immediate goal was to shift British resources from the European enemy to the Pacific War against Japan since the war in Europe was almost over but was still raging in the East. The artistically crafted colored map left behind shows the extent of the British Empire in 1945 and the use Britain made of its territory to place communication intelligence stations all over the world.[1]

If we fast-forward to 2013, there is another remarkable map showing SIGINT stations and fiber optic cables around the world, but this time it is drawn by the US National Security Agency. It was meant to remain secret for a long time, but the whistleblower Edward Snowden secured it and passed it on to journalists. Like the British before them, the United States now had the world covered with signals intelligence capabilities sixty-eight years later. Britain had passed the global espionage torch to the United States.

This chapter tells the story of what happened between the British Round the World SIGINT tour in 1945 and the Snowden-acquired map in 2013 to shift the center of gravity and power from Britain to America

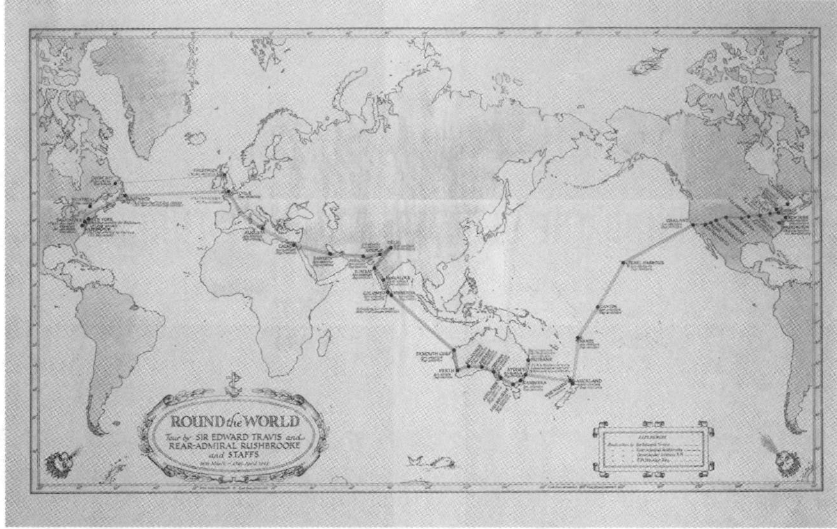

Figure 7.1 A map showing the route of the around the world communications tour by Sir Edward Travis and colleagues in 1945, which led to the creation of the UKUSA alliance. *Permission granted by Clarissa Lloyd, estate of Sir Francis H. Hinsley. Illustration located in Walter L. Pforzheimer Papers. General Collection, Beinecke Rare Book and Manuscript Library, Yale University*

in global communications technology and from radio intercept stations to satellite intercept stations and fiber optic cables. US intelligence had grown from a pupil sitting at the feet of their British teachers during World War II to a global hegemonic SIGINT power by the early Cold War. The chapter describes how Britain passed the torch of global electronic espionage to the United States as it lost its colonies abroad by trading territory for technology and money.[2]

The United States powered its global espionage empire by technology. Whether by means of spies in the sky, underground, in the mind, or in the ether, technology helped create the superpower and secure its global hegemony. As we have seen, using technology as the major tool to collect secret information began in the 1950s and continues to this day. When President Eisenhower supported scientists' call to develop spy planes and spy satellites by agencies like the CIA traditionally tasked with human intelligence, he helped create an American way of spying. Unlike the CIA, it was not surprising that the NSA and its forerunners used technology, as communications intelligence is based on technology. Combining Britain's

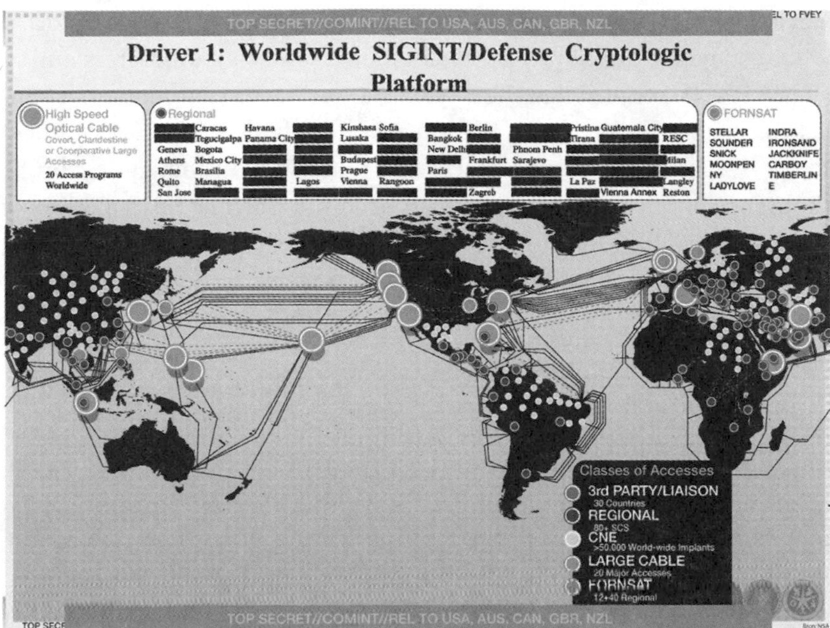

Figure 7.2 National Security Agency SIGINT platforms, 2013, including fiber optic cable routes. *National Security Agency*

real estate with American global aspirations helped create a technology that covered the globe from world-circling satellites from above to fiber optic cables under the ocean.

Round the World Tour

The Round the World map charts the British code breaker's journey through the hot spots of the British Empire as the trail swoops to the East from Great Britain to the Middle East to India to the Pacific to the United States, then back to Great Britain. The 1945 British communications intelligence entourage literally went around the globe highlighting the Pacific Theater. During their first stop in Cairo, Egypt, the delegation sought to decommission a station already winding down while moving the resources farther east.[3]

The longest stop—from March 18 to April 5—took place in the British colonies of India and Ceylon (now Sri Lanka). The group toured SIGINT stations there; the largest, the HMS Anderson, was located near Colombo,

Ceylon. Harry Hinsley, Travis's assistant, a code breaker and a historian who worked for the Government Communications Headquarters during World War II, recalled that the Ceylon station was "a cantonment of bungalows with thatched roofs in which hundreds of WRENS [Women's Royal Naval Service members] working under naval commanders broke thousands of Japanese signals." It had been the wartime headquarters of the Combined Bureau Far East (CBFE), previously located in Hong Kong and Singapore. From there the delegation traveled to Australia, where it planned to transfer more resources to the SIGINT agencies in Melbourne and Brisbane.

On April 17, the group left Australia for the United States via New Zealand and Pearl Harbor. While Rear Adm. E. G. N. Rushbrooke, director of naval intelligence, traveled to the Canadian SIGINT agency, Travis, Hinsley, and Cmdr. Clive Loehnis, from the Admiralty Operational Intelligence Center, arrived in Washington, DC, at the end of April to talk to officials from the Army, Navy, and State Departments about future Anglo-American SIGINT collaboration. Hinsley was pleased to see that the wartime interdepartmental rivalry between the navy and the army had decreased, but the United States was still not interested in forming a transdepartmental agency like the British GCHQ.[4]

From BRUSA/UKUSA to the Five Eyes

The world signals intelligence tour was one brick in the foundation of post–World War II cooperation between Britain and the United States. Anglo-American intelligence cooperation had actually already begun many years before, some say as early as 1940. The United States had a lot to learn about intelligence, and the British were eager teachers. They had also set up major intelligence organizations in the United States like the British Security Coordination, based at the Rockefeller International Center in New York City, to facilitate cooperation. It seems fitting that there is a huge bronze statue of the Greek god Atlas holding up a globe in front of that building. When the Art Deco statue was created in 1937, the sculptor did not intend for it to symbolize imperialism but rather to represent an international ethos. Even so, the statue is a nice symbol of Britain's imperial reach at the time and the notion that it is holding the world together like the mythical Atlas.

Outside of the realm of intelligence, Anglo-American cooperation had

Figure 7.3 Atlas at Rockefeller Center holding up the globe. *Wikimedia Commons, Another Believer*

already begun with the sharing of war technology in summer 1940 when Churchill was anxious to trade British radar technology for American technology. Sir Henry Tizard, an English chemist and inventor, was sent to neutral America at the end of the summer as part of the British Technical and Scientific Mission—dubbed the Tizard Mission—with his briefcase full of radar and sonar secrets.[5]

As part of this opening of technical cooperation between Great Britain and the United States, Britain sent Alan Turing, the famed British cryptographer, to America to visit Bell Labs to procure super-secret scrambling technology. At first, American officials were suspicious and would not let him into any laboratories, especially Bell Labs because its work was top secret, but after much back and forth between Gen. George Marshall and Churchill's representative, Sir John Dill, in Washington and Bell Labs and the navy, he was allowed to visit the lab, in part because he also had access to British secrets the Americans were anxious to acquire. The exchange highlighted American and British concern that the parties were not sharing all their technical secrets. The geographer Jason Dittmer also points out that Turing was allowed to cooperate on decryption but not encryption. Unlike decryption, so the argument goes, encryption protects a state's own secrets and thus should not be shared with other countries.[6]

At the time, the British kept their prized signals intelligence close to the chest. Code breakers sequestered in the stately brick mansion Bletchley Park, about eighty miles from London, had succeeded in breaking the Germans' seemingly impenetrable Enigma cipher machine. The machine looked like a cross between an old portable typewriter and a telephone switchboard, but every time an operator pressed a key it enciphered letters with a series of rotors. The British had, in fact, been able to break the Luftwaffe's codes by spring 1940.[7]

By October that year, Churchill had learned that the United States had broken the Japanese Purple code. William F. Friedman, America's foremost code breaker during both world wars, had led the team that tackled the Purple code and was selected to travel to Britain to share that secret with the British. Unfortunately, the trip was delayed because he suffered a nervous breakdown from overwork.[8]

Several years after he recovered from the nervous breakdown, in April 1943, Friedman flew to Great Britain on a C-54 government airplane. He traveled to Bletchley and told the British that his group in army signals intelligence had broken the Japanese diplomatic code Purple. The British were surprised that he shared this secret knowledge, but it opened up the possibility that they would also share their breakthroughs. In fact, Friedman wrote in a memorandum, "We are now exchanging Japanese Army intercept material with the British. . . . [T]he fact should constitute some

basis for establishing similar exchanges as regards German Ar
Force intercepts."[9]

Friedman was right. The coveted German army and air forc
had been part of the so-called Ultra (for ultra-secret) program. British code breakers' success led to a flow of material that helped the British anticipate the Germans' tactical moves. Of course, the British were reluctant to let this secret out to anyone because it would be successful only as long as it remained secret.

Friedman developed warm relations with British cryptographers, especially with Edward Travis. Although Travis was considered "gruff, rough and burly" by colleagues, he was cordial to Friedman, whom he wanted to cultivate. By 1943, Travis, also known as "Jumbo" to friends, and his staff provided Friedman with an in-depth tour of Bletchley Park. For the first time, Travis's boss opened "wide the gates of the Inner Sanctum," according to Friedman. This relationship continued into the post–World War II period until Travis's death in 1956.[10]

Informal cooperation between the United States and the British led to a formal agreement known as BRUSA (British USA), signed by Travis and George Strong, a major general in the US Army intelligence division, G-2, who represented the US War Department, in June 1943. Hinsley recalls that he came up with the acronym and was worried that the Americans would object to the British name coming first, but they did not. Along with admonishments about maintaining the strictest secrecy, the core of the agreement stipulated that both parties agreed to "exchange completely all information" about the detection and solution of Axis codes and ciphers. It was known as "special intelligence" and coded with an "ULTRA" prefix. The agreement emphasized that both parties would intercept only enemy military agencies or secret services like the Abwehr, not neutral or nonmilitary communications. The agreement divided the labor so that the United States was mainly responsible for reading Japanese military and air codes and Britain would handle the German and Italian ones, codifying each side's strength. It also stipulated that Britain would help the United States gain experience by allowing its agents to work on breaking keys in Britain, using British machines.[11]

The friendship between Travis and Friedman had become so close that by VE day, May 1945, they shared a celebratory dinner at Bletchley Park. The menu included Potage Ultra, Poulet Arlington, Legumes a choix random, and, for dessert, Dolce Americo-Britannique à la mode Brusa. Of course, Ultra soup referred to the Ultra secret; chicken Arlington, to Arlington Hall, the US code-breaking building; random cold vegetables, to radomes; and the sweet dessert American-British à la mode Brusa, to the British-US agreement.[12]

Although Canada, Australia, and New Zealand were included in the BRUSA agreement, initially the United States was not allowed to cooperate with those commonwealth countries without British permission. The BRUSA agreement and its successor—the UKUSA—were finally declassified and released by the NSA and the UK National Archives in 2010 after much speculation and curiosity about what was in them. At first glance, the files seem like dry legal agreements between two parties, with endless revisions of appendixes and details. Some interesting themes do emerge, however. There was constant tension between the two countries regarding the sharing of secret material. There was suspicion from both sides about withholding secret material. The documents also help chart the evolution of the relationship with the so-called British dominion countries like Australia and New Zealand. During the early years the agreement was between the London Signal Intelligence Board and the US Army-Navy Communication Intelligence Board; later the UKUSA agreement was between the GCHQ and the NSA. The British files also reveal that Travis played a dominant role in drafting the first iteration of the agreement. He shaped the direction of the alliance by pointing out that during World War II the British-US collaboration dealt to a large extent with "technical developments."[13]

The agreement was updated periodically with endless appendixes and mind-numbing details. In 1954, the cooperative agreement was renamed UKUSA (United Kingdom United States of America); by then, the agreement was between the British GCHQ/Communications entities and the American NSA, although Canada, Australia, and New Zealand played important roles. Sometimes UKUSA is used as an acronym to include all five countries, but according to the 1955 agreement, Canada, Australia, and New Zealand were only considered "UKUSA-collaborating countries." This was certainly an improvement over the 1946 agreement, which dismissed them as "dominions."[14]

As cooperation among all five countries—the United States, the United Kingdom, Canada, Australia, and New Zealand—increased and the Anglo-American countries began to collaborate more closely in the 1960s, the term *Five Eyes* began to appear, a more appropriate term than "UKUSA countries." The term comes from the British secrecy classification system whereby material stamped "Eyes Only" meant that it was secret—and that only an approved "eye" should read the material ("Five Ears" might be a more appropriate term). The term eventually received the acronym "FVEY"; this meant that the secret file could be read by one of the five countries. With the increasing input of Canada, Australia, and New Zealand through new installations and bases, the Five Eyes agreement had become an alliance or consortium that became a breathtakingly global espionage operation.

The NSA: Birth and Global Expansion

Unlike the United Kingdom, the United States had no unified communications intelligence agency in the early postwar years. When North Korea invaded South Korea on June 25, 1950, and caught US intelligence officials by surprise, this stimulated the US intelligence community to create a better and more unified communications intelligence (COMINT) agency. As a result, President Harry S. Truman approved a top-secret order to create the National Security Agency and abolish its forerunners, including the American Forces Security Agency (AFSA), in 1952.[15]

During the 1950s, the NSA more than doubled in size, from 30,000 in 1952 to 65,000 in 1960. Only about 10,000 of these people worked at the NSA's Fort Meade, Maryland, headquarters.[16] The rest manned stations on ships in the ocean, conducted surveillance from aircraft, tapped underground cables from submarines, and worked at bases scattered across the globe.

Along with personnel expansion, the NSA constructed over seventy intercept stations and COMINT units around the world at the cost of millions of dollars. Together with the thirty-five intercept stations operated by Canada, Australia, New Zealand, and the United Kingdom, the Five Eyes countries created a global communications empire encircling the Soviet Union and the Eastern Bloc, the People's Republic of China, and North Korea.[17]

As the NSA scholar Matthew Aid notes, if you add the twenty-five intercept stations of the NSA's third-party collaborators in West Germany, Austria, Norway, Denmark, Italy, Greece, Turkey, Pakistan, Thailand, Nationalist China, Japan, and South Korea to the mix, "one can make the argument that the UKUSA partners possessed the largest and geographically best Sigint collection system in the world."[18]

Passing the Torch

While the NSA was expanding, the British Empire was contracting. It was time to give up its colonial territories. After the defeat of Nazi Germany in World War II, Britain was bankrupt. It could no longer afford a sprawling empire. Simultaneously, British territories began to rise up against colonialism. Many of the territories, however, were amenable to the English maintaining bases; others evicted them.

During the Suez Crisis in 1956, the British and French, with the support of Israel, invaded Egypt after the Egyptian president, Gamal Abdel Nasser, nationalized the Suez Canal, which the British had built. Scared of a Russian invasion, Eisenhower urged Prime Minister Sir Anthony Eden to withdraw. He did, but the episode became known as his "imperial escapade." Not only was Britain forced to leave its stations in Egypt but, as a result of this fiasco, other countries evicted the British as well.

The most devastating eviction occurred in Ceylon, in the Indian Ocean, off the coast of India. As mentioned, during World War II, the British ran the HMS Anderson Station in Colombo, but they were asked to move to another part of the country because the Ceylonese wanted to use the area for themselves. Consequently, Britain planned and financed a large aerial farm of four hundred acres in Perkar, Ceylon, in the middle of the island. Once the Ceylonese heard of Eden's imperial escapade in Egypt, they assumed the British had stopped to refuel their ships in Ceylon on the way to Egypt and asked them to get out of Ceylon. This request came after Britain had already invested 2 million pounds in the project. The two parties finally reached an agreement whereby the British would be allowed to stay another five years.

Island Espionage

Cyprus

As the British were kicked out of country after country, and with the loss of Egypt and other Middle Eastern bases in Iraq and Palestine, the British moved their personnel and facilities to an old colonial stronghold, Cyprus. Cyprus was an ideal listening post for Middle East operations because of its easternmost position in the Mediterranean Sea, facing Lebanon and Syria on the east, Turkey in the north, and Israel and Egypt in the south. The location also offered superb intelligence on Soviet strategic weapons.

Cyprus, a British colony since 1914, quickly became a "refugee camp" for SIGINT personnel from Iraq, Egypt, and Palestine, as GCHQ expert, Richard Aldrich, notes. The British set up tents that housed a thousand workers at RAF Pergamos. Ayios Nikolaos, a key SIGINT installation, housed another thousand personnel.[19] By 1960 Cyprus had also achieved independence, but the British were allowed to maintain two Sovereign Base Areas on the island covering one hundred square miles. The Western Sovereign Base Area (WSBA) in Akrotiri included the village as well as the Limassol Salt Lake and two main base areas for RAF Akrotiri and Episkopi. The Eastern Sovereign Base Area (ESBA) in Dhekelia Cantonment included an electronic intelligence base in Ayios Nikolaos, just north of the UN buffer zone.[20]

Cyprus was a key SIGINT foothold for Britain and the United States. The United States had a listening post north of Nicosia in Yarallakos. But in general Americans had to keep a low profile because the postcolonial agreement was between the Cypriots and Britain. Americans disguised their presence by wearing yellow shorts, T-shirts, and baseball caps in order to look like tourists whenever they visited the British Sovereign Bases.[21]

One of the earliest UK-US joint projects started in the late 1950s focused on developing SIGINT and over-the-horizon (OTH) radar in a highly secret facility on Cyprus. The equipment bounced radio waves off the upper atmosphere, and these radio waves then reached targets beyond the horizon up to two thousand miles away. This meant that operators could view missiles, aircraft testing areas, bomber bases, and rocket sites as far away as southern Russia.[22]

The British had launched work on a prototype, code-named Zinnia, for surveillance of airplanes, but when the CIA's Office of Science and Technology began to cooperate with the British, the range was extended to rockets. Zinnia was then able to provide a measure of warning of surprise attack as part of Project Sandra.

When Project Sandra became operational in late 1961, it provided early warning for all of NATO and had a top-secret link to the US Navy in the Mediterranean, the Sixth Fleet. By 1970, America began its own project called "Cobra Shoe," which was a more powerful and modern version of

Sandra that included an early missile-warning system. To further disguise American presence on the island, the British Royal Air Force ran the project for the US Air Force.[23]

Cyprus was a powder keg because the island was split between Turkish Cypriots in the north and Greek Cypriots in the south, but it was actually London that threatened the busy aerial farms on the island. By summer 1974, the "sprawling nature of sigint sites" became hard to defend as more troops were deployed to Northern Ireland. The British wanted to leave Cyprus even though they knew it could provoke strong resistance by the intelligence community lobby in Washington, DC.[24]

When Cabinet Secretary Sir John Hunt traveled to Washington, DC, to break the bad news to Henry Kissinger, James Schlesinger, and William Colby, Kissinger swore at him at the meeting. Kissinger thought that the British should "continue to occupy this square on the world chessboard" and that withdrawal would destabilize the Middle East. London eventually backed down because of the "global importance of working closely with the Americans."[25]

It turned out the British may have been bluffing in order to get the United States to pay for the installations. Yet again America forked out the money. One of the reasons the United States wished to increase its presence in Cyprus was the deteriorating relationship with Turkey. Turkey had closed down the US military bases in Turkey, which meant the loss of a mother lode of intelligence-gathering facilities that had cost tens of millions of dollars to build.[26]

By the 1980s and 1990s, fiber optic cables started to augment satellite surveillance. Satellites are expensive and have limited amounts of bandwidth. Older wires and communication cables could be tapped easily because they emitted electromagnetic radiation, but fiber optic cables were a different breed. The signals fiber optics release are light pulses, not electricity: dozens of strands of glass are encased in a stainless-steel tube wrapped in more steel and cables. This ensures that they are not as easy to tap.[27]

Even so, the Snowden documents revealed that Britain's GCHQ was tapping hundreds of fiber optic cables by 2013 in an operation codenamed Tempora. The contents of internet traffic and telephone calls were all stored and then passed on to the NSA in programs grandiosely called Mastering the Internet and Global Telecoms Exploitation.[28]

Cyprus became one of the largest and most important hubs for fiber optic cables. Code-named Sounder, the Cyprus base was Britain's third largest internet surveillance hub after GCHQ headquarters in Benhall and a GCHQ station called Bude in Cornwall. Reportedly, fourteen fiber optic cables washed up from the ocean onto the Mediterranean island.[29]

Diego Garcia

While the British managed to stake out the two large bases in Cyprus, what they really wanted was a return to colonial power and its associated real estate. An opportunity came up in the most unlikely and forsaken place: the middle of the Indian Ocean. The British thought they could solve the problem of local resistance to colonial rule by finding territory with no indigenous people. When the Indian Ocean colonies of Mauritius and Seychelles began to clamor for independence, surprisingly, Britain complied with their demands. To do this, Anthony Greenwood, colonial secretary, flew to Mauritius and made a deal. He offered the islanders independence and a parting gift of 3 million pounds if they would let the British have the Chagos Archipelago, a group of seven atolls making up sixty tropical islands in the middle of the Indian Ocean between eastern Africa and Australia. The authorities in Mauritius agreed, and the British soon announced the creation of a new colony in 1965: the British Indian Ocean Territory (BIOT).[30]

British neocolonialists and American base planners were particularly interested in the island of Diego Garcia, on the southern end of the Chagos Archipelago. On a map, Diego Garcia looks like a marooned "Fantasy Island," isolated as it is in the middle of the Indian Ocean. It is a horseshoe-shaped atoll with dreamy turquoise water pooled in the center. Fluffy white clouds hover over the atoll like cotton balls on a ledge of glass. The closest continent, India, is some one thousand miles away, as is Seychelles. Africa, to the west, is even farther. Maldives, a popular tropical resort destination, is the closest island at about 730 miles away. But Pentagon military strategists weren't planning a holiday. They saw its geopolitical importance, not its beauty. In particular, it was a civilian naval planner, Stuart Barber, who recommended the Pentagon acquire the island as a military base. A thin, bespectacled dreamer, Barber cooked up the "Strategic Island Concept," to which Diego Garcia was central.[31]

Barber advised the Pentagon to acquire Diego Garcia. US officials approached the British about establishing a communication station on the island in about 1963. The United States reached an agreement with the

Figure 7.4 Aerial view of Diego Garcia. *US Navy, Wikimedia Commons*

British by the end of December 1966, and a station was built in 1970.[32] Technically, the United States only leased the island from the British for fifty years, even though it was truly a joint venture. But there was one major problem.

The island was not deserted; it was occupied by an Indigenous population of about two thousand. Britain agreed to pay to move these people to Mauritius if the United States covered the costs of the installations. As Simon Winchester writes, "The British government, obeying with craven servility the wishes of the Pentagon," removed "every man, woman and child from the islands." However, the costs of removing the Indigenous population kept escalating, and Britain could not pay the 10-million-pound expense. As a result, the United States agreed to cover the rest of the resettlement costs. Since paying outright would represent neocolonial activity, the United States let the British deduct the costs from the Polaris missiles they sold to them.[33]

The British civil servant Sir Paul Gore-Booth characterized the British neocolonial activity in a 1966 memo: "The object of the exercise was to get some rocks which will remain *ours*; there will be no indigenous population except seagulls."[34] Joining the indigenous seagulls, though, would be around four thousand foreign US servicemen and contractors.

Once the prized island was "swept clean" and the area made "sterile," as the US Navy described the process, the NSA could set up its new facility. By spring 1973, fourteen intercept stations were set up on the atoll, whose area comprised no more than thirty-four square miles. The navy was pleased with the natural coral lagoon that lay between the thin arms of the horseshoe; it looked like it could be sunk underwater with the next big wave since it was only four feet above sea level.[35]

This was not the first island the US government had "swept clean" and made "sterile" for military purposes. As part of Barber's Strategic Island Concept, numerous islands around the globe, especially in the Pacific Ocean, underwent a similar process. In fact, the Pacific Islands had already been turned into "stepping stones" for the US military during World War II and before. By the Cold War, islands like the Azores and Kwajalein also displaced indigenous people in order to replace them with technological systems that became part of the US global network of power. Kwajalein then became a lab for US nuclear and ballistic testing.[36]

The Diego Garcia station, often called "the Rock," was one more jewel in the crown of the forty to fifty joint Five Eye Ocean Surveillance intercept and high-frequency direction-finding (HF-DF) signals intelligence facilities operated around the globe. The installation was code-named Bullseye and the satellite ground station located on the northwestern tip of the atoll, Classic Wizard.[37]

The Diego Garcia station is not shy about the joint US-British nature of its activities. The emblem displayed on its website shows a US flag and a British flag flying side by side over the filament-thin island with the motto, "One Island, One Team, One Mission and US Navy Support Facility, Diego Garcia, B.I.O.T." The website also provides a map of the downtown area that includes a gym, tennis courts, a swimming pool, an officers' club, a bike shop, BIOT headquarters, Paradise Alley Bowling Center, and American Forces Radio (AFN). The water tower near the harbor entrance welcomes visitors with huge letters, "Welcome to the Footprint of Freedom," referring to the island's leg shape, with a foot at the bottom and toes facing south.[38]

When Simon Winchester tried to visit the island on a sailboat as a civilian, he was turned away and told to leave the next morning. During his night there, the island was lit up—the ships adorned with deck lights, the "airstrip" glowed "with sodium vapor lamps, and the satellite dishes" scanned "the skies bathed in a soft white glow." Antennas winked "red and white, strobe lights" flickered, "the barrack blocks and the security fences" were "bright in the blue of the kliegs." As his boat sailed the next morning, Winchester could hear AFN radio advertising aerobic workshops, US Savings Bonds, and drug abuse programs. His sailboat then entered the darkness of the Indian Ocean and American radio faded.[39]

Secrecy restrictions on the island did not prevent espionage, however. Jerry Whitworth, a naval radioman, was stationed on Diego Garcia twice, once as supervisor of technical control (1974–75). He was part of the John Walker Family Spy Ring (see chap. 4) and passed on material that supplemented the electronic material seized from the US ship *Pueblo* in 1968, allowing the KGB to read all cryptographic traffic between US Navy Headquarters and ships around the world, one of its greatest achievements. Whitworth was arrested in 1985 and sentenced to life in prison.[40]

Ascension Island

Over the centuries, the British Empire had collected a number of strategic islands, some of which they returned to the original islanders during the process of decolonization. But there was one island that was a mirror twin of Diego Garcia. Ascension Island, like Diego Garcia, was a speck of an island in the middle of the vast, dark ocean, but it was located on the other side of the globe, in the middle of the Atlantic Ocean between Africa and Brazil. Unlike Diego Garcia, though, it did not have an Indigenous population to get rid of. It was part of the British Overseas Territory (BOT).

Ascension Island, a volcano, has been used as a communication hub ever since its founding on Ascension Day, 1501. Sailors used to leave letters on the island for pickup by a ship sailing in the other direction. There is apparently still a letterbox available to drop messages for passing vessels. But the island only became a truly global colonial outpost in 1899, when the Eastern Telegraph Company brought one end of the cable its ships had dragged from Table Bay, Virgin Island, to Jamestown, in St. Helena. As more cables were sunk in the sea, Britain expanded its empire. By World War I, Ascension Island became a hub for the telegraphic system. The British Crown officially took control of the island from the navy in 1922. As Winchester aptly characterized it, "The British saw cables as the vital synapses of the Imperial nervous system."[41]

Figure 7.5 Cat Hill on Ascension Island. *Wikimedia Commons, Jerrye and Roy Klotz, MD*

The cable terminal men were soon joined by ever-evolving modern communications systems. In 1934, the Eastern Telegraph Company changed its name to Eastern Cable and Wireless to indicate its changed focus. The British electronic spies descended on the island through the British Composite Signals Organization, a mysterious foreign branch of the Government Communications Headquarters. Pretty soon aerial farms decorated the island, along with ground control stations and other eavesdropping equipment. The US Air Force built a target tracking radar station in 1960–61, and the site, known as Cat Hill, became a joint GCHQ-NSA facility.[42]

According to Snowden documents secured by the Uruguay media, island eavesdroppers spy on military and civilian communications in Brazil, Argentina, Colombia, and Venezuela. After the discovery of oil in the British Falkland Islands, the spy island monitored communications about oil as well.[43]

American Outposts

The establishment of signals and communication intelligence in Cyprus and Diego Garcia grew out of Britain's imperialist past and postwar attempt to retain some "rocks" as it decolonized. In Cyprus, Britain was able to hang on to one hundred square miles of territory, and in the Indian Ocean region it was able to acquire the Chagos Archipelago and the prized island of Diego Garcia as a new colony. Slowly America aided Britain financially in retaining the Cyprus bases while establishing a covert presence of its own. In Diego Garcia, the United Kingdom supplied the territory, while America built and ran the station.

The United States also began to stake out bases and installations in allied countries around the world. Most noteworthy were those in the Five Eye countries and Germany, including Menwith Hill in Great Britain; Bad Aibling in Germany; the SIGINT station in Misawa, Japan; the Waihopai Station in New Zealand; and Geraldton and Pine Gap in Australia.

One of the most striking images visitors come away with at the Menwith Hill Station in North Yorkshire is the number of super-sized white golf ball–like structures dotting the lush green landscape. It is a jarring juxtaposition: the bucolic landscape with sturdy stone houses against the backdrop of a ghost-like moonscape of giant white globes. These golf ball structures both disguise and protect the satellite dishes and aerial antennas. The white Kevlar-like plastic skin covering the aluminum frame protects the equipment from the elements while also disguising the direction and angle of elevation of the satellite dish. Visitors approaching the station see the radomes proliferate, first one, then four, then eight. By 2011, there were at least thirty domes packed together on the hill, white against the green landscape surrounded by barbed-wire fencing and grazing cows.[44]

In the midst of what the British call cow country sits the largest secret intelligence–gathering station in the world outside the territory of the United States, and it is operated by the United States. This time the terrain belonged to the British; the land was bought by the British Crown in the 1950s and leased to the US Department of Defense. The cover story was that the installation was initially jointly run by the Royal Air Force (RAF) and the US Air Force, but Kenneth L. Bird, who was stationed there in the 1960s, writes that it was initially operated by the US Army Security Agency (USASA) and then handed to the civilian NSA in 1966 because the NSA had more qualified engineers and technicians who could operate the new digital computers and space-based signals intelligence.[45]

The station was "leased" to the NSA by a NATO Status of Forces Agreement (SOFA) between the United States and the United Kingdom whereby the United States could use the land for twenty-one years. This arrangement was renewed several times, until the United States was given an "unlimited timeframe" to use the land.[46]

Like Diego Garcia, and US military bases around the world, the Menwith Hill Station is a self-contained mini US city complete with housing, schools, a grocery store (PX), a pub, a sports center, a chapel, a playground, a running track, a baseball diamond, and a bowling alley amid the buildings where operators listen to intercepted communications. When it opened, Menwith Hill was viewed by the locals as just another US military installation that dotted the English and Scottish landscape after World War II; it didn't bother them initially, but in recent times there have been protests by antinuclear groups. Even so, the station was disguised, and the sign outside the front read, "RAF Menwith Hill," until very recently. There were no British airplanes in sight.[47]

Lesser known is the fact that much of the work of the station was underground during the Cold War, giving it the nickname "mushroom farm." Nevertheless, the Russians could still count the cars in the parking lot to determine how many people worked there. If there was a crisis, they could see the number of cars in the lot increase. More people worked there than publicity revealed.[48]

Despite the fact that Menwith Hill is an open secret and that the radomes provide visual proof of spy satellite activity, as late as 2005 a classified document from the Snowden cache cautioned employees, "Any reference to satellites being operated or any connection to intelligence gathering is strictly prohibited."[49]

The US-run Menwith Hill base became an anchor for the Five Eyes global surveillance network. During the Cold War, its chief target was Soviet and Eastern Bloc communications. The base monitored high frequency radio signals in Eastern Europe and taped the voices on Ampex-like tape recorders; the conversations were then transcribed by analysts on a typewriter.[50] By the 1980s, Menwith Hill contracted with Lockheed Martin to develop the Big Bird satellite (the K-9 Hexagon satellite operational from 1971 to 1986) to capture communications. After 9/11 Menwith Hill's global reach matched the territorial needs of the so-called Global War on Terror. It also kept up with the globalization of telecommunications in general.

By the late 1980s, the NSA thought fiber optic cables would make satellites obsolete, but this was not the case, even though fiber optic signals move much faster—at the speed of light—and are cheaper than satellites.

Unlike fiber optic cables, satellites allowed the NSA to monitor communications of countries in remote parts of the world that do not have fiber optic cables. Moreover, a commercial satellite existed that could monitor unencrypted Digital Network Intelligence (DNI) traffic. This technology helped haul in an enormous amount of information. A 2006 report acquired by Edward Snowden stated, "This data source alone provides more data for Menwith Hill analysts to sift through than our entire enterprise had to deal with in the not-so-distant past."[51] Of course, this was not necessarily a good thing. Too much data became a problem, but the NSA would soon find a solution for this problem, or so they thought.

Satellites proved useful in the war on terror, and Menwith Hill could target trouble spots like the Middle East and North Africa. After 9/11, the base was used to target terrorists and extremist groups like al-Qaeda in areas like the Afghanistan-Pakistan border, Somalia, and Yemen.[52]

According to the Snowden documents, the NSA developed a powerful technology to geolocate terrorists, code-named Ghosthunter. The technology could pinpoint the exact location of terrorists while they accessed the internet at internet cafés in the Middle East and North Africa. Menwith Hill was at the forefront of these new technological developments and provided 99 percent of the FORNSAT (Foreign Satellite Collection) data for Ghosthunter. FORNSAT allowed Menwith Hall operators to intercept foreign satellites' transmissions. This technology apparently provided "near-global coverage" and could reach countries as far away as China and Latin America.[53]

But early in the war on terror the most significant targets were in the Middle East and North Africa. Using this technology, Menwith Hill operators could locate the "targets" as soon as they logged onto the internet. This led to "a significant number of capture-kill operations against terrorists."[54]

According to *The Intercept*, Ghosthunter succeeded in pinpointing the location of a suspected al-Qaeda "facilitator" in Lebanon who was considered "highly actionable." In other words, he was considered a target to kill or capture. Ghosthunter also identified a "weapons procurer" in Iraq named Abu Sayf because he regularly logged in to his Yahoo accounts at the Super Net Cafe about two hundred miles from Baghdad four days in a row. The US Marine Corps arrested Abu Sayf in 2007 using the "locational information" from Menwith Hill "that was based on tips received from

NSA Georgia." The National Geospatial Intelligence Agency (NGA) cell at Menwith Hill provided imagery to help the marines target him. Task Force 16 raided two apartments; they found Abu Sayf and his associates in one and his father and two brothers in the other. The NSA thought the capture would lead to "a diminished flow of weapons and insurgents into Iraq."[55]

A slide provided by Snowden shows a list of seven terrorists allegedly either caught or killed because of SIGINT information. Reportedly, another three hundred terrorists were caught or killed because of SIGINT.[56] Ghosthunter's geolocation abilities also reflected a shift in strategy and responsibilities of agencies. During the Cold War, Menwith Hill just provided the information; by 2007 they acted on it.

Collect It All: Elegant Chaos

On June 16, 2008, Lt. Gen. Keith Alexander, who had been director of the NSA since 2005, visited Menwith Hill. During his time there, he discussed the interception of foreign satellite emissions and told workers that he had "a good summer homework project for Menwith Hill: Why Can't We Collect All the Signals All the Time?"[57]

This challenge led to a joint British-US project appropriately named Elegant Chaos. On the PowerPoint slide about this project, the word *Elegant* is spelled in flowing, elegant font, whereas the word *Chaos* is printed to look chaotic. The US flag is flying alongside the British flag over the Menwith Hill emblem depicting a lion and a castle. Both the phrase and the presentation of the project suggest an elegant mathematical solution to an overabundance of data.

This was a new "collection posture" for the base, with the goal to "collect it all, process it all, exploit it all." This suggests that along with heeding Keith Alexander's "collect it all" approach, Menwith Hall thought about how to process the data. Analysts developed a six-step process starting with "sniff it all," whereby they would "maximize" their "receiving capabilities." In the next step, "know it all," they would keep their pulse on the whole environment using automated FORNSAT data; then in the "collect it all" step they would increase the volume of signals; in "process it all," they would find the data in the signal; and in "exploit it all," they would find the intelligence in the signal using an automated process ("automate, automate, automate," was their chant) with query-focused datasets (QFD), the inspiration for Elegant Chaos. Finally, they would "partner it all," by collaborating with the GCHQ on techniques while sharing with bases like the one in Misawa, Japan.[58]

Given the "collect it all" mentality, it is not surprising that the NSA built a new steel-girded (750 tons, they boasted) concrete operations building at Menwith Hill between 2009 and 2011, spending over $40 million on an enormous, 95,000-square foot structure code-named Project Phoenix. The data center occupied about 10,000 square feet of this space. It took another year to "fit-up" the building with all the bells and whistles any SIGINT analyst could wish for (this cost another $40 million): 182 miles of cable and fiber (enough to stretch from the station to Edinburgh Castle), new computers, teaching technology for the ten new classrooms, and collaborative desk environment furniture. The station was especially excited about its first two-hundred-seat auditorium to host classified and unclassified lectures and conferences, its first equipment room with "redundant power" and cooling supplies, and its first open office floor plan in a base that prized secrecy.[59]

Now Menwith Hill possessed a new building to house the ever-increasing volume of data. Alexander's directive was a curious one as his predecessor, Michael Hayden, and NSA employees recognized that there was a problem analyzing the reams of data collected by satellites and fiber optic cables. In fact, Hayden testified in front of the Judiciary Committee that the volume, velocity, and variety created by modern communications threatened to overwhelm the NSA.[60]

Menwith Hill had also been concerned about the volume of data several years before Alexander arrived at the base. In a 2006 document, "Too Much of a Good Thing," the Customer Outreach and Advocacy unit at Menwith Hill Station launched a new project called Countrystore to "make the sorting, storage and retrieval of data more efficient and effective." They asked how to sort through the "gigabytes of data" they collected daily to determine what to keep that will help them understand or find "new targets." They had already learned that they could not keep it all, and even if they did, they did not have the tools or technology to sift through it. The reporter anticipated the adage, "More data is a good thing, right?" Just as a Google search hauls up a lot of data, often fatiguing the searcher, so too was this the case with SIGINT collection. Too much data does not necessarily lead to good information. Project Countrystore may have stalled after Alexander's visit and the launch of Elegant Chaos.[61]

PINE GAP

In 1966, around the same time Menwith Hill was taken over by the NSA, another satellite ground station was being built on the other side of the hemisphere in the Australian Outback, the Red Center. The base was nineteen kilometers west of Alice Springs and called Pine Gap. While Menwith Hill was cold, lush, and green, Pine Gap was Martian red, hot, and dry. While the NSA ran its largest base outside of America in Great Britain, the CIA ran its largest base in the world in Pine Gap. But both sites shared the moonscape radomes amid remote nature. And both used visible radome-encrusted dishes and radar to send and receive information from satellites.

A few months before construction began in 1966, Robert Mathams, head of the Scientific Branch of Australia's Joint Intelligence Group, and three CIA men from its Division of Science and Technology (DS&T) drove out to Pine Gap to celebrate. After passing some low hills, they sat on the ground and opened a case of red wine. The three men from the CIA—Bud Wheelon, head of DS&T; Carl Duckett, his deputy; and Leslie Dirk, a staff member—made a toast to Pine Gap. They were celebrating the amazing new site for the ground station using an innovative intelligence satellite. The science fiction writer Arthur C. Clarke first suggested the idea of communicating from a ground station to a satellite and then back to another ground station with a geostationary satellite in 1945, but it was only science fiction at the time. [62]

Clarke's idea and a NASA-DoD syncom satellite captured the imagination of the CIA, and Bud Wheelon launched a group to explore the feasibility of the idea. Lloyd K. Lauderdale, a US Navy graduate and Johns Hopkins PhD, was selected to manage the program, named Rhyolite. It was Lauderdale who transformed the idea into reality.[63]

Pine Gap came out of the shadows and into the limelight when Christopher Boyce, a cipher clerk at TRW Aerospace Company in Redondo Beach, California, was caught and convicted in 1977 of selling satellite secrets to the KGB. One of those secrets was information about the revolutionary new satellite, the Rhyolite, also called Bird 1, that was rolled out in 1970 as part of a four-satellite contract with TRW in 1966. It was a geostationary SIGINT satellite built for the CIA and the National Reconnaissance Office that could intercept telemetry—the technical data given off from radio signals during missile tests—for missile detection.

"Geostationary" means that it stays over one place on earth and rotates with earth as it moves.[64]

A visitor to Alice Springs, a tiny town with a population of about twenty-five thousand in 2011, including base personnel, has to drive sixteen hours simply to get there from Adelaide, the closest city on the southern coast of Australia. Planners originally thought workers at the base could commute from Adelaide to Pine Gap, but instead workers opted to live in Alice Springs. The remote location ensured that the Soviets could not eavesdrop on, or intercept signals from, the base. Not only is the location remote, but the base is in a valley between the MacDonnell Ranges and is a naturally quiet environment for electronics. In addition, it has a seven-square-mile buffer zone to reduce surveillance. When the base first went public in Australia at the height of the Cold War in 1966, it was pitched as a joint space research center. Visitors have to be cleared to enter the facility. Many curious people who venture as far as the entrance will encounter a sign at the beginning of a dead-end street designating it as "Joint Defense Facility Pine Gap" and cannot travel any farther. In fact, it is a CIA- and NRO-run base that passes information on to the NSA as well.[65]

Unlike Menwith Hill and Diego Garcia, the American presence is more muted, at least in Alice Springs, where there is a baseball diamond in a sports complex and Oreo cookies and Dr. Pepper are available at the supermarket.[66] But this lower-key presence belies that fact that American contractors built and equipped the facility with all the high-tech bells and whistles. Along with the TRW satellites in the air, Ford Aerospace and Communications Corporation provided two satellite ground terminals in order to communicate with TRW in Redondo Beach and the CIA in Langley. Other contractors included the Collins Radio Company from Texas; E-Systems, responsible for the management and operation of the computer room; and IBM. IBM provided most of the computers at Pine Gap, along with some Digital Equipment Corporation (DEC) VAX computers. The computer room was the largest of its kind in the world at about six thousand square feet when it was built, and by 2015 the floor space in the new Operations Building was the size of three and a half football fields. By 2016, it was twenty-thousand square meters, and analysts wore headphones to communicate with each other because it was too far to walk, even to grab a cup of coffee. All American supplies and equipment were airlifted to the Alice Spring airport on Starlifter planes twice a week. The information recorded on reel-to-reel tapes was then airlifted back to the

United States for analysis by the CIA and the NSA. According to the Australian defense minister there was no "significant Australian-made equipment" at Pine Gap. Like Menwith Hill and Diego Garcia, the British and Australians provided the land and the United States provided the money and technology.[67]

After Pine Gap's exposure by Boyce, Australian officials assured the public that the station was used to verify arms control agreements. But the Australian SIGINT expert Desmond Ball claims that only about 40 percent of the information from the satellites is used for that purpose. Moreover, he explains that the station was built before the arms limitation talks got under way and before the United States and the Soviet Union agreed that each side could monitor the other side using "national technical means of verification" (NTMVs).[68]

During the early years, the CIA and the NRO shaped the mission of the base, and its primary purpose was to target Soviet ELINT (electronic intelligence) in order to detect signs of Soviet missiles and other Soviet strategic nuclear weapons. Even though the CIA was tasked with human intelligence, it had an office for SIGINT and ELINT because its chief target was the Soviet Union and it had trouble recruiting human spies. Pine Gap was seen as a sister station to Menwith Hill because it collected mostly ELINT, while Menwith Hill was tasked with SIGINT.

In the 1990s, Pine Gap became increasingly militarized. The civilian CIA and NRO were no longer the main inhabitants of the base, although it remained the CIA's most important and largest source of technical intelligence collection in the world. According to the Australian specialists Desmond Ball and Richard Tanter, by 2013, 66 percent of the US personnel at Pine Gap were from the US Air Force, Army, or Navy. Since the 1990s the military personnel went beyond the former tasks of the station and began working on FORNSAT/COMSAT (foreign satellite/communication satellite) collection like Menwith Hill. They scoured the internet via these communication satellites instead of fiber optic cables and monitored emails, website searches, and chat rooms to provide intelligence in support of intelligence operations in Iraq and Afghanistan.[69]

The Snowden documents reveal that the NSA had started to play a much bigger role at Pine Gap by 2005. The unclassified cover term for the NSA's activities at the Joint Defence Facility Pine Gap (JDFPG) was Rainfall, whereas all the activities at the site were referred to as JDFPG. It was top secret that the National Reconnaissance Office had a Mission Ground

Station at Pine Gap. Along with the Mission Ground Station Menwith Hill, Pine Gap processed signals from Mission 7600 satellites that covered "the majority of the Eurasian landmass" and Africa; they were "military COMINT targets." Once Pine Gap personnel collected the signals, they were passed on to the NSA in the United States for analysis.[70]

Even more powerful was the Mission 8300 system. It was a four-satellite geosynchronous earth orbit system that supported US military combat operations and was designed to collect, process, record, and report SIGINT information. It covered the former Soviet Union, China, South Asia, East Asia, the Middle East, Eastern Europe, and land in the Atlantic Ocean.[71]

Both missions had geolocation capabilities to "help pinpoint airstrikes." There was a section known as the "geopit" equipped with tools for geolocations that allowed the station to geolocate cellphones from the "Pacific to the edge of Africa," and it may have assisted in the "controversial US drone strikes."[72]

All these revelations were intriguing if not disturbing—a secret US spy base in the red center of Australia conducting global surveillance using state-of-the-art high-tech gadgets. Therefore, it wasn't surprising that Netflix and the Australian Broadcasting Company (ABC) developed a thriller about Pine Gap's activities. Despite the locale and the spy theme, the show lasted for only six episodes and received a desultory review in *The Guardian*. The reviewer's assessment was that the show contained a lot of "yakkety yak interspersed with occasional scenes of bonking." He found it was a good cure for insomnia.[73] At least viewers learned that electronic spying from a desert lacks the glamour of a James Bond thriller. Despite these shortcomings, the opening sequence of the film is quite dramatic and nicely depicts the global reach of the NSA as the camera scans the globe and pinpoints three satellite facilities that American global power relies on to collect intelligence: Buckley Air Force Base in Colorado, Menwith Hill, and Pine Gap.[74]

Waihopai Valley, New Zealand

When the farmers Donald and Jonnie MacDonald advertised 36 hectares (88.95 acres) of land for sale in Waihopai Valley, the heart of Marlborough wine country, they found a buyer in 1987 who was not interested in planting grapes or tending sheep. Instead, the buyer, the Government Communications and Security Board (GCSB), the New Zealand equivalent of the NSA, wanted to build a new satellite station to target the Intelsat (International Telecommunications Satellite Organization) hovering above the island of Kiribati, just north of New Zealand at the equator. Founded in 1964, Intelsat sent its first satellite into orbit in 1965. By 1999, it maintained about nineteen satellites above the equator and around the world.[75]

The GCSB had been looking for a suitable piece of land for quite some time. Unfortunately, it could not convert its antenna station in Tangimoana on the North Island to a satellite station because the ground was too sandy to support the structures. They also needed land near a military base for backup support, along with a broad, quiet sky for good reception. The peaceful Waihopai Valley, twenty minutes from Blenheim, fit the bill. The government bought the land for a mere 210,000 New Zealand dollars.[76]

By the time the spy station opened shortly before the fall of the Berlin Wall in 1989, it had cost over $26 million to build. A satellite station, with a big full moon satellite dish along with antenna and buildings, in the middle of a vineyard is hard to keep secret. And the government did not try to attempt to hide the installation. As a result, the station attracted the attention of peace activists, anti-bases campaigners, and journalists, who protested it because some thought it was being built to spy on civilian communications "mainly for the benefit of Australian & US secret service agencies" at an exorbitant price. A brochure handed around by the Anti-Bases Campaign (ABC) depicted Uncle Sam pointing and spouting, "I want you to shut up and pay for the secret spy satellite base at Waihopai." Although New Zealanders paid for it, the GCSB was seen as a "subsidiary" of the NSA in the Pacific.[77]

Once the station was built, some protesters and journalists were able to sneak in and see the machinery inside the building. Nicky Hager's description in his remarkable, eye-opening book on New Zealand's role in the international spy network UKUSA is like looking over his shoulder and peering into the controls room: "Inside Waihopai's buildings, in a room almost twice the size of a basketball court, is the heart of the station—the secret operations centre." Most of the time there are no people in the huge operation room: "Banks of very sophisticated equipment and spaceship-like control areas run themselves. The only movement comes from the constellations of small blinking red, green, orange and white lights. The equipment is supplied by allies and wholly integrated into their system—you could just as well be in the United States."[78]

The Waihopai station, code-named Ironsand, is one of five satellite stations placed strategically around the globe by the United States, Britain, Australia, and New Zealand that target Intelsat satellites as part of the UKUSA alliance. Unlike Pine Gap or Menwith Hill, these are not ground stations but rather intercept communications from information relayed by the Intel satellites that are located above the equator and ring the world transmitting most of the world's international phone calls and messages from faxes, telexes, and emails. When these stations were opened in the 1970s, the NSA had become the leader of the UKUSA alliance. Two of the stations located in the United States are run by the NSA: Sugar Grove in the mountains of West Virginia, which targets the Intelsat that services the Atlantic and North and South America, and the Yakima Training Center, opened in 1973, in Washington State, that covers the Pacific. The UK station in Morwenstow, Cornwall, was established in 1971 by GCHQ in close collaboration with the NSA and sits high above the cliffs, targeting the Atlantic, Europe, and the Indian Ocean. The two other stations were the newer ones built in the late 1980s: sister stations in Geraldton, Australia, and Waihopai, New Zealand, both of which were designed to target the Pacific.

Although New Zealand considers itself a small island nation in the Pacific, its geographic location makes it an outsize partner. When the base opened with one satellite dish in 1989, technicians targeted the IS-701 satellite located at 180 degrees east, Intelsat's main satellite responsible for the Pacific Ocean countries and islands. By 2012, the station had two dishes and the IS-701 satellite was replaced with the much more powerful IS-18. Both satellites had global beams but IS-701 from a western hemisphere perspective and IS-18 from a southern hemisphere perspective, according to a document collected by Snowden.[79]

All these stations supported the UKUSA's global eavesdropping program called Echelon and were established to "collect and process Intelsat communications during the height of the Cold War."[80]

ECHELON: Global Surveillance Exposed for the First Time

In 1988, long before the Snowden revelations of 2013, Duncan Campbell, a tenacious British investigative journalist, penned an article titled

"Somebody's Listening" for the *New Statesman*. In it he unveiled a "top-secret new global surveillance system" that could "tap into a billion calls a year" and "spy on whom they wish, when they wish." Not only that, US, British, and allied intelligence agencies were embarking on a "massive, billion-dollar expansion."[81]

His main source was a disaffected Lockheed Martin employee, Margaret Newsham, who had worked at Menwith Hill as a software manager where she operated dozens of VAX computers that supported the system. While there she was appalled to learn that eavesdroppers listened to US senator Strom Thurmond's phone conversations as well as Russian conversations. She spilled the beans about the P415 global surveillance system developed at Lockheed Martin Space and Missile Corporation in California. The powerful system was designed to scoop up the ever-expanding telecommunications traffic. She accused the company of overcharging and corruption.[82]

These accumulated revelations of global eavesdropping on communications like phone calls, fax messages, and, later, emails spurred the European Parliament into action. All the major players involved in the Echelon program, journalists who exposed it, and experts on the NSA like James Bamford were asked by the parliamentary committee to testify and write reports. Despite his sensationalistic salvo in the *New Statesman* article, Duncan Campbell wrote a sober report, "Interception Capabilities 2000." He described how the Five Eye COMINT organizations penetrated most of the world's international communications using systems to "access, intercept and process every important form of communications." This was possible because, he claimed, "UKUSA nations" operated "at least 120 satellite collection systems."[83]

In the report, Campbell also made the surprising statement that the NSA did not have a key word capability as outlined in hysterical TV shows like *60 Minutes* that reported key words like *bomb* could be picked up by the system: "Contrary to reports in the press, effective 'word spotting' search systems automatically to select telephone calls of intelligence interest are not yet available, despite 30 years of research."[84]

It wasn't until after the Snowden document dump that it was possible to verify and learn more about the Echelon system. It turned out that Echelon was, in fact, part of a dual-pronged NSA-UKUSA program called Frosting established in 1966 "for the collection and processing of all communications emanating from communication satellites." The other project, code-named Transient, targeted all the Soviet Union's communication satellites, while Echelon collected and processed Intelsat communications. The NSA had wasted no time. Intelsat had sent its first satellite into orbit in 1965.[85]

Meanwhile, as US intelligence became more global in signals and communications intelligence, so too did the telecommunications industry. The globalization of the telecommunications industry became a threat to the NSA. Once a leader in innovating communications technology, it began to lag behind. Gen. Michael V. Hayden, who had been director of the CIA and the NSA, opined in 2000 that "our technological adversary is not a nation state but the global telecommunications industry." He felt that during the Cold War the United States was "always technologically superior," the "stream of money" steady, and the target focused.[86] As a result of his directives, the NSA started to outsource a lot of their technology. There was a dramatic increase in the use of contractors, and in-house technology was rejected in favor of contractor technology in order to innovate more quickly so as to digest the massive amounts of information ingested. This led to the Trailblazer surveillance system to collect and process information. But there was one problem.

The NSA could no longer ingest and analyze all the information it collected. This had been a perennial problem but came to a head by the 2000s. At a 2009 Signals Development (Sigdev) conference, a presenter stated, "Collection is outpacing our ability to ingest, process and store to the 'norms' to which we have become accustomed."[87] Aside from the harm of Alexander's "collect it all" mentality, the NSA, like other US agencies that relied on technology to conduct intelligence, had become a victim of its powerful technologies of collection.

NSA intelligence analysts were painfully aware of this information overload problem and did not necessarily agree with the director's "collect the whole haystack" approach. The agency apparently had, and presumably still has, a department called the Research Directorate's Coping with Information Overload Office (R6). Not much is known about the program, but it seems related to a $48.6 million line item in the black budget Snowden provided to journalists in 2013, also called "Coping with Information Overload." The program was also referred to in a telling 2006 document written by NSA analysts from the "Human Language Technology" department who reminded readers that "analysts have been drowning in a tsunami of intercept whose volume, velocity and variety can be overwhelming" and "the speed and volume . . . will increase . . . almost beyond imagination." The analysts described their ability to find "huge amounts of data, much of which is not what we really want." One of the SIGINT challenge slides in the Snowden documents includes a photograph of a haystack with a needle piercing it.[88]

In addition to comparing information overload and analysis to tsunamis and needles in haystacks, analysts also circulated a parable at the NSA about two people who go to a farm and buy a truckload of melons for a dollar each. They also sell the melons for the same price. When they realize they are not making a profit, they ask whether they "need a bigger truck?" In this case, more is just more. The "metadata coffers get full." The author felt he needed to capitulate with a white flag because, "We need COLOSSAL data storage . . . (aka **we need a bigger SIGINT truck**)."[89] It is no wonder that the NSA began to build enormous facilities like the Utah Data Center, essentially a hard drive in the desert, to store information.

Edward Snowden's explosive entrance onto the world stage in 2013 called attention to global surveillance 2.0. Although he is widely known for exposing domestic snooping by the NSA, most of the material he collected and brought out of the NSA vaults was about global eavesdropping and bulk collection.[90] His material showed that Echelon was superseded by other internet spying programs like XKEYSCORE and Prism whereby the NSA and its Anglo alliance could access data stored by Google, Facebook, and Microsoft.

Telegraph Network Redux

As we have seen, by the 1980s, fiber optic cables began to complement and sometimes supplant satellite communications. Undersea cables were thought to be more secure than satellite and radio communications and not as easy to intercept or tap. They were also less visible. Unlike the moonscape architecture of gigantic dish satellites dotting vineyards or mountaintops, cables were hidden at the bottom of the ocean.

Most of the fiber optic cables reproduced the same routes of the old telegraph network as well as telephone infrastructures replicating Anglo-American geopower. In addition to the two maps displayed at the beginning of this chapter, the British telegraph line map is another telling visual representation of British imperial power. In the nineteenth century the telegraph helped the British rule their colonies and keep trade well oiled.

The British also used their island colonies and coaling stations to establish landing zones. Just as the telegraph cables were the "vital synapses" of the British Empire's nervous system, so too were the fiber optic cables the backbone of the UKUSA communications body politic, an empire that enabled American hegemony in the late twentieth and early twenty-first centuries.

Fiber optic cables weren't limited to the islands of Cyprus and Ascension, as discussed previously, nor were US and UK activities limited to tapping. The cable map acquired by Snowden shows that the NSA also installed malware to wreak havoc on enemies' communication centers.

The worldwide SIGINT map (see fig. 7.2) illustrates the NSA's collection efforts around the world. It shows where the NSA and Five Eyes countries installed their twenty high-speed optical cable access and interception points (big blue dots), with four dotted along the US west coast. But most important were the yellow computer network exploitation (CNE) dots. CNE was a technique used to install malware in devices. The NSA bragged that it had over fifty thousand implants worldwide. The majority of the implants seem to be clustered in Asia and Russia. By installing implants, the NSA can "own the computer" and see every key tapped and screen opened. It can enter and alter data in the computer even if it is not connected to the internet.[91]

Collecting information from fiber optic cables as data flowed by was called "upstream" collection, whereas information collected directly from the servers of internet behemoths like Google, Facebook, Yahoo, and others received the code name PRISM and widespread exposure when the Snowden files made headlines in 2013. A top-secret NSA slide describes these two types of collection and includes a bubble stating, "You Should Use Both," with arrows pointing to both collection methods.

The emblem for Special Source Operations (SSO), the unit responsible for fiber optic collection, depicts an eagle with its claws clenching fibers draped over the globe. Although the *Washington Post* thought it looked like a parody, the image is another in a long line of grandiose seals used by US intelligence to represent global aspirations and activities.[92]

According to Snowden, SSO was the NSA's "crown jewel." The SSO team defined themselves unabashedly as the embodiment of "Big Data." They collected so much data that a 2006 report boasted that they were ingesting "one Library of Congress every 14.4 seconds." An NSA slide further reported that SSO provided "80% of collection for NSA." This was

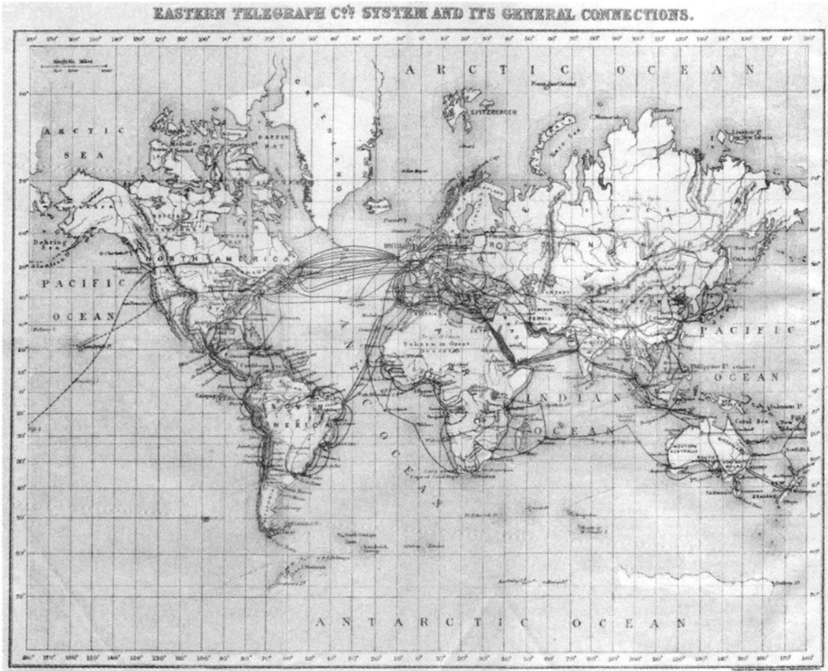

Figure 7.6 Eastern Telegraph Company submarine telegraph cable routes, showing the global reach of telecommunications, 1901. *Wikimedia Commons, From* A.B.C. Telegraphic Code, 5th ed., 1901

all made possible by leveraging key corporate partners in commercial telecommunications companies. The companies carried code names like Blarney, Stormbrew, and Fairview. Although Fairview and Stormbrew were not identified in the secret papers, intrepid journalists were able to follow leads from the Snowden files and identify Fairview as AT&T and Stormbrew as Verizon, two of the largest US telecoms.[93]

Fairview/AT&T and Stormbrew/Verizon were considered top producers in the NSA's corporate portfolio. Both companies produced SIGINT successes by "living on the global intelligence network." According to another top-secret PowerPoint presentation on Special Source Operations, cable sources provided 61 percent of the information during the first half of 2010 used in preparing the President's Daily Brief (PDB).[94] The PDB was a digest of intelligence information prepared for the president of the United States by the director of national intelligence and selects information from major intelligence organizations like the CIA and the NSA.

NSA's global operations seemed boundless by 2013. Using data-crunching technology, the NSA produced a heat map with the telling name "Boundless Informant" to chart and quantify the amount of information it acquired through internet data, Digital Network Intelligence (DNI), and telephone data, Digital Number Recognition (DNR). This map represented the NSA's "Global Access Operations" and provided managers with information on how much metadata was collected in each country. In the thirty days depicted on the map, ninety-seven billion items were collected, of which three billion were from the United States, a fact brought to light by Snowden and the journalist Glenn Greenwald.[95]

What emerges from the Snowden NSA files is a sprawling technological powerhouse that exploded after 9/11. Programs like Trailblazer, a costly internet data-mining program, proliferated. By 2008 even more powerful programs like XKEYSCORE and the GCHQ Tempora emerged that helped sift through the ocean of data hauled in through the lightning-fast fiber optic cables.

One of the NSA's most important partners was Germany. While Bad Aibling in southern Germany was the key listening station of the United States during the Cold War, by the Global War on Terror, with that moonscape, radome-studded facility winding down, the European Cryptologic Center (ECC) in Darmstadt took center stage. Located in building 4373 within the "Dagger Complex," a US military base, it is nestled among vineyards and farmland like so many other NSA facilities. This center was responsible for "consuming metadata garnered from XKEYSCORE (XKS).[96]

The capabilities of XKEYSCORE and the German locale inspired an NSA newsletter author to pen an inspired piece in 2012 titled "Dragons, Shrimp, and XKEYSCORE: Tales from the Brothers Grimm." The article shows how the twelve-headed dragon challenge of XKEYSCORE was demystified through "speed-dating" training. While analysts used very large shrimp nets to haul in anything it caught, XKEYSCORE gave them the capabilities to just use a handheld goldfish net for more targeted fishing.[97]

> We are like Forrest Gump on his shrimping boat[,] . . . pulling in a boot, toilet seat, seaweed, and there they are . . . three shrimp! We burn up a lot of resources getting those shrimp, those reportable documents or metadata used to expand target knowledge, and we deal with tons of toilet seats. . . . XKS has become so important because with it, analysts can downsize their gigantic shrimping nets to tiny, handheld goldfish-sized

> nets and merely dip them in the oceans of data, working smarter and scooping out exactly what they want.[98]

XKEYSCORE software offered access to terabytes of content and metadata per day. All the analyst needed was an email address to query the target's communications. It was the NSA's Google for private communications and one of its most powerful global and technological tools. It could store full-take content for three to five days. The NSA map illustrating XKEYSCORE depicts operations coming from NSA headquarters and radiating out to the rest of the world with 125 sites. Another illustration shows an analyst sitting at his desk spying on a possible terrorist sitting at his computer in Pakistan, rifle by his side, looking at London on Google Earth. The analyst could target the man because he had his email address, stylized as "badguy@yahoo.com."[99]

An Empire of Signals

Historians have spilled quite a bit of ink arguing about whether the United States was an empire during the Cold War. In the end, the discussions become semantic, about definitions of words like *empire*, *colonial*, and *neocolonial*, or a catalog of how the United States viewed colonial activity since the turn of the century.[100]

History records that the United States avoided "colonial" activity because it condemned the British colonial empire. By the Cold War, instead of landgrabs, the United States established military bases dotting the globe while maintaining some of its territories like Guam. These bases and territories are often seen as a manifestation of US "power projection." Officially, planners wanted to avoid neocolonial activity. Or as Daniel Immerwahr describes in his lively book, the United States was a disguised empire made up of long-forgotten or overlooked territories at the periphery of, or even well beyond, mainland United States (the "logo" map), like Hawaii or Puerto Rico or the US Virgin Islands.[101]

Yet critics like Chalmers Johnson argue that while the United States was an "informal empire" during World War II, in part because of the paucity of colonies, by the post-9/11 period it emerged as a full-blown nonterritorial empire and began to "openly . . . spread its imperial wings." For Johnson, the "military juggernaut intent on world domination" is enough to designate it a "militarized empire" or a "military empire."[102]

There is no doubt that the United States led the pack in establishing a secret communications empire. Just as over 725 military bases dotted the globe during the Cold War, so too did hundreds of SIGINT stations straddle the globe in strategic locations, sometimes on the military bases themselves or near them for support. There were so many secret espionage stations abroad that Michal Moran of NBC news opined in 2001, "Today, one could throw a dart at a map of the world and it would likely land within a few hundred miles of a quietly established US intelligence-gathering operation."[103]

As the United Kingdom passed the global espionage torch, the United States took the lead in establishing these communication intelligence stations around the world to support American global empire activities while also creating its own signals empire. In fact, the United States sustained its global power by controlling communications around the world while becoming the leader in signals intelligence activity in the process.

The UKUSA alliance was not just a formality; it was a friendship forged during World War II. That friendship was celebrated at Friedman's and Travis's SIGINT-themed dinner and many times thereafter. In 1996, the GCHQ presented a plaque to the NSA that hangs on the director's wall; it reads, "50 years of friendship and cooperation, BRUSA-UKUSA."[104]

The British had taken the lead during World War II, but by the Cold War era, the leadership torch was passed on to the United States. The process began by trading technology for territory while helping perpetuate vestiges of British colonial rule. As the Cold War progressed, America replaced land with technology. It did not need vast land territory to achieve global hegemony. Instead, the Five Eyes shared all their territory, and allied countries could use that land for installations in strategic places like the United Kingdom, Australia, and New Zealand. Or there were installations in former, or soon to be former, British colonies like Cyprus and Hong Kong, or countries that the United States had occupied during the early Cold War, like West Germany and Japan, where land was made available for military and intelligence bases. In the end, though, it was global technological capabilities that helped create and sustain American empire.

Notes

1. I would like to thank Christopher Andrew for directing me to the Walter L. Pforzheimer Papers at the Yale University Archive, which provided me with

a reproduction of the Beinecke Library, GEN MSS 187, broadside folder 137. It is not clear when the map was created or by whom, but it was in Sir Francis H. Hinsley's papers. Permission was granted by Clarissa Lloyd, Hinsley Estate. See also Christopher Andrew, "The Making of the Anglo-American SIGINT Alliance," in *In the Name of Intelligence: Essays in Honor of Walter Pforzheimer*, ed. Hayden B. Peake and Samuel Halpern (Washington, DC: NIBC Press, 1995), 103–6.

2. Richard H. Aldrich, *GCHQ: The Uncensored Story of Britain's Most Secret Intelligence Agency* (London: Harper Press, 2011), 7.

3. Andrew, "Making of an Anglo-American SIGINT Alliance," 103.

4. Andrew, 104.

5. David Zimmerman, *Top Secret Exchange: The Tizard Mission and the Scientific War* (Toronto: McGill-Queen's University Press, 1996); and James Bamford, *The Puzzle Palace: A Report on America's Most Secret Agency* (New York: Penguin, 1983), 393–94. The NSA UKUSA material released in 2010 documents British interest in trading technology. It contains an aide-mémoire by the British embassy dated July 1940. See www.nsa.gov/Portals/70/documents/news-features/declassified-documents/ukusa/early_papers_1940-1944.pdf.

6. For correspondence related to Alan Turing from December 2 to December 12, 1942, see www.nsa.gov/Portals/70/documents/news-features/declassified-documents/ukusa/early_papers_1940-1944.pdf. See also Jason Dittmer, *Diplomatic Material: Affect, Assemblage, and Foreign Policy* (Durham, NC: Duke University Press, 2017), 49.

7. Bamford, *Puzzle Palace*, 393.

8. Bamford, 394.

9. National Archives, College Park, MD, Record Group 457, NSA Historic Cryptographic Collection, NR 2820, "Memorandum to Colonel Corderman from William F. Friedman, Headquarters Arlington Hall Station, 8 February 1943." Now available online: https://www.nsa.gov/news-features/declassified-documents/ukusa/assets/files/early_papers_1940-1944.pdf.

10. William Friedman to Edward Travis, August 20, 1943, NSA, William Friedman Papers, www.nsa.gov/Portals/70/documents/news-features/declassified-documents/friedman-documents/correspondence/ACC35864/41780849081991.pdf; Ronald Lewin, *ULTRA Goes to War: The Secret Story* (London: Hutchinson, 1978), 136; and D. R. Nicholl, "Travis, Sir Edward Wilfrid Harry (1888–1956)," *Oxford Dictionary of National Biography*, https://doi.org/10.1093/ref:odnb/61098.

11. Memorandum for the Chief of Staff, June 10, 1943, Agreement between British Government Code and Cipher School and U.S. War Department in regard to certain "Special Intelligence," www.nsa.gov/news-features/declassified-documents/ukusa/assets/files/spec_int_10jun43.pdf. Declassified 2010.

12. Bamford, *Puzzle Palace*, 399.

13. For NSA release of files, see www.nsa.gov/News-Features/Declassified-Documents/UKUSA/. For UK National Archive files, see https://discovery

.nationalarchives.gov.uk/browse/r/h/C18031, the HW 80 files. Travis quote from HW 80-1.

14. See www.nsa.gov/News-Features/Declassified-Documents/UKUSA/. The 1954 and 1955 agreements in the NSA documents.

15. Aid, "National Security Agency and the Cold War," 36.

16. Aid.

17. Aid.

18. Aid.

19. Aldrich, *GCHQ*, 162.

20. For information on the Sovereign Base Areas, see their website, www.sbaadministration.org.

21. On Cyprus, see these documents from the Snowden Archive, July 2010: https://snowdenarchive.cjfe.org/greenstone/collect/snowden1/index/assoc/HASH70c7.dir/doc.pdf. See also John Goetz, Frederik Obermaier, and Nicky Hager, "Cyprus: Isle of Spies," *Süddeutsche Zeitung*, November 5, 2013.

22. Aldrich, *GCHQ*, 322.

23. Aldrich, 322–23.

24. Aldrich, 329.

25. Aldrich, 329–30.

26. Aldrich.

27. Patrick Radden Keefe, *Chatter: Dispatches from the Secret World of Global Eavesdropping* (New York: Random House, 2005), 73.

28. Ewen MacAskill, Julian Borger, Nick Hopkins, Nick Davies, and James Ball, "GCHQ Taps Fibre-Optic Cables for Secret Access to World's Communications," *The Guardian*, June 21, 2013, www.theguardian.com/uk/2013/jun/21/gchq-cables-secret-world-communications-nsa.

29. Nick Squire, "British Military Base Used to Spy on 'Middle East,'" *Telegraph*, November 5, 2013; and Nicky Hager and Stefania Maurizi, "Cyprus: The Home of British/American Internet Surveillance in the Middle East," *L'Espresso*, November 5, 2013.

30. Simon Winchester, *Outpost: Journeys to the Surviving Relics of the British Empire* (New York: Harper Perennial, [1985] 2003), 26; David Vine, *Island of Shame: The Secret History of the U.S. Military Base on Diego Garcia* (Princeton, NJ: Princeton University Press, 2009); and Aldrich, *GCHQ*, 335–39.

31. Vine, *Island of Shame*, 4–5, 197–98. See also David Vine, *Base Nation: How U.S. Military Bases Abroad Harm America and the World* (New York: Henry Holt, 2015), 65–67.

32. Aldrich, *GCHQ*, 335.

33. Aldrich; Winchester, *Outposts*, 30.

34. Vine, *Island of Shame*, 91; emphasis in original.

35. Jeffrey T. Richelson and Desmond Ball, *The Ties That Bind: Intelligence Cooperation between the UKUSA Countries—the United Kingdom, the United States of America, Canada, Australia, and New Zealand* (Boston: Allen & Unwin, 1985), 205–6; Bamford, *Body of Secrets*, 165; and Winchester, *Outposts*, 31.

36. Ruth Oldenziel, "Islands: U.S. as a Networked Empire," in *Entangled Geographies: Empire and Technopolitics in the Global Cold War*, ed. Gabrielle Hecht (Cambridge, MA: MIT Press, 2011), 18–22.

37. Richelson and Ball, *Ties That Bind*, 202.

38. For a map of Diego Garcia, see www.navymwrdiegogarcia.com/others/downtown-map. See also Winchester, *Outposts*, 28.

39. Winchester, *Outposts*, 52–53.

40. Peter H. Sand, *United States and Britain in Diego Garcia: The Future of a Controversial Base* (New York: Palgrave Macmillan, 2009), 44.

41. Winchester, *Outposts*, 124–25.

42. Sue Steiner, Robin Liston, Richard Grundy, and Mike Hentley, *St Helena: Ascension, Tristan Da Cunha* (Chalfont St. Peter: Bradt Travel Guides, 2007).

43. Nikolas Kozloff, "Welcome to Remote U.S.-U.K. Spy Island," *Huffington Post*, November 11, 2013, www.huffpost.com/entry/welcome-to-remote-us-uk-s_b_4254732.

44. Yorkshire CND, "Lifting the Lid on Menwith Hill: The Strategic Roles and Economic Impact of the US Spy Base in Yorkshire," Report, 2012, 2, www.cnduk.org; and Keefe, *Chatter*, 3–4.

45. Kenneth L. Bird, "Menwith Hill Station: A Case Study in Signal Intelligence Gathering during the Cold War," *Monitoring Times* 16, no. 2 (February 1997): 16–19.

46. Yorkshire CND, "Lifting the Lid," 32; and Bird, "Menwith Hill Station."

47. Keefe, *Chatter*, 4.

48. Confidential source.

49. Snowden document published by *The Intercept*; and Ryan Gallagher, "Inside Menwith Hill: The NSA's British Base at the Heart of U.S. Targeted Killing," *The Intercept*, September 6, 2016, https://theintercept.com/2016/09/06/nsa-menwith-hill-targeted-killing-surveillance/; http://www.documentcloud.org/documents/3089521-Menwith-satellite-classification-guide.html.

50. Bird, "Menwith Hill Station."

51. "Too Much of a Good Thing," www.documentcloud.org/documents/3089505-Too-much-of-a-good-thing.html.

52. Gallagher, "Inside Menwith Hill."

53. Ghost Hunter Snowden document links: www.documentcloud.org/documents/3089523-Ghosthunter-only-capability-of-its-kind.html; www.documentcloud.org/documents/3089512-Ghosthunter-and-the-geolocating-of-internet-cafes.html; www.documentcloud.org/documents/3089508-Ghosthunter-goes-global.html; https://www.documentcloud.org/documents/3089492-Ghosthunter-tasking-process.html.

54. "Apparition Becomes a Reality," www.documentcloud.org/documents/3089509-APPARITION-becomes-a-reality-new-corporate-VSAT.html. Cited in Gallagher, "Inside Menwith Hill."

55. On the capture, see "SIGINT Target Package Leads to USMC Capture of

al-Qa'ida Weapons Procurer," https://assets.documentcloud.org/documents/3089506/SIGINT-target-package-leads-to-USMC-capture-of.pdf.

56. "SIGINT Target Package."

57. "MHS Initiatives: Maximizing Our Access," https://www.documentcloud.org/documents/3089503-MHS-initiatives-maximizing-our-access.html. See also "Elegant Chaos: Collect It All, Exploit It All," https://theintercept.com/document/2016/09/06/elegant-chaos-collect-it-all-exploit-it-all/.

58. "Elegant Chaos."

59. "Work Is Progressing on Menwith Hill Station," www.documentcloud.org/documents/3089513-Work-is-progressing-on-Menwith-Hill-Station-s.html; and "New Ops Building at MHS Completed, Fit-Up Begins," www.documentcloud.org/documents/3089515-New-ops-building-at-MHS-completed-fit-up-begins.html.

60. Testimony of General Michael V. Hayden, July 26, 2006, www.judiciary.senate.gov/imo/media/doc/hayden_testimony_07_26_06.pdf.

61. "Too Much of a Good Thing."

62. Richelson, *Wizards of Langley*, 109–10; and http://lakdiva.org/clarke/1945ww.

63. Richelson, *Wizards of Langley*, 111.

64. See Desmond Ball, *Pine Gap: Australia and the US Geostationary Signals Intelligence Satellite Program* (Sydney: Allen & Unwin, 1988).

65. Keefe, *Chatter*, 23–24. The rest of the information is based on viewing a good map image of Alice Springs.

66. Jackie Dent, "An American Spy Base Hidden in Australia's Outback," *New York Times*, November 23, 2017.

67. Ball, *Pine Gap*, 59–60; and Desmond Ball, Bill Robinson, and Richard Tanter, "Management of Operations at Pine Gap Nautilus Institute for Security and Sustainability, 24 November 2015," http://nautilus.org/wp-content/uploads/2015/11/PG-Managing-Operations-18-November-2015.v2.pdf; and Debra Killalea, "Pine Gap: Nautilus Institute Explores Alice Springs Joint Defence Facility," www.news.com.au/technology/innovation/inventions/pine-gap-nautilus-institute-explores-alice-springs-joint-defence-facility/news-story/4cb8906c915e2df71b61c0c24babc1c9.

68. Ball, *Pine Gap*, 84.

69. Desmond Ball, Bill Robinson, and Richard Tanter, "The Militarisation of Pine Gap: Organisations and Personnel," NAPSNet Special Report, August 14, 2015, http://nautilus.org/?p=46638.

70. S. Ryan Gallagher, "The U.S. Spy Hub in the Heart of Australia," *The Intercept*, August 19, 2017, https://theintercept.com/document/2017/08/19/m7600-m8300-sigint-guide.

71. Gallagher.

72. Gallagher.

73. Luke Buckmaster, "Pine Gap Review–Lots of Yaketty Yak and Occasional Scenes of Bonking," *The Guardian*, October 11, 2018, www.theguardian

.com/tv-and-radio/2018/oct/12/pine-gap-review-lots-of-yakkety-yak-and-occasional-scenes-of-bonking.

74. Netflix, opening sequence: www.netflix.com/title/80195198.

75. On Intelset, see www.intelsat.com/about-us/history/.

76. Bronwen Reid, "Chatters of State," *NZ Listener*, May 21, 1988; and Nicky Hager, *Secret Power: New Zealand's Role in the International Spy Network* (Nelson, NZ: Craig Potton, 1996).

77. National Library of New Zealand, Owen Wilkes Collection, brochure.

78. Hager, *Secret Power*, 258, 260.

79. GCSB Update, March 21, 2012, COMSAT Advisory Board, http://static.stuff.co.nz/files/GCSBMarch2012.pdf.

80. "YRS Gears Up to Celebrate 40 Years," *Northwest Passage* 3, no. 7 (July 2012), Snowden Archive, https://snowdenarchive.cjfe.org/greenstone/collect/snowden1/index/assoc/HASH8bd1.dir/doc.pdf.

81. Duncan Campbell, "Somebody's Listening," *New Statesman*, August 12, 1988, 10–12.

82. Campbell.

83. Duncan Campbell, "Interception Capabilities 2000," https://fas.org/irp/eprint/ic2000/ic2000.htm.

84. Steve Wright, "An Appraisal of Technologies of Political Control," 1998, www.statewatch.org/news/2005/may/steve-wright-stoa-repdf; and Campbell, "Interception Capabilities 2000," 5.

85. "YRS Gears Up to Celebrate 40 Years."

86. Lloyd Salvetti, "An Interview with NSA Director Lt. Gen. Michael V. Hayden," *Studies in Intelligence* 44, no. 1 (January 2000): 5.

87. Sigdev Conference, from a slide reproduced in Glenn Greenwald, *No Place to Hide: Edward Snowden, the NSA, and the U.S. Surveillance State* (New York: Metropolitan Books, 2014), 151.

88. "Dealing with a 'Tsunami' of Intercept," https://www.eff.org/files/2015/05/26/20150505-intercept-sidtoday-tsunami-of-intercept-final.pdf. See Peter Maas, "Inside NSA, Officials Privately Criticize 'Collect It All' Surveillance," *The Intercept*, May 28, 2015, https://theintercept.com/2015/05/28/nsa-officials-privately-criticize-collect-it-all-surveillance. This article also includes twelve documents related to the topic appended with the complete original document in PDF format. These documents are used in this section. For the Black Budget, see "Resources Exhibit No. 13," "Coping with Information Overload," under "Mission Processing and Exploitation," https://grid.glendon.yorku.ca/items/show/8; https://www.washingtonpost.com/world/national-security/black-budget-summary-details-us-spy-networks-successes-failures-and-objectives/2013/08/29/7e57bb78-10ab-11e3-8cdd-bcdc09410972_story.html.

89. "Signal vs. Noise Column: Do We Need a Bigger SIGINT Truck?," from a SID*today* column, https://www.documentcloud.org/documents/2088978-do-we-need-a-bigger-sigint-truck. Boldface in original.

90. For a quantitative analysis of how much information Snowden collected

about domestic spying was leaked to the press, see the unpublished thesis by Patrick F. Barton, "Edward Snowden Unauthorized Disclosures and Press Publication of Classified Intelligence Information: A Case Study" (Diss., North Central University, Arizona, 2016).

91. Greenwald, *No Place to Hide,* chap. 3.

92. Barton Gellman, "Edward Snowden, After Months of NSA Revelations, Says His Mission Is Complete," *Washington Post*, December 23, 2013.

93. Gellman. For "Big Data" and 80 percent figure, see "SSO Corporate Portfolio Overview," slides 5, 67, Snowden Archive. For AT&T and Verizon exposés, see Julia Angwin, Charlie Savage, Jeff Larson, Henrik Moltke, Laura Poitras, and James Risen, "AT&T Helped U.S. Spy on Internet on a Vast Scale," *New York Times*, August 15, 2013.

94. "Special Source Operations: The Cryptologic Provider of Intelligence from Global High-Capacity Telecommunications Systems," slide 5, Snowden Archive.

95. "GAO: Global Access Operations: Boundlessinformant," PowerPoint presentation, 4 pp., Snowden Archive.

96. Snowden Archive, https://snowdenarchive.cjfe.org/greenstone/collect/snowden1/index/assoc/HASH7dcc.dir/doc.pdf.

97. Snowden Archive.

98. Snowden Archive.

99. "X-KEYSCORE as a SIGDEV Tool," 2009, Snowden Archive, https://snowdenarchive.cjfe.org/greenstone/collect/snowden1/index/assoc/HASH586f.dir/doc.pdf; and Morgan Marquis-Boire, Glenn Greenwald, and Micah Lee, "KEYSCORE: NSA's Google for the World's Private Communication," *The Intercept*, July 1, 2015.

100. See, e.g., Maier, *Among Empires*.

101. Immerwahr, *How to Hide an Empire*.

102. Johnson, *Sorrows of Empire*, 4.

103. For bases figure, see Johnson, *Sorrows of Empire*, 4; Michael Moran quote on 155. See also Michael Moran, "G.I. Joe as Big Brother," MSNBC, April 6, 2001.

104. James Bamford testimony, European Parliament, quoted in Keefe, *Chatter*, 205.

8

CRYPTO AG

In February 2020, the *Washington Post* broke an explosive story. It reported that the CIA, in partnership with West Germany's intelligence service, had secretly bought Crypto AG, a Swiss company that manufactured and sold code-making machines, in June 1970. Not only did these intelligence agencies become owners of the company, but the cypher machines were doctored to be read easily by them. By now it will not be surprising that the CIA was interested in controlling encryption technology. As early as the 1950s the CIA had invested in building the Berlin Tunnel signals intelligence operation to tap Soviet communications. Despite its charge to conduct espionage using human sources, the CIA continued to use large-scale technical systems like spy planes, satellites, and drones to acquire secret information throughout the Cold War and the so-called Global War on Terror. Obviously, spy agencies did not have the facilities to build these technologies themselves. Instead they partnered with private industry and military agencies to facilitate big technological projects. However, none of those stories was as audacious as buying a company, doctoring the machines, and easily reading the weakly encrypted messages of 120 foreign countries, primarily in the global south. It created global information inequality and information dominance by a core of northern countries. It was a kind a techno-imperialism within the larger spy-tech empire. Most important, the operation allowed the United States to be a global espionage power as early as the 1970s and to use the capability to influence foreign policy until the company was sold in 2018.[1]

In the secret ninety-six-page CIA history, not yet available to the public, and on which the *Washington Post* based its story, the CIA gloats about its achievement: "It was the intelligence coup of the century, foreign governments were paying good money to the US and West Germany for the privilege of having their most secret communications read by at least two (and possibly as many as five or six) foreign countries."[2]

Crypto AG was founded and owned by the Russian exile Boris Hagelin since 1950. The company started out in Sweden, Hagelin's new home, but he moved it to the neutral tax haven Switzerland. Hagelin had been a close friend since the 1930s of the famed cryptographer William Friedman, who was also of Russian descent and who worked for the NSA. They bonded over their common heritage and mutual interest in encryption. At the Cosmos Club in Washington, DC, in 1951 they shook hands over dinner and made a "gentleman's agreement" that they would restrict the sales of cypher machines to "friendly" countries the United States approved of; all other countries would "get older, weaker systems."[3] The relationship between the NSA and Hagelin eventually became rocky because the NSA placed restrictions on sales and did not share important information with Hagelin. The NSA withdrew from their partnership with him in the late 1950s. The NSA also did not think they needed such an operation because they could easily crack the codes of the Third World countries themselves. Instead, the CIA formed a licensing agreement with Hagelin. After negotiations in 1969 and other countries like France expressing an interest in buying Crypto AG, the CIA together with the BND bought it. The operation was known initially as Thesaurus; the code name was then changed to Rubicon in 1987. The purchase of the company now code-named Minerva included the transfer of all their global clients.[4]

By the mid-1960s the United States found a way to doctor the machines. With the spread of electronic circuits, Hagelin's old-fashioned mechanical machines were becoming obsolete. Hagelin let the United States step in to create a new electronic model, the H-460, developed entirely by the NSA. This new circuit-based electronic system could make the seemingly randomly generated numbers repeat themselves quickly, allowing NSA experts to crack the code.[5]

The two agencies also brought in high-tech companies to advise them on technical and business issues. The Germans cooperated with Siemens, a corporate giant in telecommunications, and the United States later integrated Motorola into the enterprise in order to assist Crypto AG with technical issues.[6] This followed a trend for the United States. Intelligence agencies without the resources of high-tech companies partnered with them to achieve their goals. As early as the 1950s the CIA had partnered with Lockheed Martin to build the vaunted U-2 spy plane. The National Reconnaissance Office was, and continues to be, surrounded by a business park featuring the cream of American industry like Boeing and Booz Allen Hamilton. Finally, the NSA also has a "National Business Park" (NBP) less than a mile from headquarters that includes companies like Booz Allen Hamilton and Lockheed Martin.[7] The Edward Snowden revelations also featured the way in which the NSA teamed up with global corporate giants like Verizon, AT&T, and Google to master their global operations vision.

The doctored machines allowed US intelligence to achieve a number of foreign policy successes during the 1970s and 1980s according to the internal history. Before President Jimmy Carter brought Israel's prime minister Menachem Begin and Egyptian president Anwar Sadat to Camp David to negotiate peace accords in 1978, the United States was listening to Sadat's communications with allied Arab countries in real time. This allowed Carter to learn what he could accomplish and where he might back down. The peace accords helped stabilize the Middle East.[8]

As we saw in chapter 6, the encrypted communications obtained in the Rubicon operation allowed the United States to successfully negotiate the release of American hostages held in Iran in 1979, the year after the Camp David Peace Accords. The United States could read the encrypted communications of both Iran and Algeria, which was acting as a mediator, because they both used Crypto AG cipher machines. Bobby Ray Inman, the NSA's director at the time, regularly got calls from President Carter for an update on how the Khomeini regime was responding to the latest messages. Inman could reply about "85 percent of the time," according to the CIA history. Inman began to call Carter his telephone pal because of the frequency of the telephone exchanges.[9]

During the 1980s, Crypto AG's clients reflected the global hot spots of the time, including countries like Saudi Arabia, its biggest customer, as well as Iran, Italy, Indonesia, Iraq, and Libya. After La Belle, a West Berlin disco popular with American servicemen, was bombed in 1986, the United States quickly implicated Libya. Two US soldiers and a Turkish woman died. President Ronald Reagan ordered retaliatory strikes ten days later after reading intercepted communications. When Reagan announced the strikes, he said he had direct and precise evidence. He even went as far as to relate that Libya's East Berlin embassy received orders to undertake the attacks. The day after the bombing, said Reagan, "they reported back to Tripoli on the great success of their mission." Reagan's comments nearly exposed Operation Rubicon, and any attentive listener could guess that the United States intercepted Libyan communications.[10]

Reagan was not the last person to jeopardize the secrecy surrounding Operation Rubicon. In 1992, Hans Bühler, a salesman for Crypto AG, traveled to Iran to visit his clients. He had been traveling there for many years, but this time he was detained. He was released nine months later after the BND secretly paid a ransom of $1 million. The CIA declined to contribute because of the US policy against paying ransom for hostages. Bühler had not been aware that the CIA and BND owned the company and rigged the machines. But after his return to Switzerland he learned more and started talking about his new knowledge to the press. Crypto AG terminated his contract in March 1993. This publicity led to digging by the press and shed new light on clues that had been ignored earlier, like references to the "Boris project" in the Friedman files donated to the Virginia Military Institute after he died in 1969. By 1995, the *Baltimore Sun* published an article titled "Rigging the Game." Although the authors were right about the "rigging" of the machines, they implicated the NSA in the project, not the CIA, and did not know the details later revealed through the acquisition of the CIA history. But still, the publicity led a number of Crypto's clients like Argentina, Italy, Saudi Arabia, Egypt, and Indonesia to cancel their contracts by 1996. It is no wonder that the project was code-named Hydra. Because of this adverse publicity, the BND decided to pull out of the project in 1993, and the CIA bought their share of the company for $17 million. As a result, the Swiss Crypto AG company was owned and controlled by the CIA from 1994 to 2019, when the company closed.[11]

It was not just the Bühler affair that led to the downfall of the Crypto-CIA partnership. Globalization and more general developments in communications technology like public key cryptography gave governments other options to secure their communications. Robert Dover and Richard Aldrich also suggest, based on private interviews, that the CIA pressured US computer companies to rig desktop computers to make up for the loss of access when Operation Rubicon started to decline in 1996. This is not surprising given the Snowden revelations about the NSA's relationship with private companies that they pressured or collaborated with to gain access to private communications, the internet, and big data.[12]

Years after Operation Rubicon was over, Bobby Ray Inman told journalists that he had no qualms about running the Operation Rubicon program:

"It was a very valuable source of communications on significantly large portions of the world important to US policymakers,"[13] reflecting the totally amoral, if not immoral, attitude of most intelligence officials and the enterprise of spying in general. How the operation is viewed in society might be variable, but the political implications are clear: the CIA-BND-Crypto alliance was both part of the techno-spy empire and an enabler of US empire.

Notes

1. Greg Miller, "The Intelligence Coup of the Century," *Washington Post*, February 11, 2020, www.washingtonpost.com/graphics/2020/world/national-security/cia-crypto-encryption-machines-espionage.
2. Miller.
3. See the live link to the Cosmos Club agreement in Miller, "Intelligence Coup of the Century."
4. This chapter is based heavily on a special issue of the journal *Intelligence and National Security* on Operation Rubicon as well as on Dover and Aldrich, "Cryptography and the Global South." There is also an excellent German ZDF documentary that helped launch this wave of scholarship: https://vimeo.com/456864505. For information in this paragraph, see Melina Dobson, "Operation Rubicon: Germany as an Intelligence 'Great Power'?," *Intelligence and National Security* 35, no. 5 (2020): 608–22.
5. Miller, "Intelligence Coup of the Century."
6. Dobson, "Operation Rubicon."
7. Author site visits and Google Maps.
8. Dover and Aldrich, "Cryptography and the Global South," 1909. Their examples are based on the unavailable CIA history.
9. Miller, "Intelligence Coup of the Century"; see the tab on the Iran hostage crisis linked to the CIA history.
10. Miller.
11. Miller; and Scott Shane and Tom Bowman, "Rigging the Game," *Baltimore Sun*, December 10, 1995, www.baltimoresun.com/news/bs-xpm-1995-12-10-1995344001-story.html; Dover and Aldrich, "Cryptography and the Global South," 1911.
12. Dover and Aldrich, "Cryptography and the Global South," 1912.
13. Miller, "Intelligence Coup of the Century."

9

GLOBAL EYES

In October 1957, shortly after the Soviet Union launched Sputnik into orbit, Lyndon B. Johnson, then Senate Majority Leader, spoke about the event with great rhetorical flourish.

> The Roman Empire controlled the world because it could build roads. Later—when moved to sea—the British Empire was dominant because it had ships. In the air age, we were more powerful because we had airplanes. Now the Communists have established a foothold in outer space. It is not very reassuring to be told that next year we will put a better satellite in the air. Perhaps it will even have chrome trim and automatic windshield wipers.[1]

To Johnson, Sputnik's launch into outer space threatened American global and technological supremacy. He considered it the technological equivalent of Pearl Harbor. Not only did the event spark a space race between the two rival superpowers that permeated the Cold War, but it also reignited interest in supporting research on a "world-circling spaceship," as RAND called a satellite in its 1946 proposal. Before long, in January 1958, the United States launched its own civilian satellite, Explorer 1, into orbit, followed by GRAB (Galactic Radiation and Background), a US Navy ELINT satellite, in July 1960 and Corona, a CIA imagery reconnaissance satellite, in August 1960.

By its very nature, a satellite is a global technology. It circles the earth in a steady orbit, like the earth orbiting the sun. During the early years of the development of reconnaissance satellites, however, the CIA, the air force, and the navy were not interested in viewing the whole globe. Instead, they focused their satellite sights on a large swath of the Soviet Union—so-called denied territory—to track missiles, bombs, radar, and nuclear technology. Rather than lofty discussions about using a global-encompassing technology, the early history of reconnaissance satellites is riddled with nasty turf battles between the CIA and the air force involving control of the National Reconnaissance Office and the satellites themselves. Even so, the global scope of the program quickly expanded through the needs of mapping agencies like the Defense Mapping Agency and the United States Geological Survey (USGS). These agencies needed good maps to launch and target ICBMs, for example. As these needs increased, the NRO modified the Corona search satellite and the Gambit surveillance satellite to create the Hexagon mapping camera, which combined increased resolution with a wider view in order to create better maps. Using reconnaissance satellite imagery to create global maps was an unintended consequence of the reconnaissance satellite program.

It wasn't until after the Cold War that the NRO programmatically admitted, and self-consciously proclaimed, its aspirations to cover the globe with its satellites. Its new 1996 vision statement described the NRO as "freedom's sentinel in space, one team revolutionizing global reconnaissance." Keith Hall, an intelligence bureaucrat and then acting director of the NRO, explained that the new statement reflected "the expanding role of intelligence" and the "importance of achieving global information superiority."[2]

Even with the delay in announcing a conscious global imperative until after the Cold War, the United States had already expanded its global reach. Since the targeting of Soviet war technology in the late 1950s and 1960s, the United States expanded its global ground stations, which included the visible radomes, radar dishes, and vast antenna farms. These facilities mushroomed around the globe, from Buckley Air Force Base in Colorado to Menwith Hill in Great Britain to Pine Gap in Australia. During the Cold War, overhead reconnaissance and surveillance satellites began to discover and monitor every military and economic development that could have an effect on the United States, from agriculture in foreign countries to their industrial base and access to oil and gas. The 1960s saw the foundation of US reconnaissance and surveillance satellites.

While the initial founding of the NRO on August 25, 1960, grew out of the Eisenhower administration's support for spy technology, its official opening in 1961 coincided with John F. Kennedy's presidency. Unlike Eisenhower's open approach, Kennedy wanted to "cloak" air and space reconnaissance in "utmost secrecy." The Kennedy administration "wanted to avoid the appearance" of using high-tech equipment to spy on other countries, especially less developed ones, "from the safety of space." Kennedy also did not want the Soviet Union to develop countermeasures to reconnaissance satellites, as it did with the U-2 spy plane.[3]

The very existence of the NRO was top secret; the organization was born secret. Unlike the CIA, the NSA, and other spy agencies, the NRO existed officially, but it did not exist publicly. According to a declassified memorandum dated 1963, "The title NRO is classified SECRET and the existence of a classified National Reconnaissance Program within the US government is classified TOP SECRET."[4] The NRO was so secret that it did not officially acknowledge its existence until 1992, despite leaks by newspapers in the 1970s that made it an open secret. Its office was housed in a suite of rooms 4C-956 in the Pentagon under the cover name Office of Space Systems behind an unmarked door. Even the NRO logo—a spherical satellite orbiting the earth—was classified.

By the time the NRO was an open secret in the 1970s, President Carter announced that overhead reconnaissance had become essential in monitoring arms control agreements through so-called national technical means. Satellites began to be seen as peacekeepers during the Cold War. Some NRO in-house histories even went so far as to claim that overhead reconnaissance had kept the Cold War from becoming hot.

U-2 Information Explosion

In previous chapters, I examined the origins of the U-2 spy plane in the mid-1950s and its role in discovering the medium-range missiles on Cuba. Of course, initially the main target of U-2 overhead reconnaissance missions was the Soviet Bloc, but targets expanded in the 1950s and 1960s to include the Middle East, China, India, Latin America, Africa, Korea, Vietnam, and Southeast Asia. With the expanding missions came an expanding global reach, but more problematic, the proliferation of missions produced an overwhelming number of photographs.

Arthur C. Lundahl, director of photointerpretation at the CIA, who had a good working relationship with President Kennedy, explained to him in one of his early briefings that the U-2 camera could photograph a

Figure 9.1 Seal of the National Reconnaissance Office. *National Reconnaissance Office*

swath of about 125 nautical miles wide and 3,000 miles long on over 10,000 feet of film. He invoked the image of Sherlock Holmes scanning evidence with a large magnifying glass. "Imagine a group of photo interpreters on their hands and knees scanning a roll of film that extended from the White House to the Capitol and back," said Lundahl in his typical easy-to-understand way. Kennedy always remembered this analogy and asked Lundahl to repeat it when other officials were briefed at the White House.[5] But those figures referred to only one mission. Imagine how many thousands of feet of film were produced by two hundred or five hundred missions in a year. Investigators would barely have time to crawl on their hands and knees from the White House to the Capitol and back. And those images only came from the U-2 spy plane. As intelligence agencies turned to satellite imagery after 1960, the volume of images increased exponentially.

On August 18, 1960, at 7:57 p.m., a fiery roar shattered the stillness of the beachside launch pad at Vandenberg Air Force Base in California as a Thor booster rocket mated to an Agena spacecraft launched a Discoverer XIV satellite into space in a polar north-south orbit. The Discoverer was described as a scientific satellite on a mission to collect scientific data for the public, but in fact that was an elaborate cover story for the very secret reconnaissance satellite program code-named Corona at the CIA. This was the fourteenth launch and the first totally successful one; it had been preceded by thirteen failures over the past year and a half that cost billions of dollars. The failures were plagued by the following problems: either the spacecraft Agena failed to orbit or it fell in the Pacific, or the Thor booster self-destructed, the satellite recovery vehicle (the capsule) was lost in Spitzbergen, was shot too high in orbit, was lost in reentry, failed to separate, or was destroyed in reentry. Mission 9009 (as Discoverer XIV was known) was also the first satellite that had a camera attached to it and the first capsule that was successfully snagged in the air by a cargo plane. This mission alone brought back more photographic information than all the U-2 missions combined.

David Doyle, an imagery analyst and manager at the National Photographic Interpretation Center, commented, "When the film from Mission 9009 arrived at the Steuart Building at 5th and K Streets in northwest Washington, it was the start of a new era. That mission gave us more coverage than all the U-2 missions. And that was to be repeated on every day a Corona satellite was in orbit. So, over a year's time, it was a tremendous amount of information at our disposal."[6]

According to the first report penned by NPIC, Mission 9009 covered 1.5 million square miles of the Sino-Soviet Bloc. The authors stressed the novelty of examining imagery from satellites, noting that it represented "one of man's first attempts to produce an intelligence report from satellite photography."[7] The excitement was even more palpable at the Corona/Discoverer XIV briefing led by NPIC director, Arthur Lundahl, who announced with "dramatic flair" that it was "something new and great we've got here." When his deputy opened a curtain that showed a map, there were multiple bands of vertical stripes emanating from the North Pole across the Soviet Union and extending west to Greece. This was a dramatic difference from the one squiggly line across the map the U-2 spy plane had covered. Discoverer XIV's camera had scanned those stripes in the Soviet Union and took photographs of military sites; the interpreters cheered when they saw the map.[8]

The take from Mission 9009 alone filled dozens of reports and documented thirteen categories of militarily significant sites like airfields, atomic energy facilities, missile sites, ports, and harbors. The photointerpreters were overwhelmed with information but managed to identify the Kapustin Yar Missile Test Range more extensively than they had with the U-2 spy plane images; they also identified twenty new surface-to-air missile sites and a new nuclear weapons research and development center, among other military-related items.[9]

By the end of 1960, the Corona satellite had hauled in 271,317 linear feet (51 miles) of film. But this paled in comparison to the peak year of 1964, when it brought in 3,261,324 linear feet (617 miles) of film. This would mean that a photointerpreter would have to analyze film that stretched from Washington, DC, to Boston to New York City. Obviously, all this information could not be analyzed or used.[10]

Even so, Corona targets quickly expanded to mirror world events. According to Dino Brugioni, a senior manager at NPIC and lead photointerpreter, some of the events captured on film included the Russian and Chinese nuclear programs, the Six-Day War between Israel and Arab nations, the Soviet invasion of Czechoslovakia, the Soviet race to the moon, the Chinese-Soviet border conflict, the India-Pakistan war, the Vietnam War, the Kystym nuclear incident, the building of the Berlin Wall, the Chinese takeover of Tibet, and the remains of the Gulag Archipelago.[11]

Global Mapmaking

But more important for the emergence of US global coverage was the impact of satellite imagery on mapping. Even if strategic targets were confined to so-called denied areas like the Sino-Soviet Bloc during the early years, analysts quickly saw the potential for the creation of global maps. This meant that the satellites, initially intended for foreign intelligence, began to photograph places in the United States like Washington, DC.[12] Elaine A. Gifford, a photogrammetrist at NPIC, admitted in an interview that the "CORONA system wasn't initially designed for mapping purposes. . . . [N]evertheless, it quickly evolved into supporting mapping capabilities." Not only that, but they quickly realized that "what we needed to do was survey the entire earth from space." As a result, they developed a "satellite with a calibrated camera, a precise orbital position, and exact camera attitude." In short, they used reconnaissance satellite imagery to create a civilian and military global mapping system.[13]

As the geographer John Cloud notes, this development created a new synergy between civilian and military personnel in a new "codeword mapping community." This community had grown out of World War II and early Cold War needs. One of the most important training grounds for

NPIC photogrammetry (the science of dimensions and spatial relationships in images) and other photo analysts was the Ohio State University Mapping and Charting Research Laboratory (MCRL). The work there was mostly funded by the Department of Defense, and the staff worked with classified contracts and secret reports. By 1954, the air force's St. Louis Aeronautical Chart Plant in Missouri employed over three thousand people.[14]

This St. Louis installation rapidly went through an acrobatic series of name, acronym, and mission changes during the Cold War and the post-9/11 era. In 1947 it was renamed the Aeronautical Chart and Information Center (ACIC); by 1972 it had become part of the newly formed Defense Mapping Agency (DMA), and when that bureaucracy became part of the National Imagery Mapping Agency (NIMA) in 1996, St. Louis was included. The largest name and mission change came in 2003 when NIMA became part of the National Geospatial-Intelligence Agency; the St. Louis facility then became NGA West. With such an enormous expansion, NGA decided that the St. Louis facility needed more space. As of 2022, the government is hard at work building a new $1.7 billion building slated to be completed by 2025.[15]

Hexagon

The Corona program ended in 1972. It had provided the intelligence community with over a decade of eye-popping satellite imagery. Although its KH-4 camera provided excellent mapping imagery, it was the enormous, bus-sized Hexagon satellite that was designed and manufactured to be a dedicated mapping satellite. The Hexagon was a synthesis of the KH-4's ability to provide "continuous stereoscopic ground coverage" and the Gambit's KH-7 camera's resolution. The NRO Hexagon history describes it as "the ultimate design for a mapping system" because it could provide simultaneous coverage of "large, contiguous areas of the earth at large scale."[16]

During the early years when the famed Corona reconnaissance satellite was collecting images, the information on film came to earth via the bucket-catching system. This seemingly primitive film-return method of getting the information grew out of the US experience using enormous camera-carrying balloons to view the Eastern Bloc and the Soviet Union during the 1950s. The idea was to catch the film that had been released into a gold-plated bucket attached to a parachute before it landed in the water. Big cargo planes would swoop down and haul in the bucket using winches secured to the floor near the opening.

Real Time

The problem, of course, with the film bucket return system was the delay in receiving and evaluating the material. In many cases, the photographic documentation of international crises was seen on satellite cameras after the fact. The most glaring example of this was the Soviet invasion of Czechoslovakia in 1968.

Although US satellite engineers had attempted to develop real-time satellite systems in the 1950s, their efforts had failed, and the intelligence community decided to opt for the elaborate, time-consuming, and unreliable film return bucket system instead. Efforts during the 1960s and 1970s to develop a real-time reconnaissance satellite that could send images to earth finally came to fruition in December 1976 with the launch of the KH-11, code-named Kennan, a project spearheaded by the CIA and its California contractor, Lockheed.

The new revolutionary spy satellite was the first to use a CCD, a charge-coupled device, a technology first invented at Bell Labs in 1969 by George E. Smith and Willard Boyle, who created a new memory circuit that was used for signal processing and imaging. Although the CCD had been used by astronomers in telescopes since 1975, it wasn't applied to satellites until the KH-11.[17]

Images started to beam back to America on the same day Jimmy Carter was inaugurated as the thirty-ninth president of the United States, January 20, 1977. Early that morning, before the 9:00 a.m. senior staff meeting at Langley, just hours before Carter was officially inaugurated, the CIA received its pictures. E. Henry "Hank" Knoche, then acting DCI, was so excited about the images that he was tempted to present them to Carter on that very day but instead made an appointment to see Carter and his national security adviser, Zbigniew Brzezinski, the next afternoon at 3:15 at the White House. Knoche brought along a handful of six-inch-square black-and-white photographs that did not show military hardware developments in the Soviet Union but rather "provided an overhead perspective" of Carter's inauguration the day before. When Knoche spread the pictures on the table in the map room Carter "shook his head in amazement" and said, "Of course . . . this will also be of value to our arms control work."[18]

As the reconnaissance satellites improved, the US intelligence community decided to reduce manpower and HUMINT in favor of buying machines. This meant that there were fewer people available to analyze the ever-increasing amount of data. The bucket film return system hauled in plenty of information to analyze, but it wasn't until the revolutionary real-time image from the KH-11 Kennan satellite that analysts were overwhelmed with data. The physicist Jerry Nelson recalled, "The information coming down from these things is just going to choke you. . . . [I]t gets awful real fast. You can't get big enough computers to process it. You can't buy enough programmers to write the codes or look at the result or interpret them. At some point you just get saturated and that defeats your whole purpose."[19] Unlike the film return satellites, the KH-11 sent back images every hour and every day.

The National Photographic Interpretation Center

Machines replaced many humans in the intelligence community, but the massive amount of data the machines hauled in required human analysts as well as computers. The NPIC was the major office for imagery analysis in the early years. Originally a small photointerpretation division within the CIA staffed by a handful of photointerpreters, it slowly grew in an attempt to match the increasing technical capabilities of spy planes and satellites and their product. Before Eisenhower left office in 1961, he created the NPIC, an amalgamation of the CIA photo division and agencies in the Department of Defense like the Defense Mapping Agency.

Arthur C. Lundahl founded imagery analysis at the CIA. A navy veteran of World War II aerial reconnaissance, a geologist, and a hobbyist photographer, he was poached by the CIA from the navy, where he worked as second in command at a photography unit from 1946 to 1953. He was the right man at the right time in the right place. Colleagues considered him "imaginative, outgoing, [and] perceptive," with a firm grasp of the technology of photographic interpretation. He also had a gift for "reporting' its achievements. According to his colleague Dino Brugioni, he earned the "complete respect, admiration, and devotion" of the "twelve apostles" who worked with him. A vigorous advocate of aerial reconnaissance, he became the public face of imagery analysis during the Cuban Missile Crisis. He raked in all the national security awards in the United States, and the United Kingdom awarded him the Order of the British Empire in 1974, the year after his retirement.[20] His iconic status is memorialized in the Arthur C. Lundahl Auditorium inside the National Geospatial-Intelligence Agency in Springfield, Virginia, dedicated in 2011.

Lundahl moved the CIA's Photographic Interpretation Center into the decrepit Steuart Motor Car Company building near downtown Washington, DC, in 1956, the same time the U-2 spy plane became operational (see chap. 1). He code-named the project to interpret the photographs collected from U-2 missions HTAUTOMAT, after the then-popular New York City automated cafeterias. He envisioned that "as all the data flowed in, people would be coming in on weekends, holidays, and in the middle of the night—just like the Automats in New York City where people are eating turkey dinners at 3 a.m."[21] With the flood of information from the U-2 spy planes and spy satellites, staff had increased to three hundred and then to thirteen hundred, but that was still not enough to analyze the copious material.[22]

In many ways, the seven-story Steuart Building, located in a slum, provided ideal cover for a secret operation. NPIC inhabited only the top four floors, while the Ford dealership took up the bottom three floors, using the ground floor as a showroom. It wasn't only the increase in staff that led to a move to a bigger and better building in 1963. As photointerpretation gained in importance in the intelligence community, government leaders like the attorney general and the secretary of defense started to pull up in their shiny black limousines at the Steuart Building. The opulence of the cars and men in stiff suits contrasted sharply with the squalor of the neighborhood. The story goes that when Robert "Bobby" Kennedy visited the building, he had to walk over a sleeping drunk to get in. The Kennedy administration made it a priority to find a better building in 1962. The $17 million renovations (two-thirds of that year's NPIC budget) of Building 213, a former gun turret factory that stored steel blanks, at the Washington Navy Yard in southeast Washington, were already furiously under way when the Cuban Missile Crisis broke out in fall 1962.[23]

With the move into the enormous Building 213 in January 1963, the NPIC's floor space increased from 50,000 to 400,000 square feet.[24] To Lundahl, the move "seemed like a dream come true. . . . Walking through the gates and seeing Building 213 in its white splendor, it almost looked like the Taj Mahal." Unofficially, the building became known as the "Lundahl Hilton."[25]

As the stream of information from satellites increased, so too did the need for photo interpreters. Even with substantial hires in 1963 and 1964, the center had trouble keeping up with the increasing volume of information produced by the Corona satellite's KH-4a camera and the higher-resolution KH-7. After each mission, there was information overload at Building 213.[26]

Once the imagery from the planes or satellites was processed, it was written up in NPIC reports, variously called TALENT reports (the code word for imagery analysis), TALENT-KEYHOLE for imagery including satellites, Joint Mission Coverage Index (JMCI), Detailed Photographic Interpretation Report (DPIR), and more. OAK reports focused on imagery from the KH-4 Corona satellite. OAK may be a random code word, or it could signify that the material was "one of a kind"; no one seems to know the origin of the acronym. These reports covered subjects like airfields, electronic communication, industry, military targets, nuclear sites, shipyards, missile sites, and storage, transport, and pipeline systems for target countries.[27]

By the late 1950s, graphic images started adorning the covers of the reports. One of the most striking and ubiquitous is an image of an elongated globe studded with symbols of reconnaissance planes and their imagery targets. The center of the globe depicts a mushroom cloud. To the right, there is a plane flying over a factory toward an enormous missile launching in the air; other missiles are ready to launch on their trailers. To the left of the mushroom cloud, there is an image of a laboratory depicted by test tubes and beakers as well as a large round radar collector ground station.[28]

It wasn't until the mid-1960s that NPIC developed its own emblem for internal and external use, years after it took that name in January 1961. The seal depicts the head of an unhappy-looking eagle wrapped in endless spools of photographic negatives. The film-choked eagle, as the staff called it, is embedded in a blue sky with ten stars. The image is surrounded by compass markings and the title of the center: National Photographic Interpretation Center. Like the CIA seal, it is red, white, and blue, the colors of the United States, and also like the CIA seal, it includes an eagle, America's national bird.

This increasing flow of information led to the creation of new photo-

Figure 9.2 Seal of the National Photographic Interpretation Center. *Wikimedia Commons*

interpretation departments at the CIA and the Defense Intelligence Agency (DIA), as recommended by the CIA's Inspector General and the Department of Defense in 1965. The Committee on Overhead Reconnaissance also created the National Tasking Plan and two different kinds of targets: national and departmental. When a target was designated as national, it was shared with the whole intelligence community. With an inverted sort of logic, targets were so important that "duplication of effort was deemed necessary."[29]

Even with new photointerpretation departments in the intelligence community, the NPIC served as a clearinghouse. It was responsible for creating and maintaining a computer database on all national targets that was available for all intelligence consumers. By the end of the Corona satellite run in 1972, the database grew to ten thousand targets.[30]

Even with the availability of primitive computers, the NPIC kept track of these targets using low-tech methods: shoeboxes and stories. "Shoeboxes" were government-issued wooden boxes that could hold 5-by-8-inch index cards. Instead of cards, photointerpreters filled their boxes with images. Because computer memory was expensive and unreliable, photointerpreters retained historical memory by telling stories. While the database contained brass tacks information like latitude and longitude, an identifying number, and target name, it did not include relational information or track changes over time. This was done through contextual and operational storytelling about findings from missions. Even with the flood of information to interpret from the satellites' films, storytelling continued to be a way to retain and impart knowledge.[31]

Lundahl had impressed the president, Congress, and policymakers with his storyboards. He would tell the story behind the images pasted on the board. The Cuban Missile Crisis storyboards are the most well-known and famous ones, but this was standard practice for the NPIC. Its main focus was Soviet missile and nuclear capabilities. Most of the targets found, identified, plotted, and compared with other activities were in the Soviet Union. Missile test centers like Tyuratam were related to the nuclear test area in Semipalatinsk, for example.[32]

While light tables and microscopes were the bread-and-butter technology for photointerpreters, what the NPIC really needed to cope with this flood of information was more high-powered computers. By 1973 the NPIC had 120 terminals connected to a Sperry 494 mainframe computer they had acquired from the NSA, another agency dealing with information overload. But they complained that these computers were not powerful enough to store and analyze all the information.[33]

The Corona satellite cameras had produced a flood of images, but it wasn't until the Hexagon satellite's KH-9 camera brought back photographs that combined broad areas with excellent resolution in 1973 that the NPIC could no longer cope. The KH-9 camera delivered twelve buckets of film a year, which translated into more than 189 miles of film. Each bucket contained 90 to 160 cans of film and came to the NPIC Navy Yard building by the truckload. The NPIC struggled to handle this "overwhelming amount of information." Leaders estimated that they would need twenty-five hundred people to look at all the film. According to Jack O'Connor, a former NPIC photointerpreter, the "huge volume of KH-9 imagery meant that rapidly reviewing all incoming film became nearly impossible."[34]

Hexagon, the last film-return satellite, had delivered material every couple of weeks, but the NPIC's real coping nightmare would come with the KH-11, or Kennan, the first real-time imagery camera. The Kennan covered the whole world in hourly orbits that progressed from east to west. Because of this, analysts were now organized by specialties all over the world. An analyst covering missiles or nuclear targets would focus not just on the Soviet Union but the whole world. Although the NPIC had tried to prepare for this digital real-time imagery by installing a more powerful computer in 1977, the new Sperry 1100 with three hundred Delta Data terminals, it continued to be overwhelmed.[35]

Xanadu Collocation

The NRO had spearheaded the development of the Corona, Hexagon, and Kennan satellites in concert with contractors largely based in California and Massachusetts. By the 1980s it had secured an officially invisible but dominant and expensive role in the intelligence community. Since its existence was still secret, the NRO's budget was buried in air force expenditures and to a lesser degree in CIA and navy programs. According to William Burrows, during the 1980s, the NRO/air force ate up about 15 percent, or $30.8 billion, of the $200 billion national intelligence budget. And the CIA spent another $2.9 billion on research and development on satellites; the Navy Space Project spent $1.89 billion on the White Cloud ocean reconnaissance satellite project. And these figures don't include the NSA's space reconnaissance SIGINT programs. Between 1980 and 1989, the NRO/air force spent about $14.8 billion on procurement for the satellites and the boosters on which they are propelled into orbit and $11 billion on research and development. Burrows estimated that the "total tab" for technical collection in the 1980s came close to $50 billion, twice as much as it cost to send men to the moon ($5 billion in 1985 alone).[36]

The 1980s ended with the fall of the Berlin Wall in 1989, the collapse of communism, and the end of the Cold War. Congress cut defense and military budgets by as much as 25 percent of their Cold War levels, which had peaked in the 1980s. Even so, the NRO, with its industry relationships and funding, managed to find a way to save money and make big plans.

In 1989, NRO officials started to discuss creating an enormous new office building in northern Virginia to consolidate its staff and contractors. The proclaimed end of the Cold War did not stop them. Even President Bill Clinton's successful effort to declassify the existence of the NRO in 1992 did not deter the NRO from moving forward with the building as it stepped officially into the public arena.

By 1994, the building was almost done. But there was one big problem. NRO leaders had not informed Congress or received approval for the $347 million budget. The Senate Select Committee on Intelligence was upset. Despite the senators' respect for the NRO's contribution to national security, they thought the building's price tag and excessive size and appearance was "silly" and "wasteful" for taxpayers. Sen. Howard Metzenbaum of Ohio argued that there was "enough room for two NRO's" on the site and that it was "far too lavish."[37]

The "gold-plated pleasure" dome inspired Sen. Max Baucus of Montana to quote Coleridge's poem because he thought the project was inspired by poetic fantasy.

In Xanadu did Kubla Khan
A stately pleasure dome decree
Where Alph the sacred river ran,
Through caverns measureless to man
Down to a sunlit sea.
So twice five miles of brittle [fertile] ground
With walls and towers were girdled round

Baucus thought Xanadu was equivalent to northern Virginia; Kubla Khan, to the intelligence community; and the Alph, the Potomac River and the situation with the National Reconnaissance Office: a million square feet with a "gigantic, walled-off," area including a fountain and a sauna (the fountain and sauna were cut after the uproar).[38]

By 2013, the NRO's budget request was $10.2 billion a year. It ranked third in terms of the intelligence community's budget allocations and was only slightly behind the big hitters: the NSA's $10.8 billion budget and the CIA's $14.7 billion, of a $52.6 billion intelligence budget pie, according to documents secured by Edward Snowden.[39]

"Revolutionizing Global Reconnaissance"

It's not surprising that the seal created to represent the National Reconnaissance Office depicts an NRO satellite circling the globe. After all, it is an accurate depiction of a satellite's orbit. Unlike NASA's emblem, which emphasizes outer space, the NRO's emblem depicts a gaze toward earth. Even as an appropriate image, the emblem represents US power to surveil the world.

The secrecy surrounding the NRO is reflected in the evolution of the design of the emblem. In its first iteration, the NRO was still a very secret organization housed in the Department of Defense. When the NRO director, Brockway McMillan, retired in 1965, he was awarded a certificate containing a seal from the mythical "Special Academy for Space Progress" designed by the Air Force Special Projects Office. The image of the earth with a tiny round satellite orbiting it was perched on a skunk on its hind-legs. The skunk, of course, depicted "Skunk Works," a nickname for the Lockheed Company in California led by Kelly Johnson that produced the U-2 spy planes. The skunk on the seal disappeared by the early 1970s, but the seal remained the same.[40]

By 1973, the name on the seal was replaced with "Office Secretary of the Air Force, Space System," and it became the unofficial seal of the NRO's Pentagon headquarters. The seal now depicted a satellite orbiting the earth against a dark-blue star-studded firmament, yellow continents, and a yellow band surrounding the whole emblem. It wasn't until the mid-1980s that the real name of the organization, the National Reconnaissance Office, replaced the old cover name. The globe was now embedded in a black starry background, and this design served as the penultimate emblem; it studded classified NRO publications until 1994, the year the current emblem (2019) began to be used. By 1994, the NRO no longer denied its existence and went public. The last emblem is similar to the one that preceded it, but it replaced the black starry sky with white, the continents are green, and "United States of America" is printed at the bottom.[41]

Surprisingly, it wasn't until after the Cold War that the NRO became truly global. During the Cold War the NRO concentrated on so-called denied areas covering about a quarter of the earth's landmass. By 1996, the NRO told Congress that the "globalization of the threat" forced them to shift their "efforts towards the entire world." In 1996 the NRO proudly changed and proclaimed its vision and mission statement. Its motto became, "Freedom's Sentinel in Space: One Team, Revolutionizing Global Reconnaissance." The NRO told Congress in 1998 that it had changed the motto to reflect the "importance of achieving global information superiority." The National Security Council's "redirection of national intelligence" and its expanding role enabled them. Leaders started to focus on new "transnational" threats like drugs, terrorism, and vanishing resources.[42] The NRO had become an agency looking for problems. It had solutions that perpetuated the existence of the organization.

Keith R. Hall, a large man sporting a mustache and short dark hair and invariably wearing a white shirt and suit and tie, had been director of the NRO (DNRO) since March 1997 and was a career bureaucrat. His intelligence experience began when he led two overseas army intelligence units and continued when he held senior management positions in Washington like the Senate Select Committee on Intelligence and the CIA. He also played a role in merging US imagery and geospatial organizations in the National Imagery and Mapping Agency.[43]

Hall admitted when he assumed his role as DNRO that the NRO needed to improve its "bedside manner." During his previous fifteen years in the intelligence community, he often heard colleagues from other agencies comment, "We do not like those guys. They are arrogant." They thought the NRO was "a very high performing organization, but boy, are they a bunch of SOBs," they said. Hall gave the NRO a "C" on bedside manner.[44]

When the NRO consolidated its operations at the Chantilly, Virginia, headquarters, the idea was to unify disparate parts, to merge L.A. with Langley, the armed forces with the CIA. But the four six-story towers, separated by walkways, continue to segregate employees. While the CIA, the army, and the navy left cultural legacies that continued in the Chantilly headquarters, industry, the "lifeblood for the NRO," surrounded the NRO campus like moths to a flame. Google Maps, and a drive around the area, reveals that the NRO is surrounded by an enormous business park, rivaling that of the NSA, including industry big hitters like Boeing, the Aerospace Corporation, Perspecta, SAIC/ Leidos, and Booz Allen Hamilton. This close association with industry powered the NRO's technological successes and also created revolving door positions for former or retired NSO employees. Hall became senior vice president of Booz Allen Hamilton after he left the NRO in 2001.[45]

For much of the Cold War the tagline "Freedom's Sentinel" was the NRO's motto. This phrase was often attached to the emblem, pasted on NRO T-shirts, or affixed to official business. By the time the NRO maintained a website, its vision changed to "Supra et Ultra," Above and Beyond. For a historian of science, this motto is reminiscent of the early modern period's motto, "Plus Ultra," affixed to the image of the pillars of Hercules on the ocean. Just as the Cold War was a period of space exploration, so too was the early modern period a time of maritime exploration.

The Octopus Logo

On December 5, 2013, the Office of the Director of National Intelligence announced in a Twitter post that an Atlas 5 rocket would blast off at 11:00

p.m. carrying a classified NRO payload. Attached to the announcement was the patch for the mission, NROL-39 ("L" standing for "launch"). It depicted a globe with an angry octopus latching its tentacles onto the earth. A caption read, "Nothing Is beyond Our Reach."

There was nothing unusual about announcing the mission launch and affixing an image of the patch. The NRO had been announcing their launches for years. After all, it's hard to hide a rocket launch at their Vandenberg, California, launch site. The patch tradition was a continuation and modification of NASA's earlier practice whereby astronauts were allowed to name their mission. After that tradition was discontinued, NASA and the NRO began to allow the mission launch team to create the mission patch, which was also affixed to the rocket itself. The NRO had developed dozens of patches for classified military missions. Many of them were menacing and mysterious. Some depicted wizards, owls, or three-headed dragons. None sparked a public outcry.

But as soon as the octopus-hugging globe was released, the NRO was accused of being "tone deaf." After all, the Snowden revelations in June 2013 about US surveillance had already created public distaste for the US government's global mass surveillance. Even if the NRO was less widely known than its notorious NSA sibling in the intelligence community, a Twitter posting is bound to reach a wide audience.

The cartoon-like logo was no joke. An FOIA request for the developmental material revealed the origin of the motif, its rationale, and its approval. The idea initially arose because a cable called an "octopus harness" malfunctioned while testing the space vehicle. But as the mission team engineers thought about it, the characteristics of the octopus seemed to offer possibilities for representing the mission of the NRO itself. The octopus is an intelligent animal that uses its tentacles to capture its prey in intricate and out-of-the way spaces. Since the NRO thought nothing was beyond its reach, enemies could be reached no matter where they hide. As the mission manager, who thought the patch was "cool" and "really neat," put it in his speech, "The enemy has no where [*sic*] to run[;] . . . the octopus kind of to me represents the idea. . . . We've kind of got our fingers everywhere at any given time."[46]

The patch was approved with all the necessary signatures in February 2012. The only hint that anyone at the office had qualms about the logo is a remark written in blue ink on the approval sheet: "A little Sinister!!"[47]

The National Geospatial-Intelligence Agency

The NGA—that alphabet soup amalgam of previous acronymed agencies, DMA, NPIC, NIMA, and so on—in Springfield, Virginia, attracted media attention when it announced its new building plans. The media rightly focused on the size of the building: it is the third largest federal building in the greater Washington, DC, area, after the Pentagon and the Reagan Building. And like the Pentagon, it was built by the builder of large-scale technologies like dams and canals (and even the Berlin Tunnel), the US Army Corps of Engineers. Despite its size and its newfound importance in the intelligence and military pecking order, very few people have heard of it. When Barack Obama asked a patron at a Five Guys burger restaurant in Washington where he worked, the patron responded, "The NGA," but Obama hadn't heard of it. That was in 2009, before the NGA moved to the super-size campus in Springfield in 2011 that employs sixteen thousand.[48] Even with that number of people working on the campus, the place is shrouded by a veil of mystery and surrounded by its own police force.

Curious about the NGA and its super-sized building, I visited the in-house historian at his office in the Springfield location in summer 2019 and also toured the NGA museum. But before driving from Manassas to Springfield via I-66, I spent hours gazing at the Google Maps image of the building located at the new address and road: 7500 Geoint Drive. Google Maps revealed that a long metallic bunker/hangar-like, funnel-shaped building was adjacent to three large parking lots and had a large pool of water behind it. A Starbucks coffee icon was located right before the funnel-shaped building.

All visitors must enter through the visitor center, a clearinghouse with a security checkpoint, and have a contact with a phone number for pickup. My contact-issued parking pass served as my entry badge. As I waited, the staff thought I was a contractor, and I overheard many contractors checking in. After my contact finally got the phone call, I was picked up and escorted to the main building while passing a historical timeline that stretched along briefing boards on the sidewalk. As we approached the main building, hundreds of trapezoid-shaped windows made their appearance (the NGA fact sheet boasts 1,707 of them). Whenever we passed other people in a corridor or an open space, my escort said, "Uncleared," to warn the open floor plan workers to tone down their classified conversations. It turned out the building with the metallic cone was an enormous atrium with food courts, a hair salon, a Starbucks, and lots of tables scattered around. As I gazed up at the enormity of the space and the opulence, it seemed like a cathedral of intelligence.

Like a new suburban subdivision, the NGA campus built nine miles of new roads and planted new trees that were still immature in 2019. Although it bills itself as a LEEDS building, the campus consumes an enormous amount of energy. It includes a 105,000-square-foot central utility plant and has a cooling pool that resembles a large pond in the back for its systems. The plant produces 31,500 gallons per minute of chilled water; as the NGA fact sheet notes, that's enough to fill up an Olympic-size swimming pool every hour.[49]

The main reason the NGA got so big was that it merged and consolidated other mapping and imagery analysis agencies under one large roof. The evolution of these mergers is marked by an alphabet soup of acronyms: it started when the NPIC became part of NIMA in 1996, along with the DMA. This merger of the NPIC's intelligence-based imagery analysis with the DMA's military defense-based imagery was controversial. The decision was based on five years of debates and studies on how to organize the community's imagery intelligence resources. The bottom line was that the NGA wanted to be to imagery intelligence what the NSA was to signals intelligence. It achieved its goal. By 2013, its budget and buildings matched the NSA's in size. The NGA is one of the big three top-funded spy agencies, with a budget of $4.9 billion in 2013.

Aside from the high cost of building the satellites, the budget for the NGA and the NRO combined illustrates their importance in the intelligence pecking order as well as the appreciation of the technology itself. With the post-9/11 global reach proclaimed by the United States, what better way to monitor the world than with satellite and mapping technology? US intelligence is indeed an octopus with nothing beyond its reach.

Notes

1. *Time* 70 (1957): 18. This oft-repeated quote was originally in a speech.

2. "An Interview with NRO Director Keith Hall," *Studies in Intelligence* 45, no. 4 (2001): 2, https://www.cia.gov/library/readingroom/docs/DOC_0005378209.pdf; and FY 1998–99, Congressional Budget Justification, vol. 4, National Reconnaissance Program, February 1997, executive summary, introd., https://fas.org/irp/nro/fy98/intro.pdf.

During the fortieth anniversary of the NRO in 2001, the NRO historian R.

Cargill Hill subtitled his brief history "Ensuring Global Information Supremacy," and by the fiftieth anniversary in 2011, the NRO historians admitted that the "NRO has become a global organization managing a complex system" conducting "global operations against terrorists." Finally, an undated, more recent brochure (posted on the website in 2019) is titled "Maintaining Global Vigilance" and documents an expansion of tasks to include monitoring the "proliferation of weapons of mass destruction"; tracking "international terrorists, drug traffickers, and criminal organizations"; developing "highly accurate military targeting data"; and supporting "international peacekeeping and humanitarian relief operations" while also assessing "the impact of natural disasters." See the NRO website, www.nro.gov, for declassified documents and its in-house history based on many classified documents. For brochures, see R. Cargill Hall, "The NRO at Forty: Ensuring Global Information Supremacy," 8pp., www.nro.gov/Portals/65/documents/foia/docs/foia-nro-history.pdf; Bruce Berkowitz and Michael Suk, "NRO at 50: A Brief History," 2011, 2018, www.nro.gov/Portals/65/documents/about/50thanniv/The%20NRO%20at%2050%20Years%20-%20A%20Brief%20History%20-%20Second%20Edition.pdf?ver=2019-03-06-141009-113×tamp=1551900924364; and National Reconnaissance Office, "Supra et Ultra," n.d., www.nro.gov/Portals/65/documents/about/nro/NRObrochure.pdf.

3. Burrows, *Deep Black*, 132–34; Arthur Sylvester, Memorandum for the President, White House, Subject: SAMOS II Launch, January 26, 1961; and Director of Central Intelligence, SNIE 100-6-60, "Probable Reactions to US Reconnaissance Satellite Programs," August 9, 1960.

4. Memorandum, Subject: National Reconnaissance Office, Security Information, June 14, 1963, www.cia.gov/library/readingroom/docs/CIA-RDP75B00326R000100230009-1.pdf. For a history of NRO security breaches, see https://nsarchive2.gwu.edu//NSAEBB/NSAEBB257/19740107.pdf. See also Jeffrey Richelson, "Out of the Black: The De-classification of the NRO," Electronic Briefing Book No. 257, https://nsarchive2.gwu.edu//NSAEBB/NSAEBB257/index.htm#dco4.

5. Brugioni, *Eyeball to Eyeball*, 57.

6. Interview with David Doyle, in Dwayne A. Day, John M. Logsdon, and Brian Latell, *Eye in the Sky: The Story of the Corona Spy Satellites* (Washington, DC: Smithsonian Books, 1998), 221.

7. Joint Photographic Intelligence OAK 9009 Report, CIA-RDP78T05693A000300010002-7.pdf.

8. Interview with anonymous source as quoted in Richelson, *Century of Spies*, 297.

9. Joint Mission Coverage Index, Mission 9009, August 18, 1960, reproduced in Kevin C. Ruffner, ed., *CORONA: America's First Satellite Program* (Washington, DC: CIA, Center for the Study of Intelligence, 1995), 115.

10. An untitled historical overview of the NPIC, 1965, including a chart with linear feet of film brought in: "Mission Inputs, Fiscal Years, 1956–1970, CIA-RDP78B05167A001800060001-9."

11. Interview with Dino Brugioni, in Day, Logsdon, and Latell, *Eye in the Sky*, 226.

12. See declassified message, February 3, 1964, CIA-RDP78B04558A0018-00200005-6.

13. Interview with Elaine A. Gifford, in Day, Logsdon, and Latell, *Eye in the Sky*, 201, 210.

14. John Cloud, "Imagining the World in a Barrel: CORONA and the Clandestine Convergence of the Earth Sciences," *Social Studies of Science* 31, no. 2 (April 2001): 233–34.

15. Rachel Lippman, "A First Look at the New Headquarters of the National Geospatial-Intelligence Agency," St. Louis Public Radio, April 9, 2019. For timeline, see 181002-041_HistoryTimeline_STL_02_H.pdf.

16. Frederic Oder, *The Hexagon Story* (Chantilly, VA: Center for the Study of National Reconnaissance, 2012), 65, 165.

17. On Smith and Boyle, see, e.g., https://spectrum.ieee.org/consumer-electronics/gadgets/nobel-goes-to-boyle-and-smith-for-ccd-camera-chip.

18. The Carter description is based on Burrows, *Deep Black*, 226; and Richelson, *Wizards of Langley*, 198–202.

19. Burrows, *Deep Black*, 250–51, interview with Jerry Nelson.

20. National Photographic Interpretation Center, "Antecedents and Early Years," vol. 1, 1952–56, NPIC, December 1972, 47, www.cia.gov/library/readingroom/docs/CIA-RDP04T00184R000400070001-5.pdf; and Brugioni, *Eyeball to Eyeball*, 22. On the OBE, see Dino A. Brugioni and Robert F. McCort, "British Honors for Lundahl," www.cia.gov/library/center-for-the-study-of-intelligence/kent-csi/vol19no1/html/v19i1a02p_0001.htm.

21. See "National Photographic Interpretation Center: The Years of Project HTAUTOMAT, 1956–1958," vols. 1–6, December 1974, CIA History Staff. CREST, CIA-RDP04T00184R00040001000101; and Robert Wallace, H. Keith Melton, and Henry R. Schlesinger, *Spy Sites of Washington, DC: A Guide to the Capital Region's Secret History* (Washington, DC: Georgetown University Press, 2017), 164.

22. For these figures, see Jack O'Connor, *Seeing the Secrets and Growing the Leaders: A Cultural History of the National Photographic Interpretation Center* (Alexandria, VA: Acumensa Solutions, 2015).

23. Brugioni, *Eyeball to Eyeball*, 190–91.

24. An NPIC history writes that Building 213 was 400,000 square feet. See "Historical Development" slide, National Photographic Interpretation Center, CREST, CIA-RPD78B05167A001900300001-1. O'Connor. *Seeing the Secrets*, 56, writes that the building was 200,000 square feet.

25. Quote in Wallace, Melton, and Schlesinger, *Spy Sites of Washington, DC*, 164. For the voluminous take from satellites and the "collection revolution," see also Warner, *Rise and Fall of Intelligence*, 152, 156–64.

26. Warner, *The Rise and Fall of Intelligence.*

27. Jack O'Connor kindly contacted several former NPIC employees, none of whom knew what "OAK" meant other than being a code word.

28. These comments are based on a survey of hundreds of NPIC reports available in the CREST database: https://www.cia.gov/library/readingroom/home.

29. O'Connor, *Seeing the Secrets*, 65.

30. O'Connor.

31. O'Connor, 66–67.

32. O'Connor.

33. O'Connor, 96.

34. O'Connor, 86–87.

35. O'Connor, 95–96.

36. Burrows. *Deep Black*, 201.

37. "NRO Headquarters Project," *Hearing before the Select Committee on Intelligence of the United States Senate. One Hundred Third Congress. Second Session on NRO Headquarters Project*, Wednesday, August 10, 1994 (Washington, DC: Government Printing Office, 1995).

38. "NRO Headquarters Project," 26–28.

39. FY2013, Congressional Budget Justification, vol. 1, National Intelligence Program Summary, February 2012, https://snowdenarchive.cjfe.org/greenstone/collect/snowden1/index/assoc/HASH0134/c54a5abd.dir/doc.pdf.

40. R. Cargill Hall, "The NRO Emblem: Its Heritage and Evolution," *Space Sentinel* (Spring 2004). I would like to thank Hall for providing me with a copy of this short article.

41. Hall; and Patrick D. Widlake, "The National Reconnaissance Office (NRO) Organizational Seal, Research Note," January 18, 2018, www.nro.gov/Portals/65/documents/history/csnr/articles/docs/CSNR%20Research%20Note%20NRO%20Organizational%20Seal.pdf?ver=2019-02-28-154911-103×tamp=1551466015187.

42. Director of Central Intelligence, Congressional Budget Justification, Fiscal Year 1998–1999, vol. 4, National Reconnaissance Program, February 1997. The name of the author of the preface is redacted. Presumably it was Keith R. Hall as he was acting NRO director at the time. Quotes from introduction. Redacted document available at https://fas.org/irp/nro/fy98/index.html.

43. Editor's biographical note to "An Interview with NRO Director Keith Hall," *Studies in Intelligence* 45, no. 4 (2001): 1.

44. Editor's biographical note.

45. "Lifeblood for the NRO," from "An Interview with NRO Director Keith Hall." Google Maps image: www.google.com/maps/place/National+Reconnaissance+Office+Headquarters/@38.8819391,-77.4552933,726m/data=!3m1!1e3!4m5!3m4!1s0x89b6441908712e8b:0xb195dd4ed61c2545!8m2!3d38.8819475!4d-77.4509059.

46. Transcript of Mission Manager Speech in a fifteen-page file on the NRO logo provided to Ms. Runa Sandvik, Muckrock News, NRO, FOIA Case F14-0023, available at www.muckrock.com/foi/united-states-of-america-10/records-concerning-the -nrol-39-logo-9834/#file-23016. See also

the story by J. Pat Brown, "How an Engineering In-Joke Led to a Spy Satellite's World-Eating Octopus Logo," Muckrock News, January 19, 2016, https://www.muckrock.com/news/archives/2016/jan/19/octopus-NRO. For the Twitter post, see https://twitter.com/ODNIgov/status/408712553179533312 ?ref_src= twsrc%5Etfw%7Ctwcamp%5Etweetembed%7Ctwterm%5E4087125 531795333 12&ref_url=; and for an image of the rocket with the emblem attached, https://twitter.com/ODNIgov/status/408715995008598016/photo/1.

47. See citations in note 46. For other articles on the octopus logo, see J. Pat Brown, "The Story Behind the Comically Villainous Octopus Logo of U.S. Spy Agency," *Atlas Obscura*, January 20, 2016, www.atlasobscura.com/articles/the-story-behind-the-comically-villainous-octopus-logo-of-us-spy-agency; and Kashmir Hill, "U.S. Spy Rocket Has Octopus-Themed 'Nothing Is beyond Our Reach' Logo. Seriously," *Forbes*, December 5, 2013, www.forbes.com/sites/kashmirhill/2013/12/05/u-s-spy-rocket-launching-today-has-octopus-themed-nothing-is-beyond-our-reach-logo-seriously/#5b97ba3d6869.

48. James Bamford, "The Multibillion-Dollar U.S. Spy Agency You Haven't Heard Of," *Foreign Policy*, 2017, https://foreignpolicy.com/2017/03/20/the-multibillion-dollar-u-s-spy-agency-you-havent-heard-of-trum.

49. See Clark Construction's description of the project, "NGA Campus East: Supporting Our Nation's Military Forces," https://www.clarkconstruction.com/our-work/projects/nga-campus-east; and "National Geospatial-Intelligence Agency: Know the Earth . . . Show the Way . . . Understand the World," NGA Fact Sheet, www.nga.mil.

10

A GLOBAL KILLING MACHINE

A buzzing sound hovers in the desert sky. It has intruded into the Yemen skies before, but this time is different. It is too late for Qaed Salim Sinan al-Harethi and his five male companions in the Toyota Land Cruiser traveling on a dusty desert road in Ma'rib, a remote province, on Sunday, November 3, 2002. Al-Harethi made the mistake of using one of his five cellphones to make a call while he was bouncing around in the backseat of the white jeep. As soon as he did, an alarm went off in Room 3E132 at the National Security Agency's headquarters in Fort Meade, Maryland. Al-Harethi was a high-priority target for US intelligence; he was wanted for planning the deadly attack on the USS *Cole* two years earlier and was suspected of being an al-Qaeda operative. As a result, any time al-Harethi used one of the five phones with changing cards and numbers, an alarm went off. When an analyst compared tapes of his voice with the six-second call, he shouted, "He's in the backseat, and he's giving the driver directions!"[1]

As soon as the NSA analysts identified al-Harethi, they contacted the Central Intelligence Agency's Counterterrorism Center (CTC) team in Langley; the CIA was ready for this day. It had recently stationed a fleet of armed Predator drones south of Yemen across the Red Sea in Djibouti, Africa. Within minutes, staff in the CTC operations room alerted pilots to launch a drone to Ma'rib. And within minutes, staff members at the center, an open space of "pure frenetic energy,"[2] were watching a video feed of the car crawling across the desert. Once they verified that it was the right target, they gave the pilot in a trailer, who was remotely operating the drone, on the CIA campus an order to launch the Hellfire missile at the jeep. For a few seconds the video image disappeared as the plane swayed from the missile ejection. Once the plane steadied, CIA officials could see an incinerated jeep with six dead men in it. Body parts were everywhere. Investigators could identify al-Harethi from a mark on a dismembered leg. It was the first time ever that the CIA had the power to direct its own armed drone to kill people in a country with which the United States was not at war.[3]

It had not been an easy decision for the CIA to get into the high-tech targeted killing business. Ever since its founding, it was considered a civilian agency tasked with collecting intelligence to protect national security. This doesn't mean the agency never assassinated foreign leaders or used drones. It actually had been using drones as reconnaissance planes ever since they were developed. And before assassinations were forbidden in Gerald Ford's executive order in 1976, the CIA had attempted to assassinate foreign leaders but not using armed drones. However, it is not widely known that the CIA had developed its own reconnaissance drone as early as the 1960s. Before turning to the story of how and why the agency became a global paramilitary organization through its use of armed drones, let's turn back to the 1960s.

TAGBOARD

When the U-2 spy plane was deployed during the 1962 Cuban Missile Crisis, its days were numbered. Despite successes in reconnaissance photography, the plane had been shot down too many times. When a Soviet missile hit Gary Powers's U-2 on May 1, 1960, he ejected from the plane, tumbled out of the sky, and landed on Soviet territory. Eisenhower was devastated; his worst nightmare had become a reality. Nikita Khrushchev canceled the Geneva Summit, damaging US-Soviet relations. Khrushchev used the incident to accuse America of brazen spying, and he had proof in the form of a living pilot caught in the act.

The CIA, however, knew that U-2 spy plane overflights wouldn't last forever. Fortuitously, they had also been exploring satellite reconnaissance, and it just so happened that one of the first successful spy satellites, code-named Corona, launched in August 1960, three months after the Powers incident.

But there was another less well-known project that was a response to the U-2 incident. The CIA and the Department of Defense worked on developing a remotely piloted plane, a drone. According to recently declassified documents, Eugene Fubini, from the Department of Defense's Office of Research and Development, was talking to Kelly Johnson, the maverick U-2 spy plane developer who ran Lockheed Martin's Skunk Works in Burbank, California, in early 1962. Fubini wondered whether Johnson could develop a "pilotless" version of the supersonic spy plane A-12 (code-named Oxcart) he was working on at the time. Fubini was worried about the "international repercussions" of the U-2 incident and the fact that there was a "live pilot whose story proved . . . more politically damaging than the same mission would have provoked had the U-2 been . . . a drone aircraft." Although Johnson was initially reluctant to pursue such a plane, he said it was feasible, and it didn't take long before the drone project was under way.[4]

But like the squabbles surrounding the U-2 spy plane and reconnaissance satellites, the air force and the CIA immediately started fighting about who would maintain operational and technical control of the new drone project. The CIA thought it was the appropriate place to manage the drone project because the Oxcart was already in its bailiwick; the air force would only add operational and technical layers to the project. Besides, the CIA's Herbert Scoville argued that the secret project would then become public, and the CIA was the appropriate project manager to help maintain secrecy. But the other elephant in the room was the fact that the air force wanted to attach a bomb to the drone. At this point, arming a drone was out of the question for the CIA. The CIA's main interest was using it as a reconnaissance plane to gather intelligence. Scoville cautioned the NRO, now responsible for coordinating such efforts, that the drone could not carry more than 250 pounds of weight in any case.[5]

Although Kelly Johnson was initially reluctant to develop and manufacture drones, there were others at the Skunk Works who were fascinated by them. Engineers like Ben Rich lobbied him and jumped at the chance to attack the engineering problems of using the supersonic A-12 (Oxcart) as a mother ship on which the drone would be attached and then launched from. Rich thought it was a "pragmatic solution" for spying over enemy territory without the "political embarrassment" of a Gary Powers–type incident. Powers's plane was not the only U-2 spy plane to be shot down. Four Taiwanese U-2 planes were shot down over China, a prime US target. And during the last day of the Cuban Missile Crisis, Rudolf Anderson's U-2 was shot down and he died.[6]

The idea was to "piggyback" the drone, a dark gray, manta ray triangle shape, on top of an Oxcart-A-12 (the CIA version of the supersonic plane) or the Blackbird SR-71 (the air force version), both of which flew at a speed of Mach 3, or three times the speed of sound, about 2,301 miles per hour. The daughter ship (D-21, for "daughter") would then launch from the mother ship (M-21) with a camera attached to it, take the pictures, and drop the film package with a parachute, which would be picked up by a Hercules C-130. The drone would then self-destruct. It sounds like a science fiction story or an episode from *Star Wars* or the *Mission Impossible* films, but it was actually tried out numerous times. The Skunk Works built fifty drones at a cost of $31 million under contract with the CIA and with operational and funding support from the air force by the time the project ended in 1971.[7]

Even though the drone had no pilot, the mother ship had two human pilots in the cockpit. And that's where the beginning of the end came. As we've seen in other chapters in this book, technology rarely runs itself. On July 30, 1966, Bill Park, a pilot, and Ray Torick, the launch operator, climbed into a Blackbird SR-71 and flew over Point Mugu, north of Los Angeles.

As one can imagine, launching a piggybacked drone from a supersonic airplane is a very dangerous and tricky maneuver. Johnson was worried that the drone could fly out of control and land on a major city like Los Angeles. But what happened after three successful test launches became one of his worst nightmares. As Park and Torick reached the right altitude, they launched the drone while flying at Mach 3.2. The drone crashed into the main body of the Blackbird. The mother ship spun wildly out of control. Remarkably, both pilots kept their cool and ejected while their pressure suits were still inflated. Park landed in the water, and colleagues picked him up in a life raft in the middle of the ocean. Torick wasn't as lucky. According to Rich, he opened the visor of the suit helmet and water flooded into his pressure suit. He "sank like a stone."[8] Former International Spy Museum historian, Vince Houghton, is skeptical of that explanation. He thinks there could have been other reasons for the death of such a fit airman; he could have been hit by shrapnel from the plane, for instance, he writes in a more recent book. But as Houghton rightly points out, we might never know for sure.[9]

The death of Ray Torick on July 30, 1966, marked the end of the Tagboard project for the CIA. Johnson was so upset about the accident that he canceled the project and gave the money back to the CIA and the air force. This did not deter the air force, however. It continued the idea and started launching drones from the under the wings of a subsonic, sluggish B-52 bomber. Cyrus Vance, Lyndon B. Johnson's deputy defense secretary, supported the B-52 drone program and echoed the sentiment that he did not want a "Francis Gary Powers situation to develop." All overflights over denied territories were to be conducted with "satellites or drones."[10]

Aquiline

Meanwhile, the CIA was experimenting with a low-tech version of an unmanned reconnaissance plane in its own Office of Research Development's Applied Physics Division. The project was code-named Aquiline. David L. Christ, head of the division, and Frank Briglia worked on an eagle-sized, inexpensive plane that could carry photographic, nuclear sensing, and electronic intelligence–collection equipment. Briglia brought the concept to Douglas Aircraft Corporation, and the company developed a prototype. The plane weighed only 105 pounds, had a wingspan of 8.5 feet, and was powered by a 3.5 horsepower engine, initially developed for chainsaws, driving the two-bladed propeller.

Needless to say, it was hard to see and retrieve an object the size of an eagle. As a result, it was painted bright orange, but it was still hard to find. In addition, when the eagle drone flew into the recovery net near the ground, a wing or propeller usually broke. It would have cost another $35 million to turn it into a workable long-range reconnaissance plane. The CIA canceled the project in 1971.[11]

This did not deter a CIA employee from buying a twin-engine model plane set and attaching a TV camera to its belly. The C-130 controlled and picked up this unmanned plane, which took photographs at three feet from an object. At some point the CIA gave this technology to the army and they used it in their own Aquila RPV (remotely piloted vehicle) project.[12]

Fly like an Eagle

It's not clear how much institutional memory the CIA retains of the Tagboard episode and Project Aquiline. There is a big gap in the declassified CIA historical record between 1971, when those programs ended, and

1986, when Duane "Dewey" R. Clarridge, the newly minted CIA CTC director, started discussing using unmanned aircraft in the fight against terrorism. Even if CIA officials and staff didn't remember the CIA's previous efforts to develop and deploy an unarmed drone, the idea of drones has captivated both the public imagination and that of government officials since at least World War I. Not only that, but the military had used drones for quite some time, most notably in the Vietnam War. And on a smaller scale, as early as 1962, the US Air Force flew Fire Fly drones over Cuba during the Cuban Missile Crisis. But when the Aquiline project was transferred to the army under the code name Aquila RPV, this represented a shift to a military organization, not a civilian one.[13]

Clarridge, a cigar-chomping, swashbuckling CIA officer, had been appointed director of the new CTC by DCI William Casey after a spate of terrorist attacks in the 1980s. In 1985 alone, Americans viewed the gory details of terrorist attacks on network television. From the June terrorist hijacking of TWA flight 847 in Beirut, Lebanon, to the hijacked cruise ship *Achille Lauro* by a Palestinian terrorist where a Jewish American tourist was murdered and dumped overboard, to nineteen passengers killed at El Al ticket counters in Vienna and Rome by Palestinian gunmen, Americans were scared into canceling travel plans.[14]

Terrorism had become a global threat, and Clarridge designed the center to meet the new transnational challenge. He thought the CIA's geographically defined directorates were ill-prepared to deal with international terrorism, especially stateless Palestinians. Clarridge thought terrorism "never fits one particular piece of real estate. It is effective precisely because it spreads all over the map." As a result, he proposed a new interdepartmental center at the CIA with a global reach, a "fusion center" that would transcend the CIA's geographic boundaries. The center would include analysts from the Directorate of Intelligence and tinkerers from the Directorate of Science and Technology within the Directorate of Operations where it was located.[15]

Clarridge was an advocate of the "RadioShack" approach to using technology in operations, in particular, in countries where "electricity and flush toilets were luxuries." He couldn't wait for a "five-year development cycle for high-tech gadgets." Instead, he thought tinkerers could modify off-the-shelf technology for use within a year.[16]

On April 5, 1986, Libyan agents bombed La Belle, a West Berlin discotheque frequented by US servicemen. Two American serviceman and a

Turkish woman died, and 229 people were injured. Clarridge knew that Libya's Muammar Qaddafi was the mastermind behind the bombing because the NSA had intercepted messages from the East Berlin People's Bureau (presumably the Libyan Intelligence Bureau) to Tripoli, Libya, including one after the attack that stated that "an event" had occurred.[17]

The CIA and other agencies wanted revenge and opted for a military strike against Qaddafi. This desire was more difficult to execute than they thought. The idea was to launch a cruise missile from a submarine to hit the Libyan Intelligence Bureau building in downtown Tripoli. But the cruise missile without a nuclear warhead couldn't target one building accurately without causing serious collateral damage. Instead they opted for military targets.[18]

This event sparked Clarridge to think about more precise ways to attack enemies. He asked his CIA boss, Casey, why it was that the president authorized the military to undertake expensive air attacks with high collateral damage instead of just approving a "bullet to the head."[19]

After the La Belle disco bombing, Clarridge told Casey about an idea the CTC was working on. They brought their RadioShack approach to research and development to the problem and in just over a year had tested a "device" that would result in a "minimal loss of life for the recipients" and none for the United States. With financial help from Charlie Hawkins, then a deputy assistant secretary of defense, they had five operational "devices" at a cost of less than $8 million.[20]

Clarridge was less cryptic about this "device" in an interview with the journalist Steve Coll conducted shortly after 9/11, in December. He dubbed the highly classified effort to work on this "device"—a drone—the "Eagle Program." The drone was equipped with an infrared camera, intercept equipment, and wooden propellers. If he had used this in Libya, he would have loaded it with "two hundred pounds of C-4 plastic explosives and one hundred pounds of ball bearings." He also tried attaching small rockets to the drone to fire at targets. Clarridge's goal was to use this technology to assassinate terrorists—the "bullet in the head" fired remotely.[21]

The Predator Is Born

Terrorist attacks continued, but when Clarridge and other "hardliners" in the Reagan administration were forced to resign in 1987 because of their participation in the Iran-Contra affair, the new leaders adopted a "safer," more "bureaucratic" approach to battling terrorism. According to Christopher Fuller, "Clarridge's war-room vision" was "replaced with the cautious, analytic, report-writing culture" that William Casey and Clarridge had wanted to move away from.[22] Discussions about an in-house drone at the CIA disappeared.

This did not mean that other governmental agencies did not pursue drone technology. In fact, the Defense Advanced Research Project Agency (DARPA), sometimes called the "Pentagon's Brain," and a hotbed of innovative technology, was working on a drone that could loiter over an object for a long time—an endurance unmanned aerial vehicle—during the 1980s. The aeronautical engineer who was the brain behind the development of this drone was Abraham "Abe" Karem, an Israeli engineer who had immigrated to California and opened his own company. DARPA contracted Karem's company to build several endurance UAVs. Although Karem successfully built a drone that could loiter for thirty hours called "Amber," his company went bankrupt, and DARPA canceled the contract. Karem then sold Amber to a California defense contractor, General Atomics.[23]

That was the technical part of the drone story. But interest in using drone technology was frequently sparked by a political crisis. In 1992, Yugoslavia broke up into several different states. This newfound independence among former provinces and republics activated repressed hostility among Croats, Muslims, and Serbs and other ethnic minorities. The resulting civil war led to one hundred thousand casualties. Ethnic cleansing forced entire towns to evacuate and created millions of refugees. The Serbs tried to carve out their own territory in Bosnia, and their military laid siege to the capital, Sarajevo. After the Serbs shelled Sarajevo for many months, the United Nations intervened by sending peacekeeping troops; they declared a no-fly zone over the airport in order to deliver much-needed aid, but this didn't deter the fierce Serbians from shooting UN troops as well.[24]

Bill Clinton, who was now president, wanted to know more about what was happening in Bosnia in order to break the Serbian blockade. Intelligence agencies and the military had a hard time viewing the country using the manned U-2 spy plane or satellite imagery. There was too much cloud cover over Bosnia to view Serbian activity. Satellites also only flew over territory for several minutes a day, not enough time to get telling imagery on the rare days there were no clouds. And the United States was reluctant to use the U-2 spy plane because the pilot and the plane might get shot down.[25]

When the CIA heard about Clinton's complaint, R. James Woolsey, the new DCI, thought unmanned aerial vehicles that could loiter under cloud cover would be the perfect solution. In fact, his staff used to quip, "Whatever the problem, Woolsey thinks a UAV is the solution." Woolsey, then a balding, fifty-one-year-old, seasoned Washingtonian who had worked in the Defense Department, contacted Karem, who had impressed him as a maverick with new ideas when they worked on a missile project together.[26]

The CIA was interested in buying a couple of the drones, called the GNAT 750. In March 1993, it sent Thomas A. Twetten, CIA deputy director for operations, to the sun-drenched El Mirage Airfield near Adelanto, California, to see a drone in action. Twetten was "shocked at how loud the drone was, the engine buzzed like an untuned lawn mower." He asked the team to put a silencer on it. He was impressed, though, that it could loiter for forty hours on one tank of gas and could carry one hundred pounds of cameras and sensors. The only other limitation was that it was controlled by radio, line of sight.[27]

Work on the GNAT drone proceeded quickly. Karem was hired by General Atomics, and together with the CIA they developed an endurance surveillance drone that could loiter over Bosnia while Woolsey watched the video imagery from his office in Langley. The CIA eventually partnered with the Department of Defense, and the GNAT transitioned to the Defense Department UAV program office. General Atomics also succeeded in developing a satellite communications link between the plane and the ground control station while increasing its range and payload. With these improvements, the team decided on a new name for the drone: the Predator.[28]

After the Bosnia experience, there were debates between the CIA and the air force about how to use the Predator. The CIA argued that the drone should be used only as a reconnaissance aircraft to verify human reporting on the ground with concrete images, while the air force saw the potential to use the Predator to launch missiles as part of the "kill chain."[29]

These debates were strikingly similar to discussions between the CIA and the Pentagon during the 1950s. While the CIA embraced the flimsy, glider-like U-2 spy plane, the DoD rejected it because Gen. Curtis LeMay wasn't interested in any plane he couldn't drop a bomb out of (see chap. 1).

HUMINT and TECHINT in the War on Terror

By the end of the 1990s, terrorism had emerged again in a more insidious form than before: Osama bin Laden's activities as a financier of terrorist attacks had come to light. After two US embassy bombings in East Africa in 1998, other attacks on Americans followed, including the December 2000 attack on the USS *Cole*. In February and May 1999, CIA human intelligence sources had reported on bin Laden's presence at places cruise missiles could strike, but the CIA could not verify the information and did not act.

By this time, the debates in Washington about how to use the Predator remained unresolved. Until bin Laden appeared, that is. By summer 2000, officials started to think about how they could use the drone in their hunt for bin Laden. This transformed the debate into one about whether spy agencies should use more technology or recruit more human agents. One problem for the CIA was that technology cost a lot of money. Although the drone price tag of $3 million was cheap for the Pentagon's inflated weapons budget, the CIA couldn't afford to lose one.

But more important, the high-tech quick-fix solution minimized the CIA's prized human sources. Thomas Pickering, an influential undersecretary of state, worried that the intelligence community had a "built-in bias" for "a near-term technical solution, rather than the long-term buildup" of human agents. Jim Pavitt, CIA's deputy director of operations, shared this worry and was a strong proponent of human intelligence collection. He was concerned that money used to buy Predators would be taken from his own operations budget for HUMINT. Richard Clarke, the counterterrorism coordinator in the White House's National Security Council, who became a strong proponent of using an armed drone, replied to Pavitt's concern with his usual bluntness: "Your valuable HUMINT program hasn't worked for years. I want to try something else." Cofer Black, the new hardliner Counterterrorism Center director, agreed with Clarke, though he didn't want to tell Pavitt. Ultimately, Clarke asked Sandy Berger, White House national security adviser, to order that the Predator fly over Afghanistan.[30]

But before the CIA was on board with the decision, Charlie Allen, a "respected and resented" assistant director for collection, who worked impossible hours, convened a meeting at CIA headquarters on Memorial

Day 2000. He called air force general John A. Gordon away from a Memorial Day picnic to meet at a conference room on the seventh floor to settle the matter. The debate lasted three hours, from 10:00 a.m. to 1:00 p.m. Allen and Pavitt were at odds, but in the end the CIA authorized the unarmed Predator flights over Afghanistan, an operation dubbed "Afghan Eyes."[31]

Stalking Osama bin Laden

On Wednesday, September 27, 2000, a Predator drone took off from an American base in Uzbekistan and flew south toward Kandahar, Afghanistan, looking for Osama bin Laden's compound, Tarnak Farms. Air force captain Scott Swanson was flying the plane remotely from the ground control station (GCS) at the US Air Force Base in Ramstein, Germany; the sensor operator, Jeff Guay, who sat next to him, pointed the camera. This was their seventh flight as part of the summer project to find Osama bin Laden.[32]

As a result, Swanson and Guay were familiar with the farm compound the Taliban had provided to bin Laden, his family, and his followers. It was a typical Afghan village. Mud-brick buildings sat behind tall walls, and from the vantage of the drone hovering about fifteen thousand feet up, it looked like a huge maze to Swanson. They had both viewed it on several of the previous six flights, but their knowledge was augmented by the CIA's annotated satellite pictures and a schedule of prayer times. They were hoping the Muslims might gather for prayer, and this would provide an opportunity to photograph bin Laden.[33]

Shortly before noon, a tall man in flowing white robes walked out of a house. He was met by shorter people in dark clothing, and they gathered in a courtyard; the group surrounded him. The predator teams could also see an SUV and two trucks they thought carried security officers. There was no doubt in Swanson's mind that the tall man in white was bin Laden. Not only was he leaving his house, but the CIA had told Swanson he was 6 feet 5 inches tall. "Yeah, that's definitely the dude," he said to Guay.[34]

Swanson assumed that the bin Laden sighting would prompt orders from his superiors to launch cruise missiles from a submarine or ship located in the Arabian Sea. He kept the drone circling with its eyes on the target. But as time passed, bin Laden went back inside. The CIA wanted to keep bin Laden under surveillance, but the air force overruled the CIA and had the remote operators point the drone and camera to the Kandahar Airport, where they had seen a MiG-21 fighter plane. Although the team now had a seminal video, no cruise missiles headed toward bin Laden and his entourage that day.[35]

Charlie Allen showed the bin Laden video to George Tenet, the CIA's director, who thought the ability to see and capture him on screen was "technologically dazzling," but Tenet was frustrated because they "were not in a position to do anything about it."[36] Although Tenet had been skeptical about the Predator, the video turned him into a "convert." He carried a copy of the tape around the Hill and played it for Sandy Berger and Bill Clinton in the White House.[37] By the end of that summer the drone had caught bin Laden on camera three times.

Unsurprisingly, Clarke thought the drone camera should somehow be linked to the cruise missiles mounted on submarines in the Arabian Sea. He thought they should go for a "see it/shoot it" option. Cofer Black took this idea one step further and advocated arming the Predator itself with a surface-to-air missile to kill bin Laden if they saw him.[38] But there were still technological and legal hurdles to leap over. Besides, the CIA and the air force had to work out their budgetary squabbles.

A Hell of a Killing Machine

To air force general John P. Jumper, arming the Predator seemed like the "next logical step." When he was commander for the US Air Force in Europe, he learned that the Predator carried a laser designator along with the camera that could pinpoint targets. With this information, manned aircraft could then fire more precisely; the Predator had helped locate targets in Kosovo but did not fire at them. That is why it was the "next logical step." Instead of using two separate machines to locate and fire on targets, they could simply deploy an armed Predator.[39]

Tenet had felt frustrated that the CIA could see bin Laden on video during the summer project but couldn't do anything about it. In December 2000, Clarke came up with a solution. In a secret report on al-Qaeda he wrote, "The Spring flights may be able to incorporate a new capability: Hellfire anti-tank missiles mounted aboard the Predators," a "new capability" that "would permit a 'see it/shoot it' option."[40] He had embraced Jumper's idea. This didn't mean he could convince the CIA.

By January 23, 2001, the air force had conducted a successful "static" launch of a Hellfire missile from the Predator, three days after Clinton finished his term as president. About a month later, in February, the first successful airborne fire test worked, and this prompted changing the name of the Predator from RQ-1, a reconnaissance plane, to MQ-1, "M" meaning "multipurpose." By June 2001, the air force had a mock-up bin Laden village in Nevada that pilots successfully targeted.[41]

Instead of approaching human intelligence proponents like Pavitt to tell them about the new capabilities, Clarke contacted Charlie Allen, the CIA's deputy for operations, someone he had known for years who would embrace his point of view. This contact soon led to a meeting between air force officials and the CIA at CIA headquarters in Langley as well as divisions between proponents of an armed drone and detractors who simply wanted to use the plane for reconnaissance missions.

A debate about whether to use an armed version of the Predator dominated the summer of 2001. While Charlie Allen and Cofer Black liked the idea of an armed drone, Tenet, as DCI, questioned whether the CIA should operate an armed drone instead of the military. The fundamental question was, who should fire the shot? Allen said he would "be happy to pull the trigger," but Tenet was "appalled" and thought it was not appropriate. He told Allen he had no authority to do it, nor did he. And Pavitt was against an armed drone because it put his human sources at risk.[42] But all agreed that they would not launch a Hellfire missile against bin Laden unless there was HUMINT to confirm his location.[43]

CIA officials who opposed arming the Predator and killing bin Laden also thought it violated President Ford's assassination ban of 1976, a ban that had grown out of searing criticism of CIA tactics during the 1970s. Both Carter and Reagan had renewed the ban. After the African embassy bombings in 1998, Clinton gave the CIA authority to kill bin Laden but not specifically with an armed drone.

Another issue was financial. Who would pay for the drone if it crashed? To the air force, the CIA were spoiled children who wanted them to pay for the expensive toys. This did not remain an abstract discussion. When a plane crashed the CIA refused to pay for it, despite a bill from the air force.

As the technology for operating the drone became global, it actually became technically possible for the CIA to "pull the trigger" from its own campus. As noted earlier, the drone was initially operated by line-of-sight radio signals. By summer 2001, air force techno-scientists had made it possible to operate the drone by bouncing radio waves off satellites. All that was needed was a ground control station and access to satellite bandwidth. One could now fire the Hellfire missile and operate the Predator from halfway across the world using a remote split.

At the same time, the CIA began to scout an area on their campus to place a ground control station and a double-wide mobile home to house air force operators in case George W. Bush and the National Security Council decided to arm drones. By having the technology on campus, they could also operate a surveillance drone. On Labor Day weekend, a trailer from Ramstein, Germany, arrived and was brought to the CIA campus. Since it was a camouflage color, CIA staff picked up a couple hundred gallons of paint from Home Depot and spent the weekend painting the trailer white.[44]

At a National Security Council principals' meeting on September 4, 2001, in the White House Situation Room (Condoleezza Rice, Donald Rumsfeld, Tenet, and others), the discussion was dominated by the question of whether the president should approve their request to fly a weaponized Predator. The issue remained moot in any case because the Predator wasn't ready to launch a missile yet. Even so, Tenet thought the question of whether the military or the CIA should operate an airplane firing at US enemies, once it was ready, was crucial.[45]

One week later, planes slammed into the World Trade Center, into a Pennsylvania field, and into the Pentagon, killing over three thousand Americans. The decision to arm the Predator with Hellfire missiles became a lot easier. On September 17, 2001, Bush signed a Memorandum of Notification approving the NSC's recommendation to authorize an armed drone. Less than a month later, on October 7, Scott Swanson, an air force pilot, flew the CIA's first armed Predator remotely over Afghanistan from one of the trailers parked near the CIA's water tower. He fired a Hellfire missile at a pickup truck in which the CIA thought Mullah Omar, the Taliban's supreme commander, was sitting. He wasn't there. Instead, the missile killed two other men thought to be bodyguards.[46]

A High-Tech Global Network

Scott Swanson's first shot marked the beginning of a long global war on terror using armed drones by the CIA. This was the first time in history that a civilian intelligence agency carried out a military mission with a high-tech weapon to kill people the United States was not at war with.

It was also the first time in history that the CIA had the capability to act as a high-tech sniper from halfway across the globe. A pilot from Creech Air Force Base in Nevada could remotely kill a terrorist thousands of miles away through a high-tech kill chain spanning the globe. It was like a remotely fired version of Clarridge's "bullet in the head" with collateral damage.

Drone bases also began to dot the globe. According to an analysis conducted by Tom Dispatch, there were at least sixty drone bases operated by the US military and the CIA around the world by 2012. These new bases were usually in addition to the one thousand US military bases that already covered the globe because the drone bases had to be near target countries in the Middle East, Pakistan, and Africa. According to Nick Turse, the drone bases were the "latest development in a long-evolving saga of American power projection abroad."[47]

In the absence of US colonies, US historians often refer to the world-straddling military bases as "power projection." But the developments could also be seen as a form of colonialism or modern imperialism. As Daniel Immerwahr has noted in his book *How to Hide an Empire*, after World War II, the notion of colonialism was frowned on. As a result, the United States developed a new source of influence that did not involve colonies. Military bases were one way to extend influence abroad without formal empire.[48]

As discussed in chapter 7, the British had traded or leased some of their acquired imperial territory to the United States in exchange for technology. The drone bases were an addition to the NSA's listening stations, satellite ground control stations, and underwater fiber optic cables.

According to several news stories, some 165 people were involved in the steps it takes to launch a missile from the Predator drone and fifteen more for the deadlier Reaper drone. The pilots operating the joystick in trailers have received the most media attention; however, the largest number of people in the system are stationed at the US bases in places like Djibouti, Niger, Ethiopia, Turkey, Afghanistan, Saudi Arabia, Uzbekistan, the Seychelles, and Sicily, to name some of the most important. According to Hugh Gusterson, there are approximately seventy contractors, maintenance technicians, and pilots at the bases who maintain, fly, and land the planes at the base airports near the targets.[49]

Creech Air Force Base in Nevada and the US Air Force Base in Ramstein, Germany, are the hubs for the global high-tech kill chain. Once the pilots in the shipping-container-sized metal boxes in Nevada receive an order from Washington, Fort Meade, or Langley, the sensor operator contacts the crew at the bases who launch the drones. Once the drone is airborne, the Creech operator tilts the joystick on the operations console while tracking a target over seven thousand miles away in the Middle East, Afghanistan, or North Waziristan on the video screen. The CIA can also watch live feed in Langley and order the pilot to alter the angle or focus—what has come to be called the "unblinking stare" of the drone's sensor ball. Then the order comes to release the Hellfire missile attached to the drone.

Once the electronic pulse exits the shipping container, it travels along a fiber optic cable across the Nevada desert, over the continental United States, under the Atlantic Ocean, and over Western Europe to the relay station at Ramstein Air Force Base. The tiny packets of data are streamed to a satellite orbiting at some twenty thousand miles above the earth. This signal then bounces down to the bulbous nose of the Predator drone flying over the target. The reverse process takes place once the drone captures the image and beams it back to the United States, with a latency period of a few seconds. Once the drone drops the missile, it sways from the thrust of the missile and the image pixilates. Once the image is restored, the senior operator can view and hover over the damage caused by the missile to assess the damage.[50]

The Role of Human Agents

By 2009, the CIA had killed numerous al-Qaeda and Taliban leaders and militants, but there had been a large number of civilian deaths as well, sparking an outcry from family members and the media. To increase the precision of the strikes, the CIA started to recruit more human agents on the ground in Pakistan and Afghanistan.

Knowledge about these secret agents began to seep out of the target countries themselves after successful drone strikes. The news outlet *Pakistan Today* reported that the Taliban thought the increase in precise and successful strikes against their fighters came from an enormous stable of CIA agents on the ground. A pro-Taliban tribesman claimed, "The CIA spy network might have numbers similar to that of a militant group. I hear roughly 2,000 to 2,500 well-trained and well-equipped intelligence operatives have been active for the spy agency."[51] The CIA could probably only dream of recruiting so many spies! Even if they didn't have over two thousand spies, there is no doubt that the CIA had increased its human sources along with their drone strikes. There were apparently daily Predator drone attacks during the first ten days of October 2010.

And when Mike McConnell, in his role as the DNI, had briefed Barack Obama two days after he was elected president on November 6, 2008, about the Predator drone operations, he bragged about the CIA's "breakthrough" recruiting "human sources" through a "high-risk program over five years." Of course, the most successful way to point drones toward a target was to have spies on the "ground telling the CIA where to look, hunt and kill." McConnell also shared that the reason the United States "had scored an extraordinary intelligence coup" in the Federally Administered Tribal Areas (FATAs) was because they used both human sources and technical intelligence like communication intercepts and satellite and drone imagery.[52]

The pro-Taliban tribesman was correct when he observed that the increased precision in the numerous drone attacks in North Waziristan proved that "someone on the ground is guiding the spy planes to strike targets. The improvement in hitting accurate targets . . . is nothing but an indication that the CIA-paid agents are very much active."[53]

Al-Qaeda also noted the increase in spies and spy networks on the ground in its online book *Guidance on the Ruling of the Muslim Spy*. An al-Qaeda leader, Shaykh Abu-Yahya al-Libi, began to see spies everywhere in the FATA located in northwestern Pakistan on the border with Afghanistan. He described these spies as the CIA's "eyes to see the hidden things that they cannot see." He saw their hands "extending inside houses, in the forests up the mountains, into the valleys, and inside the dark caves in order to catch a target that their developed technology was not able to reach." Even if he couldn't see these spies, they were "killing, destroying, imprisoning, and tracking."[54]

Al-Libi even claimed that the drone missiles found their targets in Pakistan by using several different infrared homing beacons. This is why, he writes, missiles have become so accurate. They "hit their targets according to the accurate data which those spies pass on to their infidel masters." Pictures of some of the devices are included in the Arabic original of the internet-distributed book showing "chips with 9-volt batteries." According to *Wired* magazine, the nine-volt battery chips bear a striking "resemblance to the Phoenix and Pegasus models of infrared flashing beacons made by Cejay Engineering," a company the US military uses to tag people.[55]

Tribesmen claimed that the United States was pairing the high-tech devices with "old-fashioned cash" to recruit witting and unwitting spies, mostly "poor local men," to help target the enemy. In 2008–9, the United States had launched over fifty drone strikes in South and North Waziristan. US officials claimed that nine of twenty top al-Qaeda people had been killed. A Pakistani newspaper claimed that seven hundred people had been killed between 2006 and 2009, most of them civilians.[56]

Al-Qaeda began to see chip-wielding spies everywhere. No one was safe. One hundred alleged chip-planting spies were killed. The Taliban issued video confessions, including one by Habib ur Rehman, who said "the money was good." He was paid $124 to place a microchip hidden in a cigarette wrapper at a target's house and promised thousands of dollars more if the strike was a success. Instead, the video shows Rehman being shot along with three other spies.[57]

The CIA was indeed tracking the movements of targets using homing beacons to increase the accuracy of the hits. CIA spies in the FATA planted these small tagging devices in vehicles, houses, compounds, and Taliban and al-Qaeda camps. The drones would then pick up the infrared flashing signals emitted by the device and could fire precisely at the target, minimizing collateral damage.

There is no doubt that the CIA spies helped target the armed drones. Just as the U-2 spy plane's success rested on the human spies on the ground who told the U-2 plane pilot where to look, so too did the human agents help focus the Predator attacks. Even so, there were unfortunately too many civilians killed, making drones unpopular among the public while damaging the image of the United States abroad.

The CIA and the Pentagon continued their quest to increase the precision of the drone strikes for many years after the initial strikes. In 2019, the *Wall Street Journal* reported that the CIA and the Pentagon developed a "Flying Ginsu" or "Ninja Bomb" (R9X) to replace the explosion-causing Hellfire missile warhead with knives. The knife-wielding missile deploys six blades moments before impact to cut through buildings and cars before attacking the target person. It had reportedly been used half a dozen times by 2019. When the CIA used the Ninja Bomb to take out Ahmad Hasan Abu Khayr al-Masri, an al-Qaeda second in command, in February 2017, evidence remained showing a hole torn in the roof but no explosion.[58]

Notes

1. James Bamford, "He's in the Backseat!," *The Atlantic*, April 2006, www.theatlantic.com/magazine/archive/2006/04/-hes-in-the-backseat/304712/.

2. Baer, *See No Evil*, 84.

3. Mark Mazzetti, *The Way of the Knife: The CIA, a Secret Army, and a War at the Ends of the Earth* (New York: Penguin, 2013), 85–87.

4. Herbert Scoville Jr., Memorandum for Director of Central Intelligence, June 12, 1963, CIA Electronic Reading Room, www.cia.gov/library/readingroom/docs/CIA-RDP66R00546R000100090315-7.pdf.

5. Scoville.

6. Rich and Janos, *Skunk Works*, 262–63.

7. Rich and Janos, 265.

8. Rich and Janos, 266–67.

9. Vince Houghton, *Nuking the Moon and Other Intelligence Schemes and Military Plots Left on the Drawing Board* (New York: Penguin, 2019), 151–52.

10. Rich and Janos, *Skunk Works*, 267.

11. Pedlow and Welzenbach, *Central Intelligence Agency and Overhead Reconnaissance*, 352–53, appendix E. This declassified internal history contains the most complete discussion of Project Aquiline.

12. Richelson, *Wizards of Langley*, 149. See also R. C. Hall, "Reconnaissance Drones: Their First Use in the Cold War," *Air Power History* 61 (2014): 20–27.

13. Memorandum, Joseph V. Charyk, Director, National Reconnaissance Office, October 17, 1962, www.cia.gov/library/readingroom/docs/CIA-RDP69B00279R000300040022-5.pdf.

14. Steve Coll, *Ghost Wars: The Secret History of the CIA, Afghanistan, and bin Laden, from the Soviet Invasion to September 10, 2001* (New York: Penguin, 2014), 137–38.

15. Coll, 140, for quote. For information on creating the center, see Clarridge's memoirs: Duane R. Clarridge with Digby Diehl, *A Spy for All Seasons* (New York: Scribner, 1997), 319–29.

16. Clarridge, *Spy for All Seasons*, 323.

17. Clarridge, 337.

18. Clarridge, 337–38.

19. Clarridge, 339.

20. Clarridge.

21. Coll, *Ghost Wars*, 144.

22. See Christopher J. Fuller, "The Eagle Comes Home to Roost: The Historical Origins of the CIA's Lethal Drone Program," *Intelligence and National Security* 30, no. 6 (2015): 784. See also Christopher J. Fuller, *See It/Shoot It: The Secret History of the CIA's Lethal Drone Program* (New Haven, CT: Yale University Press, 2017).

23. Frank Strickland, "The Early Evolution of the Predator Drone," *Studies in Intelligence* 57, no. 1 (March 2013): 2.

24. Richard Whittle, *Predator: The Secret Origins of the Drone Revolution* (New York: Henry Holt, 2014), 70–71.

25. Whittle.

26. Strickland, "Early Evolution," 3.

27. Coll, *Ghost Wars*, 528; and Whittle, *Predator*, 72.

28. Strickland, "Early Evolution," 6.

29. Coll, *Ghost Wars*, 529–30.

30. Coll, 530.

31. Whittle, *Predator*, 147–48.

32. Whittle, 157.

33. Whittle, 157–58.

34. Whittle, 158.

35. Whittle, 158–59.

36. George Tenet with Bill Harlow, *At the Center of the Storm: The CIA during America's Time of Crisis* (New York: HarperCollins, 2007), 127.

37. Coll, *Ghost Wars*, 536.

38. Coll.

39. Whittle, *Predator*, 163.

40. Richard Clarke, "Strategy for Eliminating the Threat from Jihadist Networks of al Qida: Status and Prospects." This report was attached to a memorandum written by Clarke on January 25, 2001, to Condoleezza Rice. Both have been declassified by the National Security Archive: https://nsarchive2.gwu.edu/NSAEBB/NSAEBB147/clarke%20attachment.pdf.

41. Barton Gellman, "A Strategy's Cautious Evolution," *Washington Post*, January 20, 2002, www.washingtonpost.com/wp-dyn/content/article/2006/06/09/AR2006060900885.html.

42. National Commission on Terrorist Attacks, *The 9/11 Commission Report: Final Report of the National Commission on Terrorist Attacks upon the United States*, authorized ed. (New York: Norton, n.d.), 211. The report was published July 22, 2004.

43. Whittle, *Predator*, 188–89.

44. Whittle, 227.

45. Tenet, *At the Center of the Storm*, 160.

46. Arthur Holland Michel, "How Rogue Techies Armed the Predator, Almost Stopped 9/11 and Invented Remote War," *Wired*, December 17, 2015, www.wired.com/2015/12/how-rogue-techies-armed-the-predator-almost-stopped-911-and-accidentally-invented-remote-war/.

47. Nick Turse and Tom Engelhardt, *Terminator Planet: The First History of Drone Warfare, 2001–2050* (n.p.: Dispatch Books, 2012), 72–73.

48. Immerwahr, *How to Hide an Empire*.

49. Hugh Gusterson, *Drone: Remote Control Warfare* (Cambridge, MA: MIT Press, 2016), 30. See also David S. Cloud, "Civilian Contractors Playing Key Role in U.S. Drone Operations," *Los Angeles Times*, December 29, 2011, www.latimes.com/nation/la-xpm-2011-dec-29-la-fg-drones-civilians-20111230-story.html.

50. This description is based on the slide obtained by *The Intercept* and discussion of the kill chain in Andrew Cockburn, *Kill Chain: The Rise of the High-Tech Assassins* (New York: Henry Holt, 2015), 4–5; and Fuller, *See It/Shoot It*, 4–5.

51. Haq Nawaz Khan, "Rising Drone Attacks Hint at Strengthened Spy Network in Waziristan," *Pakistan Today*, October 10, 2010.

52. Bob Woodward, *Obama's Wars* (New York: Simon & Schuster, 2010), 6.

53. Woodward.

54. *Guidance on the Ruling of the Muslim Spy* is available as a pdf: https://fas.org/irp/dni/osc/libi.pdf.

55. *Guidance on the Ruling of the Muslim Spy*. For Arabic original with pictures, see https://fas.org/irp/world/para/libi.pdf, 146. For a translation and commentary on these chips, see Adam Rawnsley, "CIA Drone Targeting Tech Revealed, Qaeda Claims," *Wired*, August 7, 2009.

56. Declan Walsh, "Mysterious 'Chip' Is CIA's Latest Weapon against al-Qaida Targets Hiding in Pakistan's Tribal Belt," *The Guardian*, May 31, 2009, www.theguardian.com/world/2009/may/31/cia-drones-tribesmen-taliban-pakistan.

57. Walsh.

58. Gordon Lubold and Warren Strobel, "Secret U.S. Missile Aims to Kill Only Terrorists, Not Nearby Civilians," *Wall Street Journal*, May 9, 2019, www.wsj.com/articles/secret-u-s-missile-aims-to-kill-only-terrorists-not-nearby-civilians-11557403411.

CONCLUSION
INFORMATION GLUTTONS

In 2011, the National Security Agency started building a massive data repository in Bluffdale, Utah, to store the fruits of its sprawling global empire. When the $2 billion facility was completed three years later, four data halls were spread out on the compound in flat, low buildings comprising a total of one million square feet, mostly for storage. The Utah Data Center is sandwiched in a valley between Flat Top Mountain to the west, Twin Peaks Mountain to the east, and Utah Lake to the south and runs on its own power and water systems. Its 65-megawatt power substation costs $40 million a year to run, and the water facility pumps 1.7 million gallons of liquid a day while the chiller plant maintains 60,000 tons of cooling equipment to keep the servers from overheating.[1]

Some say that the center serves as a desert warehouse to store all the data, all the time. Bill Binney, a former NSA official, suspected that "they're storing everything they gather," instead of using the more targeted system he and others developed. Once the data are stored, the data mining begins. However much data the center stores, its purpose is to have a place to deposit and archive the world's communications as they are retrieved from satellites above and undersea cables below.[2]

It is not surprising that the NSA built this super storage center, given its "collect it all" mentality. One of the main themes of this book is the role of American technophilia and technophilic hubris in the launch and development of technological espionage. As we have seen, technology had the unique ability to haul in a lot of information. This led to an obsession to collect more and more information whether or not the intelligence could be used. Although technology is often expensive, there always seemed to be enough in the budgets to support it.

Analysts complained about the large amount of data from the 1950s to the 2000s, from the fruits of the Berlin Tunnel and the U-2 spy plane to spy satellites and communication interception. Instead of seeking to stem the flow of information by being more selective, most technology programs sought more staff, new computing power, and larger storage facilities to tackle and store the deluge.

Surprisingly, as early as 1966 the CIA's inspector general, John "Jack" S. Earman Jr., a thin-faced Virginian, scolded the CIA because of its omnivorous and indiscriminate appetite for information. He accused the CIA of collecting too much information, more than it could use and far more than the government needed. Since the agency did not collect the right kind of information, it flooded the system with secondary material. Apparently no one defined what the government needed from the spy agency. Because there was so much funding for technical collection, the flood of material required more and more warehouses for more and more tapes and films. The request for more storage facilities was in addition to the existing warehouses filled with miles of unprocessed satellite imagery and SIGINT tape.[3]

Earman accused the CIA of being information gluttons who had an "insatiable appetite," and this was the cause of the information explosion. He thought "a hundred bureaucratic pills to relieve the Agency's chronic indigestion" would not cure it. He advised the gluttonous CIA, "*Stop* trying to cover the whole world comprehensively and superficially."[4] Surely, the gluttony stemmed, in part, from the feeling that just one more piece of information will help an analyst gain insight into the intelligence problem. Or it could be the haul-in-the-whole-haystack mentality some leaders at the NSA espoused in the 2000s. Or it could be a form of addiction or overresearching a subject by hauling in too much information as a way to put off analysis and writing. Once collected, the information overwhelms the researcher, making it even harder to draw conclusions. As one NSA intelligence analyst quipped, it can lead to "analysis paralysis."[5]

But information gluttons are also hoarders of information. As the journalist Max Frankel noted in the *New York Times*, presidents like Richard Nixon were coached to believe that "even harmless secrets were coins of power to be hoarded." Just as one solution to secrecy hoarding is regulation, as Patrick Moynihan noted, so too could technical collection be regulated using the same cost-benefit analysis used in government bureaucracies.[6]

Earman's acerbic attack was penned in 1966. By this time the U-2 spy plane, the Berlin Tunnel, and early satellites had hauled in vast quantities of material. Their capabilities allowed them to cover the whole world, not just high-priority targets. But during the early years, there was no global rhetoric attached to programs. Despite the global capabilities of the machines, the early goals focused on so-called denied areas like the Soviet Union and Cuba—the Communist enemy. However, collection became an end in itself. This trumped the real goal of intelligence, namely, the use of the final product in policy decisions or operations.

Early CIA leaders like Richard Helms and Richard Bissell referred to torrents of information from the tunnel and raised concerns that the amount of information was counterproductive. But they did nothing to stop it. Instead, they hired more people and developed more computer power.

The early satellite system of bucket film return had already hauled in plenty of information to analyze, but it wasn't until the revolutionary real-time images from the KH-11 Kennan satellite that analysts could no longer handle drinking from the firehose of information. It is telling that the National Photographic Interpretation Center selected what some analysts called a "film-choked eagle" to represent their agency on its seal.

The National Reconnaissance Office became increasingly aware of the implications of its naturally global reach. While during the early years satellites were seen as useful because they traveled over the "denied" territory, after the Cold War, during the 1990s, the NRO explicitly described itself as "revolutionizing global reconnaissance" and achieving "global information superiority." It was turnkey ready. During the late Cold War, its machines and targets had expanded to cover the whole world. After the 9/11 attacks global terrorism became a priority. Along with expanding targets and budgets came enormous new buildings and an increase in staff.

By 2013, the globe-straddling octopus, referred to in the introduction, was an apt metaphor to represent the US intelligence community, its mind-set, and its actions abroad: nothing is beyond our reach because our tentacles cover the globe. So true but so hubristic.

By this time, the NSA espoused the "collect it all" mentality. No effort was made to focus intelligence collection. Instead, like earlier times, the strategy was to develop better computers and better data-mining techniques. But did it help?

In the wake of the 2013 Snowden revelations, President Obama asked a task force to examine Snowden's concerns about the NSA's work. All participants had security clearance and could access top-secret material. They found very few cases of success in locating and capturing terrorists and their plots using the domestic telephone metadata program. The report concluded that section 215 "only made a modest contribution to the nation's security . . . and generated relevant information in only a small number of cases." Overseas collection that resulted in perhaps thwarting about fifty-four terrorist plots was allegedly more successful.[7]

Moreover, disclosures about bulk collection of information at home and abroad, aimed at friends and foes alike, led to the loss of public trust. Not only did the NSA cross the holy boundaries by spying on its own citizens, but it outraged foreign leaders like the German chancellor Angela Merkel, whose phone was tapped by the NSA.[8]

Excessive intelligence collection also led to the erosion of strong US values like privacy and civil liberties. Snowden's exposures were not the first time that the intelligence community was scrutinized for overreach. During the 1970s, Frank Church and his Senate committees revealed similar threats to privacy and civil liberties. It seems that such exposures help rein in oversteps for a time at least, until the next crisis and excessive secrecy and the concomitant abuse of power and capabilities.

Armed drones became another hot button topic. As was the case with the NSA's signals intelligence capabilities, drones provided global coverage, especially for the so-called war on terror. From a trailer at its headquarters in Langley, the CIA could kill a terrorist in Yemen while instructing a drone to fly out of a US base in East Africa to its target. Even if there was blowback against the United States, there were no pilots shot down by the enemy, as had been the case with the U-2 spy plane. Although the drone began as a surveillance plane, attaching a Hellfire missile to the pilotless plane turned it, and the CIA, into a killing machine stalking its targets who were terrorized by the buzz of the engine.

While US technology had provided the country with immense power and reach, it also created an intelligence leviathan, unwelcome once its secret powers were unveiled. Aside from the blowback from the offensive activities, the hoarding of vast amounts of information enabled by new technologies led to information overload and ineffective analysis and use of the material. This is a lesser-known aspect of the global octopus's activities.

The emphasis on technical collection over using agents to gather intelligence material created many problems. The vaunted technology was often betrayed by humans as illustrated by the Berlin Tunnel episode and submarine espionage. As many commentators like Robert Baer noted, technical means could not get in the heads of leaders or adversaries to understand their intentions. This proved problematic when dealing with terrorists. As a result, the CIA beefed up its human resources by revamping the old Directorate of Operations and creating the new National Clandestine Service. Unfortunately, the so-called enhanced interrogation techniques, also known as torture, served as a human source method and blackened the CIA's reputation. Nevertheless, there seemed to be an increase in using human agents together with technical means, as was the case with drones in the 2000s. Whatever the merits of technical and/or human intelligence, the US emphasis on using technological means of intelligence collection produced the unintended consequence of covering the globe.

The United States did not plan to create global dominion by using technology in intelligence. The trio of geopolitics, technology, and intelligence coalesced into a global espionage empire. The empire emerged in a piecemeal but ever-evolving way with no central blueprint. In a sense it followed the law of unintended consequences, because the all-powerful technology created the perverse result of information overload.

This book has argued that technology replaced territory in the US intelligence community's ascent to becoming a global espionage power. This doesn't mean that the United States doesn't have or didn't need any land to conduct its global activities. It means that US empire should not be defined in comparison to previous empires in history that possessed large amounts of territory to pursue their hegemonic activities. Ground stations, antennas, cable stations, or server farms and other physical infrastructures of the national security state dot remote islands or allied territory to support globe-spanning satellite and undersea cable activities. Drones need to be launched from US bases. Unlike the power projection inherent in US military bases, the espionage empire is a hidden and secret one, usually out of sight and out of mind, with the exception of the paramilitary use of drones (until some of its activities are exposed by whistleblowers, historians, or journalists).

The stories in this book traverse the globe, starting small and targeted: the tunnel in Berlin (partly on allied territory) and the U-2 spy plane soaring over Soviet airspace and launched from Wiesbaden, Germany, or the US Peshawar base in its ally Pakistan, or flying over Cuba from Florida after secret agents pinpointed the precise location of the long-range missiles.

The story takes a turn for the global early on with the development of electronic eavesdropping and signals intelligence because of the World War II alliance (UKUSA) with the United Kingdom and Crypto AG. While the British geopolitical agenda was originally designed to maintain their empire and dominate global trade, when the global espionage torch passed to the United States, its agenda was to maintain global and technological supremacy.

During the Cold War, the United States was the creator of, and leader in, conducting large-scale technical espionage. Other countries had emphasized traditional human intelligence gathering. But after the Cold War when cyberspace exploded, other nations began to catch up and embrace cyber espionage. Unlike expensive spy satellites, planes, drones, and electronic eavesdropping devices, it was a cheap form of technical espionage that many countries could use.

Russia, especially, embraced cyber espionage. The US government accused Russia of meddling in the 2016 presidential election by hacking into the Democratic National Committee's servers and by manipulating social media in order to tip the election in favor of Donald Trump. According to the *New York Times*, it was "a low-cost, high impact weapon" and proved to be the "perfect weapon: cheap, hard to see coming, hard to trace."[9]

China also became a threat to US global hegemony with its own push for global power. Not only did it develop cyber capabilities and successful international telecoms like Huawei, but it also launched a massive industrial espionage campaign against the United States that the FBI considered a major threat to US economic prosperity and global power.

Artificial intelligence (AI) is another emerging technology that has changed the playing field. Intelligence agencies can use AI and its related technologies like cloud computing and big data analytics to analyze more effectively the deluge of data. But so can other countries like China, which aspires to be a world leader in AI by 2030. People who do not work for governmental spy agencies can also harness the power of AI, whether as individuals or companies. In fact, colossal companies like Google, Amazon, and Facebook are also big data players on the same level as the NSA.[10]

With the increase in publicly available data (called open-source intelligence), anyone with an internet connection can access tools and information spy agencies would have only dreamed of during the Cold War. Google Earth has proven to be an especially effective tool for citizen spying. Commercial satellites have become so powerful and affordable that spy agencies like the NRO now buy commercial satellites instead of building them. "Anyone who wants them" can use them. In particular, nuclear threat intelligence collection has become "democratized," allowing smaller countries and ordinary people to access the information.[11]

Who knows what the future will bring, but one thing is clear: the United States was unique in the way in which it conducted espionage during the Cold War and the war on terror. As a result, the witches' brew of geopolitics, technology, and intelligence created an unintended global espionage empire drowning in data.

Notes

1. James Bamford, "The NSA Is Building the Country's Biggest Spy Center (Watch What You Say)," *Wired*, March 15, 2012, www.wired.com/2012/03/ff-nsadatacenter.

2. Bamford.

3. Foreign Intelligence Collection Requirements: The Inspector General's Survey, December 1966, 2, CIA CREST Archive: www.cia.gov/library/readingroom/docs/CIA-RDP86B00269R001100040005-0.pdf.

4. Foreign Intelligence Collection Requirements; emphasis in original.

5. "The SIGINT Philosopher: Too Many Choices," https://www.documentcloud.org/documents/2088983-too-many-choices.html.

6. Max Frankel, "Top Secret," *New York Times*, June 16, 1996, 20; and Daniel Patrick Moynihan, *Secrecy* (New Haven, CT: Yale University Press, 1998).

7. Richard Clarke, Michael J. Morell, Geoffrey R. Stone, Cass R. Sunstein, and Peter Swire, "Liberty and Security in a Changing World Report and Recommendations of the President's Review Group on Intelligence and Communications Technology," 120 n.; available at https://obamawhitehouse.archives.gov/sites/default/files/docs/2013-12-12_rg_final_report.pdf.

8. Clarke et al.

9. Eric Lipton, David E. Sanger, and Scott Shane, "The Perfect Weapon: How Russian Cyberpower Invaded the U.S.," *New York Times*, December 13, 2016, www.nytimes.com/2016/12/13/us/politics/russia-hack-election-dnc.html.

10. Amy Zegart, *Spies, Lies, and Algorithms: The History and Future of American Intelligence* (Princeton, NJ: Princeton University Press, 2022), 2, 8. Zegart's important book was published as this one was being copyedited.

11. Zegart, chap. 9 and p. 234.

BIBLIOGRAPHY

Archives

CIA, Freedom of Information Act Electronic Reading Room, 2017–present, www.cia.gov/readingroom/collection/crest-25-year-program-archive.

CIA, CREST, Records Search Tool. National Archives (NARA II), College Park, MD. [To 2017]

Cold War Intelligence Online. Edited by Matthew M. Aid. Brill Online Primary Sources, 2013.

Digital National Security Archive, George Washington University. https://nsarchive.gwu.edu/digital-national-security-archive; http://www.proquest.com/dnsa/index?accountid=11107.

Dwight D. Eisenhower Library (DDEL). National Security Files.

Foreign Relations of the United States (FRUS). Intelligence Community, 1950–55. https://primarysources.brillonline.com/browse/cold-war-intelligence.

John F. Kennedy Presidential Library. National Security Files. John F. Kennedy Presidential Library and Museum.

John Marks Archive. Hard copies available at the National Security Archive, Gelman Library, George Washington University, Washington, DC.

Mary Ferrell Foundation. www.maryferrell.org/showDoc.html?docId=18191&relPageId=3.

National Archives, College Park, MD, Record Group 457, NSA Historic Cryptographic Collection.

National Library of New Zealand, Archives. Owen Wilkes.

National Photographic Interpretation Center (NPIC), National Geospatial Intelligence Agency (NGA).

National Security Agency (NSA). UKUSA Early Papers. www.nsa.gov/Portals/70/documents/news-features/declassified-documents/ukusa/early_papers_1940-1944.pdf.

National Security Agency (NSA). William Friedman Papers. www.nsa.gov/Portals/70/documents/news-features/declassified-documents/friedman-documents/correspondence/ACC35864/41780849081991.pdf.

National Security Archive. http://nsarchive.gwu.edu.

Snowden Archive on the NSA. www.https://snowdenarchive.cjfe.org.

UK National Archives, HW 80 files. https://discovery.nationalarchives.gov.uk/browse/r/h/C18031.

US Department of State, Foreign Relations of the United States, 1949, vol. 5, Eastern Europe; The Soviet Union. https://history.state.gov/historicaldocuments/frus1949v05.

US Department of State, Foreign Relations of the United States, 1950, vol. 4, Central and Eastern Europe; The Soviet Union. https://history.state.gov/historicaldocuments/frus1950v04/d532.

Yale University Archive, Walter L. Pforzheimer Papers.

Interviews

Robert Baer, 2016.

Bill Binney, 2015.

Jane Harman, 2016.

Michael V. Hayden, 2016.

John Poindexter, 2015.

Peter Swire, 2014.

Newspapers and Magazines

Chicago Daily Tribune

Chicago Tribune

The Guardian

Huffington Post

The Intercept

New York Herald Tribune

New York Magazine

New York Times

New Zealand Herald

Time

Wall Street Journal

Washington Post

Primary Sources

Chang, Laurence, and Peter Kornbluh. *The Cuban Missile Crisis, 1962: A National Security Archive Documents Reader*. New York: New Press, 1998.

McAuliffe, Mary S. *CIA Documents on the Cuban Missile Crisis, 1962*. Washington, DC: History Staff, Central Intelligence Agency, 1992.

Ruffner, Kevin C., ed. *CORONA: America's First Satellite Program*. Washington, DC: CIA, Center for the Study of Intelligence, 1995.

Steury, Donald P. *On the Front Lines of the Cold War: Documents on the Intelligence War in Berlin, 1946 to 1961*. Washington, DC: CIA History Staff, Center for the Study of Intelligence, 1999.

US Senate, *Foreign and Military Intelligence, Book I, Final Report of the Select Committee to Study Governmental Operations with Respect to Intelligence Activities.* Washington, DC: Government Printing Office, 1976.

Secondary Sources

Absher, Kenneth Michael. "Mind-Sets and Missiles: A First Hand Account of the Cuban Missile Crisis." Strategic Studies Institute, Carlisle, PA, September 2009. Pamphlet.

Aid, Matthew M. "The National Security Agency and the Cold War." *Intelligence and National Security* 16, no. 1 (2001): 27–66.

Albarelli, H. P., Jr. *A Terrible Mistake: The Murder of Frank Olson and the CIA's Secret Cold War Experiments*. Walterville, OR: Trine Day, 2011.

Aldrich, Richard J. *GCHQ: The Uncensored Story of Britain's Most Secret Intelligence Agency*. London: Harper Press, 2011.

———. *The Hidden Hand: Britain, America and Cold War Secret Intelligence*. Woodstock, NY: Overlook Press, 2002.

Allison, Graham T., and Philip Zelikow. *Essence of Decision: Explaining the Cuban Missile Crisis*. New York: Longman, [1971] 1999.

Ambrose, Stephen. *Ike's Spies: Eisenhower and the Espionage Establishment*. New York: Random House, 2012.

Andrew, Christopher. *The Defence of the Realm: The Authorized History of MI5*. London: Allen Lane, 2009.

———. *For the President's Eyes Only: Secret Intelligence and the American Presidency from Washington to Bush*. New York: HarperCollins, 1996.

———. "The Making of the Anglo-American SIGINT Alliance." In *In the Name of Intelligence: Essays in Honor of Walter Pforzheimer*, Hayden B. Peake and Samuel Halpern, 103–6. Washington, DC: NIBC Press, 1995.

Andrew, Christopher, and Oleg Gordievsky. *KGB: the Inside Story*. New York: Harper, 1991.

Andrew, Christopher, and Vasili Mitrokhin. *The Sword and the Shield: The Mitrokhin Archive and the Secret History of the KGB*. New York: Basic Books, 1999.

Baer, Robert. *See No Evil: The True Story of a Ground Soldier in the CIA's War on Terrorism*. New York: Three Rivers Press, 2002.

Ball, Desmond. *Pine Gap: Australia and the US Geostationary Signals Intelligence Satellite Program*. Sydney: Allen & Unwin, 1988.

Bamford, James. *Body of Secrets: Anatomy of the Ultra-Secret National Security Agency from the Cold War through the Dawn of a New Century*. New York: Doubleday, 2001.

———. "The NSA Is Building the Country's Biggest Spy Center (Watch What You Say)." *Wired*, March 15, 2012.

———. *The Puzzle Palace: A Report on America's Most Secret Agency*. New York: Penguin, 1983.

Barrett, David M., and Max Holland. *Blind over Cuba: The Photo Gap and the Missile Crisis*. College Station: Texas A&M University Press, 2012.

Barron, John. *Breaking the Ring: The Bizarre Case of the Walker Family Spy Ring*. Boston: Houghton Mifflin, 1987.

Barton, Patrick F. "Edward Snowden Unauthorized Disclosures and Press Publication of Classified Intelligence Information: A Case Study." Diss., North Central University, Arizona, 2016.

Bennett, M. Todd. "Détente in Deep Water: The CIA Mission to Salvage a Sunken Soviet Submarine and US-USSR Relations, 1968–1975." *Intelligence and National Security* 33, no. 2 (2018): 196–210.

Beschloss, Michael. *Mayday: Eisenhower, Khrushchev, and the U-2 Affair*. New York: Harper and Row, 1986.

Bird, Kenneth L. "Menwith Hill Station: A Case Study in Signal Intelligence Gathering during the Cold War." *Monitoring Times* 16, no. 2 (February 1997): 16–19.

Bissell, Richard M. *Reflections on a Cold Warrior, from Yalta to the Bay of Pigs*. New Haven, CT: Yale University Press, 1996.

Blake, George. *No Other Choice: An Autobiography*. New York: Simon & Schuster, 1990.

Blight, James G., and David A. Welch. *Intelligence and the Cuban Missile Crisis*. London: Frank Cass, 1998.

Bohlen, Charles E. *Witness to History, 1919–1969*. London: Weidenfeld and Nicolson, 1973.

Bon Tempo, C. J. *Americans at the Gate: The United States and Refugees during the Cold War*. Princeton, NJ: Princeton University Press, 2008.

Bower, Tom. *The Red Web: MI6 and the KGB Master Coup*. London: Aurum Press, 1989.

Brugioni, Dino. *Eyeball to Eyeball: The Inside Story of the Cuban Missile Crisis*. New York: Random House, 1991.

———. *Eyes in the Sky: Eisenhower, the CIA, and Cold War Aerial Espionage*. New York: Naval Institute Press, 2011.

Burds, Jeffrey. "The Early Cold War in Soviet West Ukraine, 1944–1948." *Carl Beck Papers in Russian and European Studies*, no. 1505 (January 2001): 1–67.

Burrows, William E. *Deep Black: Space Espionage and National Security*. New York: Random House, 1986.

Bury, Jan. "Operation Spiders: Fighting an Early Cold War Ukrainian Subversion behind the Iron Curtain." *International Journal of Intelligence and Counterintelligence* 30 (2017): 241–68.

Caddell, Joseph W., Jr. "Corona over Cuba: The Missile Crisis and the Early Limitations of Satellite Imagery Intelligence." *Intelligence and National Security* 31, no. 3 (2016): 416–38.

Clarke, Richard, Michael J. Morell, Geoffrey R. Stone, Cass R. Sunstein, and Peter Swire. *The NSA Report: Liberty and Security in a Changing World Report*. Princeton, NJ: Princeton University Press, 2014.

Clarridge, Duane R., with Digby Diehl. *A Spy for All Seasons*. New York: Scribner, 1997.

Clifford, Clark, with Richard Holbrooke. *Counsel to the President*. New York: Random House, 1991.

Cloud, John. "Imagining the World in a Barrel: CORONA and the Clandestine Convergence of the Earth Sciences." *Social Studies of Science* 31, no. 2 (April 2001): 231–25.

Cockburn, Andrew. *Kill Chain: The Rise of the High-Tech Assassins*. New York: Henry Holt, 2015.

Coll, Steve. *Ghost Wars: The Secret History of the CIA, Afghanistan, and bin Laden, from the Soviet Invasion to September 10, 2001*. New York: Penguin Books, 2014.

Corn, David. *Blond Ghost: Ted Shackley and the CIA's Crusade*. New York: Simon & Schuster, 1994.

Cox, Michael. "Still the American Empire." *Political Studies Review* 5 (2007): 1–10.

Damms, Richard V. "James Killian, the Technological Capabilities Panel, and the Emergence of President Eisenhower's 'Scientific-Technological Elite.'" *Diplomatic History* 24, no. 1 (Winter 2000): 57–78.

Day, Dwayne A., John M. Logsdon, and Brian Latell. *Eye in the Sky: The Story of the Corona Spy Satellites*. Washington, DC: Smithsonian Books, 1998.

Dean, Josh. *The Taking of the K-129: How the CIA Used Howard Hughes to Steal a Russian Sub in the Most Daring Operation in History*. New York: Dutton, 2017.

Diamond, John. *The CIA and the Culture of Failure: U.S. Intelligence from the End of the Cold War to the Invasion of Iraq*. Stanford, CA: Stanford University Press, 2008.

Dittmer, Jason. *Diplomatic Material: Affect, Assemblage, and Foreign Policy*. Durham, NC: Duke University Press, 2017.

Dobson, Melina J. "Operation Rubicon: Germany as an Intelligence 'Great Power'? *Intelligence and National Security* 35, no. 5 (2020): 608–22. DOI: 10.1080/02684527.2020.1774852.

Dorril, Stephen. *MI6: Inside the Covert World of Her Majesty's Secret Intelligence Service*. New York: Simon & Schuster, 2002.

Dover, Robert, and Richard J. Aldrich. "Cryptography and the Global South: Secrecy, Signals and Information Imperialism." *Third World Quarterly* 41, no. 1 (2020): 1900–1917.

Earley, Pete. *Family of Spies: Inside the John Walker Spy Ring*. New York: Bantam Books, 1989.

Edgette, Judith. "Domestic Collection on Cuba." *Studies in Intelligence* 7 (Fall 1963): 41–45.

Engelhardt, Tom. *Shadow Government: Surveillance, Secret Wars, and a Global Security State in a Single-Superpower World*. Chicago: Haymarket Books, 2014.

Ferguson, Niall. *Colossus: The Rise and Fall of the American Empire*. New York: Penguin, 2004.

Friedman, Andrew. *Covert Capital: Landscapes of Denial and the Making of U.S. Empire in the Suburbs of Northern Virginia*. Berkeley: University of California Press, 2013.

Fuller, Christopher J. "The Eagle Comes Home to Roost: The Historical Origins of the CIA's Lethal Drone Program." *Intelligence and National Security* 30, no. 6 (2015): 769–92.

———. *See It/Shoot It: The Secret History of the CIA's Lethal Drone Program*. New Haven, CT: Yale University Press, 2017.

G. "Turning a Cold War Scheme into Reality: Engineering the Berlin Tunnel." *Studies in Intelligence* 52, no. 1 (March 2008): 1–7.

Gaddis, John L. *The Landscape of History: How Historians Map the Past*. Oxford: Oxford University Press, 2004.

Gartoff, Raymond. "US Intelligence in the Cuban Missile Crisis." In *Intelligence and the Cuban Missile Crisis*, edited by James G. Blight and David A. Welch, 23–24. London: Frank Cass, 1998.

Garwin, Richard L. "Edwin H. Land: Science, and Public Policy." Paper presented at Light and Life, a Symposium in Honor of Edwin Land, November 9, 1991. The Irish Colleges of Physicians and Surgeons, 1993.

Gioe, David Vincent. "The Anglo-American Special Intelligence Relationship: Wartime Causes and Cold War Consequences, 1940–63." PhD diss. University of Cambridge, June 2014.

Gleichauf, Justin F. "A Listening Post in Miami." *Studies in Intelligence* 10 (Winter–Spring 2001): 49–53.

Grathwol, Robert P., and Donita M. Moorhus. *Building for Peace: U.S. Army Engineers in Europe, 1945–1991*. Washington, DC: Center of Military and History and Corps of Engineers United States Army, 2005.

Greenwald, Glenn. *No Place to Hide: Edward Snowden, the NSA, and the U.S. Surveillance State*. New York: Metropolitan Books, 2014.

Gusterson, Hugh. *Drone: Remote Control Warfare*. Cambridge, MA: MIT Press, 2016.

Hager, Nicky. *Secret Power: New Zealand's Role in the International Spy Network*. Nelson, NZ: Craig Potton Publishing, 1996.

Hall, R. C. "Reconnaissance Drones: Their First Use in the Cold War." *Air Power History* 61 (2014): 20–27.

Hecht, Gabrielle, ed. *Entangled Geographies: Empire and Technopolitics in the Global Cold War*. Cambridge, MA: MIT Press, 2011.

Helms, Richard, with William Hood. *A Look over My Shoulder: A Life in the Central Intelligence Agency*. New York: Ballantine Books, 2003. Rev. ed., n.p.: Presidio Press, 2004.

Hermiston, Roger. *The Greatest Traitor: The Secret Lives of Agent George Blake*. London: Aurum, 2013.

Hilsman, Roger. *The Cuban Missile Crisis: The Struggle over Policy*. Westport, CT: Praeger, 1996.

———. *To Move a Nation: The Politics of Foreign Policy in the Administration of John F. Kennedy*. Garden City, NY: Doubleday, 1967.

Houghton, Vince. *Nuking the Moon and Other Intelligence Schemes and Military Plots Left on the Drawing Board*. New York: Penguin, 2019.

Hughes, Thomas P. *American Genesis: A Century of Technological Enthusiasm, 1870–1970*. Chicago: University of Chicago Press, [1989] 2004.

Huntington, Thomas. "The Berlin Spy Tunnel Affair." *Invention and Technology* 10, no. 4 (Spring 1995).

Immerwahr, Daniel. *How to Hide an Empire: A History of the Greater United States*. New York: Farrar, Straus and Giroux, 2019.

Johnson, Chalmers. *The Sorrows of Empire: Militarism, Secrecy, and the End of the Republic*. New York: Henry Holt, 2004.

Jones, Milo, and Philippe Silberzahn. *Constructing Cassandra: Reframing Intelligence Failure at the CIA, 1947–2001*. Stanford, CA: Stanford University Press, 2014.

Kalugin, Oleg. *Spymaster: My 32 Years in Intelligence and Espionage against the West*. New York: St. Martin's Press, 1994.

Keefe, Patrick Radden. *Chatter: Dispatches from the Secret World of Global Eavesdropping*. New York: Random House, 2005.

Killian, James R. *Sputnik, Scientists and Eisenhower: A Memoir of the First Assistant to the President for Science and Technology*. Cambridge, MA: MIT Press, 1967.

Kinzer, Stephen. *Poisoner in Chief: Sidney Gottlieb and the CIA Search for Mind Control*. New York: Henry Holt, 2019.

Lamphere, Robert J., and Tom Shachtman. *The FBI-KGB War: A Special Agent's Story*. New York: Random House, 1986.

Laqueur, Walter. *A World of Secrets: The Uses and Limits of Intelligence*. New York: Basic Books, 1985.

Le Carré, John. *The Spy Who Came in from the Cold*. New York: Pocket Books, [1963] 2001.

Lerner, Michael B. *The* Pueblo *Incident: A Spy Ship and the Failure of American Foreign Policy*. Lawrence: University Press of Kansas, 2002.

Lewin, Ronald. *ULTRA Goes to War: The Secret Story*. London: Hutchinson, 1978.

Lewis, Jonathan E. *Spy Capitalism: ITEK and the CIA*. New Haven, CT: Yale University Press, 2002.

Macintyre, Ben. *A Spy among Friends: Kim Philby and the Great Betrayal*. London: Bloomsbury, 2014.

Macrakis, Kristie. "Technophilic Hubris and Espionage Styles during the Cold War." *Isis* 10 (2010): 378–85.

Maier, Charles S. *Among Empires: American Ascendancy and Its Predecessors*. Cambridge, MA: Harvard University Press, 2006.

Marks, John. *The Search for the "Manchurian Candidate": The CIA and Mind Control*. Reprint, New York: Norton, 1991.

Masterman, J. C. *The Double-Cross System in the War of 1939 to 1945*. New Haven, CT: Yale University Press, 1972.

Mazzetti, Mark. *The Way of the Knife: The CIA, a Secret Army, and a War at the Ends of the Earth*. New York: Penguin Books, 2013.

Mendez, Antonio J., and Matt Baglio. *Argo: How the CIA and Hollywood Pulled Off the Most Audacious Rescue in History*. New York: Viking, 2012.

Michel, Arthur Holland. "How Rogue Techies Armed the Predator, Almost Stopped 9/11 and Invented Remote War." *Wired*, December 17, 2015.

Mitchell, James E., and Bill Harlow. *Enhanced Interrogation: Inside the Minds and Motives of the Islamic Terrorists Trying to Destroy America*. New York: Crown Forum, 2016.

Moynihan, Daniel Patrick. *Secrecy*. New Haven, CT: Yale University Press, 1998.

Munson, Harlow T., and W. P. Southard. "Two Witnesses for the Defense." *Studies in Intelligence* 8 (Fall 1964): 94–98.

Murphy, David E., Sergei A. Kondrashev, and George Bailey. *Battleground Berlin: CIA vs. KGB in the Cold War*. New Haven, CT: Yale University Press, 1997.

National Commission on Terrorist Attacks. *The 9/11 Commission Report: Final Report of the National Commission on Terrorist Attacks upon the United States*. Authorized Edition. New York: Norton, 2004.

Naylor, Sean D. "Operation Cobra: The Untold Story of How a CIA Officer Trained a Network of Agents Who Found the Soviet Missiles In Cuba." *Yahoo News*, January 23, 2019.

O'Connor, Jack. *Seeing the Secrets and Growing the Leaders: A Cultural History of the National Photographic Interpretation Center*. Alexandria, VA: Acumensa Solutions, 2015.

Oder, Frederic. *The Hexagon Story*. Chantilly, VA: Center for the Study of National Reconnaissance, 2012.

Oldenziel, Ruth. "Islands: The United States as a Networked Empire." In *Entangled Geographies: Empire and Technopolitics in the Global Cold War*, edited by Gabrielle Hecht, 31–41. Cambridge, MA: MIT Press, 2011.

Peake, Hayden B., and Samuel Halpern, eds. *In the Name of Intelligence: Essays in Honor of Walter Pforzheimer*. Washington, DC: NIBC Press, 1995.

Pedlow, Gregory W., and Donald E. Welzenbach. *The Central Intelligence Agency and Overhead Reconnaissance: The U-2 and OXCCART Programs, 1954–1974*. New York: Skyhorse Publishing, 2016.

Peebles, Curtis. *The Corona Project: America's First Spy Satellites*. Annapolis, MD: Naval Institute Press, 1997.

Philby, Kim. *My Silent War: The Autobiography of a Spy*. New York: Modern Library, [1968] 2002.

Plokhy, Serhii. *The Man with the Poison Gun: A Cold War Spy Story*. New York: Basic Books, 2016.

Pocock, Chris. *Dragon Lady: The History of the U-2 Spyplane*. Osceola, WI: Motorbooks International, 1989.

———. *The U-2 Spyplane, Toward the Unknown: A New History of the Early Years*. Atglen, PA: Schiffer Military History, 2000.

Polmar, Norman, and Michael White. *Project Azorian: The CIA and the Raising of the K-129*. Annapolis, MD: Naval Institute Press, 2010.

Powers, Thomas. *The Man Who Kept the Secrets: Richard Helms and the CIA*. New York: Knopf, 1979.

Priest, Dana, and William M. Arkin. *Top Secret America: The Rise of the New American Security State*. New York: Little, Brown, 2011.

Ranelagh, John. *The Agency: The Rise and Decline of the CIA*. New York: Simon & Schuster, 1987.

Rawnsley, Adam. "CIA Drone Targeting Tech Revealed, Qaeda Claims." *Wired*, August 7, 2009.

Reed, W. Craig. *Red November: Inside the Secret U.S.-Soviet Submarine War*. New York: Harper's, 2011.

Rich, Ben R., and Leo Janos. *Skunk Works: A Personal Memoir of My Years at Lockheed*. New York: Little, Brown, 1994.

Richelson, Jeffrey. *A Century of Spies: Intelligence in the Twentieth Century*. New York: Oxford University Press, 1995.

———. *The Wizards of Langley: Inside the CIA's Directorate of Science and Technology*. Boulder, CO: Westview Press, 2001.

Richelson, Jeffrey T., and Desmond Ball. *The Ties That Bind: Intelligence Cooperation between the UKUSA Countries—the United Kingdom the United States of America, Canada, Australia and New Zealand*. Boston: Allen & Unwin, 1985.

Robertson, Ken G., and Michael R. D. Foot, eds. *War, Resistance and Intelligence: Essays in Honour of M. R. D. Foot*. Barnsley: Cooper, 1999.

Rositzke, Harry. *The CIA's Secret Operations: Espionage, Counterespionage and Covert Action*. New York: Reader's Digest, 1977.

Ruffner, Kevin C. "Cold War Allies: The Origins of CIA's Relationship with Ukrainian Nationalists." *Studies in Intelligence* (1998): 19–43.

Rumpelmayer, J. J. "The Missiles in Cuba." *Studies in Intelligence* 8 (Fall 1964): 87–92.

Salvetti, Lloyd. "An Interview with NSA Director Lt. Gen. Michael V. Hayden." *Studies in Intelligence* 44, no. 1 (January 5, 2000): 1–12.

Sand, Peter H. *United States and Britain in Diego Garcia: The Future of a Controversial Base*. New York: Palgrave Macmillan, 2009.

Schlesinger, Arthur M. "The American Empire? Not So Fast." *World Policy Journal* 22, no. 1 (Spring 2005): 43–46.

———. *The Cycles of American History*. Boston: Houghton Mifflin, 1999.

Shackley, Ted. *Spymaster: My Life in the CIA*. Dulles, VA: Potomac Books, 2005.

Sharp, David H. *The CIA's Greatest Covert Operation: Inside the Daring Mission to Recover a Nuclear-Armed Soviet Sub*. Lawrence: University Press of Kansas, 2012.

Smith, Derryfield N. "Mata Hari with a Glass Eye." *Air Forces New Letter* 24, no. 15 (September 1941): 1–4.

Smith, Richard Harris. "The First Moscow Station: An Espionage Footnote to Cold War History." *International Journal of Intelligence and Counterintelligence* 3, no. 3 (1989): 333–46.

Sontag, Sherry, and Christopher Drew. *Blind Man's Bluff: The Untold Story of American Submarine Espionage*. New York: Harper Paperbacks, 1998.

Stafford, David. *Spies beneath Berlin*. Woodstock, NY: Overlook Press, 2002.

Steiner, Sue, Robin Liston, Richard Grundy, and Mike Hentley. *St Helena: Ascension, Tristan Da Cunha*. Chalfont St. Peter: Bradt Travel Guides, 2007.

Strickland, Frank. "The Early Evolution of the Predator Drone." *Studies in Intelligence* 57, no. 1 (March 2013): 1–6.

Taubman, Philip. *Secret Empire: Eisenhower, the CIA, and the Hidden Story of American's Space Espionage*. New York: Simon & Schuster, 2003.

Tenet, George, with Bill Harlow. *At the Center of the Storm: The CIA during America's Time of Crisis*. New York: HarperCollins, 2007.

Thomas, Gordon. *Secrets and Lies: A History of CIA Mind Control and Germ Warfare*. Old Saybrook, CT: Octavo Editions, 2007.

Turner, Stansfield. "Intelligence for a New World Order." *Foreign Affairs* 70, no. 4 (Fall 1991): 150–66.

———. *Secrecy and Democracy: The CIA in Transition*. Boston: Houghton Mifflin, 1985.

Turse, Nick, and Tom Engelhardt. *Terminator Planet: The First History of Drone Warfare, 2001–2050*. n.p.: Dispatch Books, 2012.

US Senate. Select Committee on Intelligence. *The Senate Intelligence Committee Report on Torture: Committee Study of the Central Intelligence Agency's Detention and Interrogation Program*. Brooklyn, NY: Melville House, 2014.

Vine, David. *Base Nation: How U.S. Military Bases Abroad Harm America and the World*. New York: Henry Holt, 2015.

———. *Island of Shame: The Secret History of the U.S. Military Base on Diego Garcia*. Princeton, NJ: Princeton University Press, 2009.

Vogel, Steve. *Betrayal in Berlin: The True Story of the Cold War's Most Audacious Espionage Operation*. New York: Custom House, 2019.

Vogeler, Robert. *I Was Stalin's Prisoner*. New York: Harcourt, Brace, 1952.

Walker, John A., Jr. *My Life as a Spy*. New York: Prometheus Books, 2008.

Wallace, Robert, H. Keith Melton, and Henry R. Schlesinger. *Spy Sites of Washington, DC: A Guide to the Capital Region's Secret History*. Washington, DC: Georgetown University Press, 2017.

Walton, Calder. *Empire of Secrets: British Intelligence, the Cold War and the Twilight of Empire*. London: Harper Press, 2013.

Warner, Michael. *The Rise and Fall of Intelligence: An International Security History*. Washington, DC: Georgetown University Press, 2014.

Weiner, Tim. *Legacy of Ashes: The History of the CIA*. New York: Doubleday, 2007.

Welzenbach, Donald E. "Science and Technology: Origins of a Directorate." *Studies in Intelligence* 30, no. 2 (1986): 13–26.

Whittle, Richard. *Predator: The Secret Origins of the Drone Revolution*. New York: Henry Holt, 2014.

Wiener, Jon. *How We Forgot the Cold War: A Historical Journey across America*. Berkeley: University of California Press, 2012.

Winchester, Simon. *Outpost: Journeys to the Surviving Relics of the British Empire*. New York: Harper Perennial, [1985] 2003.

Wohlstetter, Roberta. "Cuba and Pearl Harbor: Hindsight and Foresight." *Foreign Affairs* 43, no. 4 (July 1965): 691–707.

Woodward, Bob. *Obama's Wars*. New York: Simon & Schuster, 2010.

Zegart, Amy B. *Spies, Lies, and Algorithms: The History and Future of American Intelligence*. Princeton, NJ: Princeton University Press, 2022.

Zimmerman, David. *Top Secret Exchange: The Tizard Mission and the Scientific War*. Toronto: McGill-Queen's University Press, 1996.

INDEX

Note: Illustrations are indicated by page numbers in italics.

ABOUT THE AUTHOR

Kristie Macrakis, the author or editor of seven books, was a professor of history in the School of History and Sociology at Georgia Tech. She was a historian of technology and science and of espionage. Her other books include *Surviving the Swastika: Scientific Research in Nazi Germany* (Oxford University Press, 1993), *Seduced by Secrets: Inside the Stasi's Spy-Tech World* (Cambridge University Press, 2008), and *Prisoners, Lovers and Spies: The Story of Invisible Ink from Herodotus to al-Qaeda* (Yale University Press, 2014). She passed away shortly before the publication of this book. www.kristiemacrakis.com.